# From Stone and Snow to Timber and Wine

*The story of the Palandri family's journey from the Apennines of Italy to the forests of Western Australia.*

## Stephen Palandri

# From Stone and Snow to Timber and Wine

*The story of an Italian-Australian family's migration, love, work, and legacy*

By

**Stephen Palandri**

Copyright © 2025 Stephen Palandri

All rights reserved.

No part of this publication may be reproduced, stored in a retrieval system, or transmitted in any form or by any means — electronic, mechanical, photocopying, recording, or otherwise — without the prior written permission of the publisher.

This is a work of nonfiction based on the author's recollections. While every effort has been made to ensure accuracy, some names and details may have been changed to respect privacy.

Some names and images appear with permission. All photos are included for historical and personal context only. This memoir is based on personal recollections. Any resemblance to persons or places not intended as factual representations is purely coincidental.

Cover design by Jake Palandri

Published by SP ARTS Press

Printed in Australia

# Dedication

For Christina, Jake, and Caleb — my greatest loves, my first readers, and my reason for writing.

And for my dear Mum and Dad — taken too soon, but never far. You taught me more than you ever knew.

This book carries on the traditions you gave us.

# Acknowledgements

This book would not have been possible without the memories, the laughter, and the gentle (and not-so-gentle) nudges from those I love.

To my incredible wife, Christina — thank you for insisting (relentlessly) that I write down my slightly unhinged childhood stories. You were right. There, I said it.

To my two sons, Jake and Caleb. Jake, thank you for giving me the time and headspace to write, and for your wise and often timely advice. Caleb, thank you for enduring the stories — again and again — and for keeping so many of our traditions alive (even the odd ones).

To my wider family — thank you for your patience, your photos, your memories, and your unfiltered commentary on early drafts. We may not always agree on the details, but the spirit of our story lives in all of us.

To those who helped gather photographs, translate love letters from another era, and read those wobbly first versions — your quiet contributions made a loud impact. Thank you.

A special thanks to those who reminded me of the most embarrassing stories I had conveniently forgotten, and to my ever-patient overseas cousins who graciously interpreted my garbled Italian messages as if they made perfect seen.

# Table of Contents

## PREFACE

Calcio d'inizio — "kick-off"

## PARTE 1: Le Radici (The Roots)

1. All'inizio (In the Beginning)
2. La nostra famiglia (Our Family)
3. Lettere d'Amore (Love Letters)
4. Nella fattoria (On the Farm)
5. Festa e Fede (Feast and Faith)
   - Parte 1: Mangiare (Eating)
   - Parte 2: Colazione (Breakfast)
   - Parte 3: Pranzo (Lunch)
   - Parte 4: Compleanni (Birthdays)
   - Parte 5: Pasqua (Easter)
   - Parte 6: Natale e Capodanno (Christmas and New Year)

## PARTE 2: Le Case e le Comunità (Homes and Communities)

6. Le nostre case (Our Homes)
7. Fede, Paura e Prima Confessione (Faith, Fear, and First Confession)
8. La montagna che ricorda (The Mountain That Remembers)
9. Legname e Vino, Margaret River (Timber and Vine, Margaret River)

# Table of Contents

## PART THREE: Growing Up (Crescere)

10. Before I Was Born (Prima che nascessi)
11. Mischief, Mayhem and Missteps (Dispetto, caos e passi falsi)
12. School Years (Gli anni scolastici)
13. From the Paddock to the Coach's Box (Dal paddock alla panchina)
14. Lines in the Water, Stories in the Wind (Lenze in acqua, storie nel vento)
15. Sausage, Tomato Sauce and Stewing (Salsicce, Salsa di Pomodoro e Stufato)
16. The Brothers and Sisters (I Fratelli e le Sorelle)
17. Show Day (Giornata della fiera)
18. The Fire, The Devil (Il fuoco, Il Diavolo)

## PART FOUR: Reflections (Riflessioni)

19. The End of Days (Gli ultimi giorni)
20. Echoes of a Life (Riflessioni adulte)

## Calcio d'inizio - "kick-off"

Calcio d'inizio—Italian for "kick-off"—is how every football match begins. A simple moment that sets everything in motion. In Italy, it's more than just a sporting phrase; it marks the start of passion, purpose, and possibility.

That's why I've chosen it to open this story. This memoir is my kick-off—the beginning of a journey into the history, heart, and humour of my family: one of six Italian families who left the little mountain town of Piandelagotti in Emilia-Romagna and made a life in Western Australia. It's a tribute to our roots, to those who came with little more than hope in their pockets, and to the legacy they built—by hand, by heart, and often by sheer grit.

My name is Stephen Palandri. I'm the youngest of six children, born to Carlo and Angelina. I grew up in Margaret River in a time and place that now feels like another world. I often compared us to The Brady Bunch—we had three girls and three boys—but that's about where the similarity ended.

We were loud, proud, messy, resilient, and raised in a home where the smell of tomato sugo mingled with eucalyptus and dark loam. Here's something I've always wondered: out of six children, why was I the only one without an Italian name? We had Ricardo, Carla, Lina, Annunziata, and Francesco… and then came me. Stephen. It never quite made sense. Maybe they ran out of names. Maybe I was so late they couldn't agree on one. Maybe—just maybe—it was an unintentional nod to the future: a bridge between the old world and the new. Still, I'm waiting for someone in the family to give me a straight answer.

Despite the English name, I'm Italian through and through—by blood, by upbringing, by culture. I now go by Steve, but this book is my way of preserving the stories that shaped me. Stories of hardship and humour, migration and memory, devotion and resilience. It's about my parents, my grandparents, and the extraordinary tapestry of family that brought the traditions of Piandelagotti into the rich dark loam of the Southwest. Our family journey began in the early 1900s, when my grandfather Giacomo Palandri left Italy to prepare a new life in Australia. In 1940, his wife Leonilda arrived with their children—

my father Carlo, and his brother Giuseppe. They were part of a quiet migration that shaped the very fabric of towns like Busselton and Margaret River.

Later, Carlo met Angelina Fontana, the woman who would become my mother. Their courtship unfolded through handwritten letters exchanged between Perth and Margaret River during wartime—a paper trail of love, longing, and laughter. I still have those letters. Reading them is like watching a slow-burning romance set against a backdrop of sacrifice and hope.

As tradition dictated, after the wedding, Angelina moved into the Palandri family home with her in-laws and Carlo's sibling. Not long after, Giuseppe—Carlo's brother—married Atilia, Angelina's sister. Yes, you read that right. Two brothers married two sisters. In a world of small towns and shared customs, this wasn't unusual—but it was beautiful. Two families, bound by love and culture, became one.

Eventually, one roof became too small. As Ricardo—the firstborn—arrived, and Giuseppe started his own family, a second home was built just a kilometre away across Caves Road. We called it La nostra Casa—our house. That chapter comes later in the book, but what you need to know is this: between my parents and Giuseppe's, there are fifteen kids. And because of how our family tree grew—two brothers married to two sisters—we were cousins by blood, siblings by heart. We shared meals, chores, secrets, and stories and nine other Italian names were given. It was noisy, chaotic, and utterly unforgettable.

This book is my way of honouring that world. Of capturing the moments big and small—the ones that shaped us, the ones that still echo today. My perspective is just the tip of the iceberg. Beneath it lies a century of sacrifice, survival, and spirit. The roots of our story stretch from the rocky, snowy slopes of Piandelagotti to the timber and vineyards of Margaret River. And our legacy, like our family, is still growing.

So, this is our calcio d'inizio—our kick-off. A story about family, food, faith, and the fierce love that held it all together. And maybe, just maybe, along the way, I'll finally figure out where "Stephen" came from.

# Part One: Le Radici
# (The Roots)

*"To know where you're going, you must first understand where you came from."*

# Chapter 1

# All'inizio (In the Beginning)

*"Ogni inizio ha la sua magia."*
– Hermann Hesse
*("Every beginning holds its own magic.")*

Every story starts somewhere, but ours begins high in the Apennine Mountains—among wind-worn stones, whispered legends, and the rhythm of footsteps worn into ancient paths. It's a story born of grit and survival, of mothers and fathers who carved a future from soil, snow, and sacrifice. Before of Margaret River, before the timber and the wine, there was Piandelagotti. And before me—Stephen—some crossed oceans not for wealth or glory, but to give us something enduring: a name, a home, a chance.

## The Mountain Remembers

Tucked high in the Apennine Mountains, where Emilia-Romagna brushes the edge of Tuscany, lies a village forgotten by time. Piandelagotti, a place where the wind remembers names, footsteps grooves into ancient paths, and firewood doesn't burn-it speaks. Contrarily, here memory is not just preserved; it breathes through snow, stone, and silence.

This tiny village, like so many dotting Italy's mountainous backbone, has ancient roots. Piandelagotti rose on the Via Bibulca, a Roman road that once echoed with the boots of legionnaires and the prayers of medieval monks. The nearby "Fonte del Silvano" spring—documented as far back as 781 AD—offered rest and water to travelers. Did my great-grandparents pause there, kneeling by that spring, tracing the same path with tired feet? The hospice of San Geminiano, later replaced by a modest oratory, stood not just as a marker of devotion but of survival.

Today, it remains a living palimpsest, its narrow lanes and steep rooftops whispering the stories of those who came before. When I walked down those lanes, it felt as if the stones recognized me. At 1,209 metres above sea level, the town is the western gateway to Parco Regionale del Frignano, a natural park that protects both its environment and its story. Piandelagotti is a seasonal place: veiled in snow in winter, golden with fading leaves in autumn, and fresh with chestnut green each spring. It is a place that demands respect and resilience from those who call it home. For centuries, it was a land of subsistence. Families grew what they could—potatoes, maize, a little wheat—and kept livestock when grass allowed. Forest work, charcoal making, and seasonal migration supplemented what the soil could not provide. In winter, they insulated their stone houses with hay in the walls. In summer, they walked miles to bring water, wood, or grain from neighbouring valleys. The terrain bred toughness, and the people were shaped by the land's indifference.

**Piandelagotti Circa 2000**

By the early 20th century, Piandelagotti had become a minor tourist destination, known for its clean air and untouched wilderness. City dwellers from Modena or Bologna would escape to the hills, chasing snow and simplicity. Makeshift skis and home-built sleds glided down frozen tracks long before ski lifts and gear shops arrived. In warmer months, families hiked along the paths once used by Matilda of Canossa, a medieval countess whose legacy echoed through these parts. Despite its size, Piandelagotti offered the essentials of mountain life. A bar for espresso and gossip. A butcher who knew every animal by name. A chemist, a bakery, a church, a school, and a doctor who still made house calls. Life was contained but never narrow. Families like the Lunardi, Fontana, Vignaroli, Palandri, and Zannotti formed the social spine of the village—interwoven through marriage, debt, friendship, and duty. These names are my inheritance as much as my surname.

When I visited in 2023, the names remained—etched into marble headstones, painted on shuttered shopfronts, and spoken with reverence by the few elders still living in the homes they were born in. My own name, Palandri, was still known and spoken with familiarity. Although, decades and oceans had only just settled between us, hearing my name amongst locals, shaped by the mountains, felt like stepping into a memory I'd never lived.

In our family, Piandelagotti isn't just a place. It's the beginning. It's where our story took its first breath—where our ancestors endured, dreamt, and eventually decided to leave. From these hills came all the ingredients of our life: grit, humility, laughter, stubbornness, song, silence, and strange ability to both cherish and let go. Would they recognise us now, I wonder, with our different accents and distant lives? Or would they simply see the same fire in our eyes?

The roads were once Roman, but the journey was ours.

## Giuseppe and Maria – Between Mountain and Sea

Giuseppe Fontana, known to us as *Nonnine*, was born in 1895 in the mountain hamlet of Casa Pesci, just beyond Piandelagotti. His world was one of flint and frost, of narrow paths and stone homes clinging to steep hillsides. Like all boys of the Apennines, he learned early that survival came from working the land—and working hard. He herded cows and sheep across alpine meadows, delivered flour from the family mill, and learned to read and write in both Italian and English, though he had little formal education.

At just nine years old, Giuseppe crossed the ocean to America with his father and older brothers, joining a wave of Italian migrants chasing a distant promise. He spent eight years in the United States, labouring in coal mines, shining shoes, and delivering milk. The work was relentless, the days long, and the reward simple money to send home.

Then came the letter: his father was gravely ill. His mother's plea was clear return. Giuseppe obeyed, boarding a ship back to Italy. But no sooner had he reached the coast another letter met him: he was to report immediately for military service. His time at home would last just one week.

Giuseppe was conscripted into the elite Bersaglieri light infantry regiment, where he rose to Corporal Major and became a machine gunner. In one of many cruel twists of war, his unit was captured and transported to Germany. But Giuseppe was never one to stay where he was told. He escaped, beginning a perilous, two-year journey through enemy territory. He moved from farm to farm, working in exchange for food and shelter, always watching, always hiding. Eventually, he made his way back into northern Italy—still under occupation—where he was wounded and recaptured. This time, fate gave him a gentler hand: a German officer, recognising his decorated status, sent him to a military hospital in Modena. His family was allowed to visit.

Once recovered, Giuseppe rejoined his regiment and was eventually honourably discharged. He returned not just to Piandelagotti, but to a future.

On 12 September 1920, he married Maria Lunardi—*Nonnina*—the youngest of six children from the well-known Lunardi family who ran the Albergo Alpino, the village's mountain hotel. Maria had grown up in the rhythms of hospitality: preparing meals, tending guests, cleaning, working from sun-up to sundown. She was strong and quiet, the sort of woman who could hold a family together with one hand and stir polenta with the other.

Together, they built a life from the remnants of war and the foundations of tradition. They had two daughters: Renata in 1921, and Angelina—my mother—in 1922. Their story, like the stones of Piandelagotti, held fast through time.

By the mid-1920s, Mussolini's grip in Italy was tightening. Hope was growing scarce, especially in the mountains. Like many others, Giuseppe Fontana began to look outward— somewhere distant, and freer. In 1925, he packed what little he had and boarded the *SS Palermo*, bound for Fremantle. There were no fixed plans, no jobs waiting—just a letter, a contact named Mr. Molinari, and a raw courage of a man who had already crossed oceans once in his life. Sometimes I wonder if that same restlessness runs in my blood.

## Across Oceans, Through Salt and Fire

Giuseppe's first nights were spent in a Fremantle boarding house. From there, he travelled south to Busselton, found comfort in familiar faces—Amadio and

**Nonnina and Nonnine early in Australia.**

## Across Oceans, Through Salt and Fire

Annunziata Palandri, also from Piandelagotti, who now owned the Ship Hotel. Their hospitality offered more than shelter; it offered continuity. It makes me think how vital small acts of welcome still are for those who arrive in new places. Through them, and other like-minded individuals, a small unofficial enclave of mountain, Italians began to form. The Zanotti, Zanni, Meleri, and Piacientini followed. Each family adding bricks to the transplanted village growing quietly in the southwest of Australia.

Giuseppe laboured wherever work could be found, deep in the coal shafts of Collie, dragging timber in the forests of Jarrahwood, or cutting roads through the tangled hills of Nannup and Pemberton. But time was shifting. A great flood destroyed one of his worksites, and with the spread of automobiles, the era of horse teams began to end. Giuseppe sold his horses, moved to Perth,

and began anew—this time in a market garden. Eventually, he secured work with Swan Portland Cement, and in Queens Park, he bought a home on three acres.

It was modest, but to him, it was a promise: something of his own in a land that was beginning to feel less foreign. Standing there decades later, looking at the buildings that are now on the site I tried to imagine what that first patch of earth must have meant to him. It was almost 100 years later that I stood in this spot.

Three long years passed before Maria could follow. On 15 February 1928, she boarded the *SS Taormina* in Genoa, flanked by her two daughters, Renata and Angelina, each clutching a corner of her skirt. She left behind everything: her mother, her siblings, the mountain air she had breathed since childhood. Her suitcase was light; her burden was not. I wonder if she ever regretted that crossing - or if she simply carried the mountains inside her, wherever she went.

For Maria, the voyage was not just across oceans—it was across realities. She traded cobbled lanes for open paddocks, the cool mist of Piandelagotti for the harsh sunlight of a flat land where the seasons felt backwards and the customs indecipherable. In this new place, food tasted different, remedies no longer worked, the rhythm of life was out of sync.

Even the mosquitoes were a mystery. In Piandelagotti, they were rare, but in Queens Park, they descended in clouds. Maria was horrified by the welts they left on her daughters' arms and legs. In desperation, she turned to instinct. Salt—*sale*—drew out the sting. Tomato juice—*succo di pomodoro*—cooled the irritation. This simple remedy would become a family tradition. Decades later, if we ever scratched at a bite, Mum would mutter: "Put some sale or pommi d'orro on it."

**SS Taormina**

Maria never boasted, never complained. She simply adapted, and in doing so, taught her children—and all of us—how to live between two worlds. Her courage didn't look like flags or medals. It looked like skin softened by salt. Like a garden coaxed from sand. Like a mother watching her daughters sleep, miles and mountains from home.

**The Fontana Family 1930s. Mum on the Left.**

## The Garden They Grew

Together, Giuseppe and Maria began the quiet work of growing deeper in unfamiliar soil. Their new home in Queens Park was a far cry from the mountain village they had left behind. The three acres surrounding the small house were overgrown and swampy. The soil was stubborn, merciless. But slowly, patiently, they cleared it—cutting back wild trees, draining what they could, and coaxing order from the tangle. They planted vegetables, bought a cow and chickens, and began long road toward self-sufficiency. Maria passed down her skills to the girls—how to churn butter knead bread, stretch milk into cheese and cream. These lessons would shape Angelina's future and lay the foundations of a life lived through food.

But fierce heat of the Australian summer brought new challenges. Butter melted. Cream soured. Milk turned quickly in the relentless warmth. A family friend, Giacomo Vigneroli, offered a solution: the Kalgoorlie Safe. This humble cabinet, cooled by damped cloth, kept food from spoiling. It was a simple invention — but it made a world of difference in a strange land, small comforts became lifelines.

The family grew. Over the next few years, three more daughters—Adelina, Atilia, and Olga—were born. Then came Ricardo, the only son. Life on the block became a collective effort. Giuseppe worked long hours at the cement works while Maria managed the home and children. Everyone pitched in, helped with the garden. Slowly, the land began to yield. Fruits on trees blossomed, vegetables flourished in patchwork rows, a modest stable rose, and more animals arrived. It was no longer merely a survival. It was a farm.

Angelina, who had arrived in Fremantle at just six years old, became her mother's bridge to the outside world. She learned to read and write in English at school, while speaking fluent Italian at home Maria, who never learned English, relied on her two daughters for everything– My mother Angelina was the second eldest daughter, from translating bills to navigating shopkeepers. By the time she was in her early teens, Angelina was already the quiet glue that held many parts of the family together.

The 1930s brought with it many hardships. Australia staggered under the weight of the Depression, and work was scarce for many. But the Fontana's endured. Angelina picked up seamstress work—altering dresses, mending trousers, earning few coins to ease the strain. She learned frugality, ingenuity, and delicate balance of duty and grace. She did all this while still attending school, helping raise her younger siblings, and managing share of the household chores.

Somehow, through it all, the family thrived. They built the first small irrigated market gardens in Perth, planted and maintained completely by hand. At the front of the property, they opened a shop, selling their produce along with essentials—cotton, pins, tobacco, even cigarettes. Moreover, a Lucerne patch was cultivated, its fragrant hay prized by racehorse owners for its healing properties.

Angelina's journey from Piandelagotti to Queens Park was just beginning. By the time war came to Australia, she was a young woman working as a seamstress in a factory, helping supply the war effort. And it was then, in the mid-1940s, that a familiar thread weave re-entered her life—a young man named Carlo Palandri, also from Piandelagotti, introduced at a gathering hosted by Innis Palandri, daughter of Amadio and Annunziata.

From that meeting, would come a new beginning, and a legacy still unfolding.

## Stone and Silence – The Story of Giacomo and Leonilda

The story of my father, Carlo, begins not with him, but with the man who shaped his world—my grandfather, Giacomo Palandri.

Born on 8 March 1890, in the rugged heart of the Apennines, Giacomo entered in a life of frost, stone, and silence. Piandelagotti, his birthplace, clung to the hills like a secret, its narrow lanes etched with centuries of hardship. There, the soil resisted the plough, and winter swept down from the mountains with a fierce, unrelenting will. The land gave little and demanded everything in return.

Giacomo's family plot was no more than two to four acres it was in Savoniero, 15 km down the slope from Piandelagotti —hardly a farm, more a test of faith. They grew wheat, a little maize, a few vegetables. Grapevines curled along a stone wall, yielding enough fruit for just a few bottles of wine. Their single cow gave milk for butter and cheese—precious commodities. Meat was rare. Sometimes, Giacomo and his brother would climb into trees, fingers numbed with cold, to steal eggs from wild bird nests. Hunger made poets and thieves of boys like them. There was no time for school. The only lessons came from calloused hands and aching backs—from rhythm set by hoe and scythe. By the age of sixteen, Giacomo knew what many before him had come to learn: the mountain held no future for its sons. In 1906, he left.

**Giacomo Palandri**

With his brother beside him, he boarded *La Provence* at the French port of Le Havre and crossed the Atlantic. They landed at Ellis Island—two mountain boys adrift in the raw appetite of America. For two years, Giacomo laboured in timber camps, on railway lines, and in stories he would one day tell us children with wide-eyed gusto. The spoke of Buffalo Bill, of Wild Bill Hickok, of dusty duels and howling coyotes. Whether it was true or not, we believed every word. But America, too, offered no permanence. In 1909, Giacomo returned to Italy. The mountains hadn't changed—but neither had the hunger. Still, something new was stirring in his life.

Her name was Leonilda. Leonilda Vignaroli was born on 13 June 1892 in Piandelagotti, into a family that bore the mountain's signature: resourceful, proud, and poor. Her father—my great-grandfather—was known by the name *Bordacca*, a jack-of-all-trades who repaired tools, roofs, and anything that could be fixed by hand. His quiet ingenuity became Leonilda's inheritance. She grew up milking the family cow, weeding a stubborn patch of vegetables, and learning to stretch nothing into something. From her mother, she learned the delicate art of willow-weaving—baskets so fine they looked like lace. She was deft with a needle, and by her teens, was already a skilled dressmaker. These weren't hobbies, but survival.

To help support her family, Leonilda left the village in her mid-teens to work in service in Milan—a world away. There, she learned precision, discipline, and polish. Yet she returned to Piandelagotti at twenty to marry Giacomo, bringing back with her a quiet elegance forged in the city and tempered by the mountain.

**Leonilda Palandri**

They married in 1913, likely in a modest ceremony in the village church with a meal shared in someone's stone-walled kitchen. Their union was unspoken strength. Perhaps they'd met under the arches of a barn or passed each other for years along the same muddy road. In the end, it didn't matter. They chose one another and built something together.

Giacomo and Leonilda lived not for comfort, but for continuity. They raised their children—Carlo among them—in a world where every loaf was earned, every stitch mattered. Their home, humble and solid, stood like they did: quiet, enduring, and full of memory.

From these two—my *Nonno* and *Nonna*—came a legacy of resilience. Their hands were worn, their language was steeped in old dialects, but their spirits were sharp. They didn't ask the world to be fair. They simply met it, day after day, with grit and grace. And from them came Carlo.

### Oceans Between Them

Just six months after their wedding, Giacomo was gone again. Leonilda, now pregnant with their first child, Gemma, stood once more to bid farewell. Giacomo crossed the sea in 1914, bound for the United States. By a twist of fate, he arrived a year before the war tore Europe apart. While the trenches filled with blood and sorrow, he was swinging axes in America's vast forests and laying railway lines across open plains.

He tried to enlist in American army, stirred by duty and same restless spirit that had always driven him. But by the time paperwork was processed, the war had ended. So, he returned—this time in 1919—to Piandelagotti. To a daughter who barely knew him. To a wife who had grown used to waiting.

Between 1919 and 1925, the family grew. Lina arrived in 1920. Then Giuseppe in 1922. And finally, Carlo—my father—in 1923. But the mountain gave little. The soil remained stubborn, and work was unreliable. And so, once again, Giacomo left. He travelled across Europe in search of work, Corsica, Germany, even parts of Africa. He sent home what he could, money and letters—thin lifelines stretched across continents.

**Nonna Leonilda and Children Late 1920s. Dad on Her Knee**

In 1925, chasing a rumour more than a promise, Giacomo tried to return to the United States. But immigration laws had changed. He was turned away. So, he gambled on another whisper: a country on the far edge of the world, where work was said to be plentiful, and forests seemed endless—Australia.

He boarded the *Città di Genova* in Genoa and stepped off the ship in Fremantle with almost nothing. No English, no money, and barely a contact to his name. But one thread connected him: a distant relation—Amadio Palandri—who, with his wife Annunziata, managed the Ship Hotel in Busselton. Years later, their path would cross with my mother's family in a twist of fate no one could have foreseen.

Giacomo did what he knew best. He went into the bush and began cutting sleepers, working alone with a broadaxe in the dense silence of the forest. Timber became his livelihood, his routine. After two years of relentless labour, he scraped together enough to buy a truck and began subcontracting with other European workers to supply the railway mills. But the Great Depression accompanied 1930 like a storm. Work dried up. He sold the truck and, once again, returned to Italy—this time with a little cash, and to a family who had barely seen him in five years.

Giacomo was often a shadow in his own household—a presence more felt in envelopes and bank drafts than beside the hearth. But his absence was not abandonment. It was sacrifice. Every departure was for his family. Each return was marked by fresh lines on his face, calloused hands and pockets never quite full.

Leonilda, meanwhile, built permanence. With the money Giacomo sent from abroad, she and one of his brothers purchased land in south of the village. They built a duplex-style home—two wings joined in stone—one for each family. And with Giacomo so often away, Leonilda raised their children largely alone. She was more than a mother; she was the mountain's daughter. She worked the land, planted vegetables, tended the vines, and raised livestock. During one of Giacomo's absences, she used his remittances to purchase a small osteria in the neighbouring home of Savoniero—a humble tavern where she poured wine, fed labourers, and kept the family anchored to something solid. Leonilda didn't wait for life to carry her forward. She seized it with rough, determined hands. While Giacomo chased fortune through forests and foreign lands, she carved out dignity from what was left behind.

## A Return, a Farewell, and the Last Voyage

In 1937, with industry stirring once again in the southwest of Australia, Giacomo Palandri returned for what would be the final time. He boarded the SS

Romolo, the same ship that had once ferried hundreds of hopefuls into new lives across distant oceans. This time, Giacomo was no longer a wide-eyed youth with empty pockets. He carried experience, a network, and an unwavering will to work.

He went back to Busselton and picked up his axe and his truck, carving out a familiar rhythm in the forests once more. He secured steady work with Bunnings, and later, with Phil Ryan at the Cowaramup Mill. Timber had become not just his livelihood but his legacy—logs hauled from the dense bush, day after day, like it was the very work he had been born to do. But areven as Giacomo toiled under the southern sun, the winds of history shifted once again. In Europe, the 1940s roared in with sirens and speeches. Tyranny and war returned to the continent like an illness not yet cured. And during that global unrest, Nonna Leonilda prepared to leave her mountain home for the last time. The decision was not easy. It never had been. But the family's future was no longer in Piandelagotti. The years of separations and remittances came to a halt. She would join her husband on the other side of the world. She boarded the SS Romolo in Genoa, just as Giacomo had done three years earlier, carrying with her not just two sons—Giuseppe and Carlo—but a suitcase packed with memory, faith, and grief. Gemma, her eldest, had already married and remained in Italy. Lina, her second daughter, won't be making the journey. She had died of tuberculosis just the year before, far from home, working as a housemaid. That loss, sharp and unresolved, must have echoed with every mile Leonilda put betweenherself and the land where she had buried her child.

The journey took nearly five weeks. Ports slipped pass under moonlight; the horizon rolled endlessly. For young Carlo, just seventeen, the voyage must have felt like a waking dream. I picture him at the ship's rail—my father—eyes wide at the vastness of the sea, listening to languages he couldn't yet understand, inhaling the dry, salty air of unfamiliar lands. How must Australia have seemed to him then? So wild. So hot. So impossibly vast. But Giacomo had taken care of the details long before they stepped aboard. He had been naturalized as an Australian citizen in 1929—a strategic decision, made not with sentiment but with foresight. Even Leonilda had been naturalized, despite never having touched Australian soil. That single piece of paper meant everything. It cleared the path for her arrival, protected her from internment, and made her—on paper at least—a citizen of this new world. As the SS Romolo docked in Fremantle, it marked the closing of one chapter and the beginning of another. Their journey—from stone houses in the Apennines to timber camps in Western Australia—was now a shared one. No longer lived in separate countries, no longer divided by oceans and decades. They would build again. Not just homes, but a new life. And though the past clung to them—through accent, habit, and memory—they faced forward, toward Margaret River, toward us. Their arrival in Australia in 1940 was, in many ways, our beginning.

## The Last Ship, the First Steps

And so, at last, the family stood together on Australian soil—not in the quiet stone village of Piandelagotti, but on the windswept edge of a strange continent, beneath sun unlike any they had known. They had crossed oceans and empires, braved war and poverty, and found each other again in the wilds of Western Australia. Nonna Leonilda could not have known, as she stepped ashore in Fremantle on 26 April 1940, how closely they had beaten history. Only weeks later, Italy declared war alongside Nazi Germany, and in response, Australia declared war on Italy. Once again, the world closed in. The fragile opening that had let them through snapped shut.

The *SS Romolo*, the very ship that had carried her and her two youngest sons across the oceans, continued its scheduled voyage up the eastern coast of Australia. But suspicion followed it like a shadow.

The Royal Australian Navy, wary of foreign vessels in their waters, began monitoring the Romolo's movements. On 5 June 1940, she departed Brisbane. Four days later, the world received confirmation: Italy had joined the war. The *HMAS Manoora*, which had briefly been called off, was sent once more to pursue the Romolo.

By the time the order came through, she was already 160 miles from her last port. The Manoora closed in quickly. Just 220 miles southwest of Nauru, the

Romolo was cornered. Her crew had no choice but to scuttle her, sending the proud ship to the ocean floor. She was the last Italian vessel to carry passengers from Italy to Australia before war severed the route for years.

My family had made it through the final window. Any later, and their story may have ended not in Margaret River, but in a detention camp or at sea. When they arrived in Margaret River, there was no welcome committee—only hard work and hard land. Giacomo had purchased 300 acres of dense bush from Francesco Tarchini. On it stood a small, rough house made of jarrah slabs and railway sleepers. It wasn't a home—not yet. It was a clearing. A start.

**SS Romolo**

For three years, they carved that land by hand. Trees came down one by one. Timber was hauled. Stones were shifted. Giacomo returned to his trade at the Cowaramup Mill, while Leonilda transformed the crude bush dwelling into something that resembled a home. She sewed, she gardened, and she cooked. She built—silently and steadily—the foundation of the new Palandri life.

Even here, the war found them.

In 1943, Carlo and Giuseppe—still not naturalised—were rounded up under wartime manpower legislation and placed into the labour corps. Two sons, fresh from war-torn Europe, now caught in another country's fear. But Giacomo, respected in the timber industry, had allies. A subcontractor at the Cowaramup Mill intervened. He vouched for the boys, and they were released to work alongside their father.

There, they learned to cut sleepers, to read the rhythm of the bush, to handle timber with precision. It was demanding work—but rooted them, body and soul, to the land. By 1945, both brothers had become naturalised Australians—no longer strangers, no longer seen as threats, but as men who had proven their place in this country. Carlo showed a natural talent for millwork, gaining a reputation for accuracy and leadership. In the dust and din of the Cowaramup Mill, a boy from the Apennines was becoming something new— an Australian man. And it was around this time, beneath the tall timber and the weight of war's ending, that fate stepped in again.

At a gathering hosted by Innes Palandri, the then owner of the Ship hotel, held in Perth, Carlo, met a young woman named Angelina. Like him, she had been born in Piandelagotti—but had emigrated with her family back in 1928, settling in Queens Park. Two mountain children, thousands of kilometres from home, now standing on the same dance floor, in a land neither had imagined. Their story was just beginning.

## A Stone House and a Thousand Letters

It was a love that did not arrive with fanfare but settled in gradually—like mist rolling in over the hills, like spring after a long, silent winter. What began with a shared dance at the Ship Hotel in Busselton–the dance was at the party in Perth. Became something deeper with every exchanged glance, and later, with every word inked in Carlo's unmistakable hand.

Theirs was a courtship shaped by distance and held together by devotion. Dozens—perhaps hundreds—of letters passed between them during those early years, each one a lifeline stretched across the long road between Margaret

River and Queens Park. Carlo's handwriting, still neat and flowing then, carried all the things he could not say aloud. In Italian, his emotions were unguarded. There was a sweetness to his prose—measured, heartfelt, full of longing. Angelina's replies were equally tender. They were young, but their letters bore the shape of a shared future.

In 1949, as their wedding approached, the Palandri family completed another kind of promise: the construction of a permanent family home. Built from granite and designed in the spirit of Piandelagotti, the new house stood proudly where the rough jarrah slab shack once stood. Every stone in its walls was selected with care. The style was unmistakably Italian, yet the materials—weathered, local-rooted—it firmly in Western Australia. Postwar scarcity made construction slow and careful. Wood was milled by hand, windows were salvaged, and mortar was mixed in batches. The craftsmanship was practical, but its endurance was poetic: the house still stands today, solid and unyielding, a legacy in limestone and granite.

The old shack was dismantled but not discarded. Every timber slab was reused—reimagined as cattle yards, sheds, and fences. Nothing was wasted. In that transformation, one saw not just ingenuity, but the rhythm of survival passed down from generations who had always known how to stretch little into much.

Carlo and Angelina were married in 1950, and with their union came the beginning of the next generation. Ricardo, their firstborn, arrived the following year, and Carla followed in 1952. The great stone house—once seeming oversized—soon began to feel smaller under the weight of babies, blankets, and generations overlapping in the same rooms. Laughter echoed down the hallways. The kitchen was filled with steam and flour. Life expanded. In 1954, Carlo used his savings from the Cowaramup Mill, and he leased the land Sussex Location 1199, a dense, untouched stretch of bushland adjacent to the family property. The land was wild, thorny, and thick with trees—but to Carlo and Angelina, it was full of promise. While Ricardo and Carla lived with the Nonno, the young couple set about clearing the land by hand, just as Giacomo and Leonilda had done before them.

**Carlo and Angelina Palandri, Married in 1950**

Every felled tree, uprooted stump, was a step closer to home. The timber they extracted was cut and milled by Carlo himself not a labourer, but now as a true builder. The new home they created on that land was more than shelter. It was a monument to commitment. It still shelters our family today. From that home, the family grew: Lina came next, then Annunziata, then Francesco. And finally—years later—me. Stephen. The outlier. The boy with strange, un-Italian name, who even now draws good-humoured ridicule from his siblings.

But names carry stories. And mine, perhaps, marks the turning point. I was born at the trailing end of something vast: a saga of mountain people turned settlers, of one family's journey from stone and snow to timber and fire, of migration and making do. By the time I arrived, our story was already sprawling across two continents and generations. I did not build the path—I was simply lucky enough to walk it.

**The Palandri and Fontana Families Together in 1951 (Nonna's Absent)**

# Chapter 2
# La nostra famiglia (Our Family)

*"La famiglia è la patria del cuore."*

– Giuseppe Mazzini

They say love finds a way—but in the story of Carlo and Angelina, love and thrived across mountains, oceans, and war. Born in the same tiny village, their paths diverged across and decades, only to converge again in a dusty, distant corner of Australia. This chapter traces how a wartime romance blossomed into a lifelong partnership, how family roots deepened in the dark loam of Margaret River, and how two Italian migrants built a home and heritage from scratch. It is the story of the first house, the first children, and the forging of a future through faith, hard work, and unshakable love.

From the last chapter we left off with Carlo and Angelina marrying in 1950. As you know, both my mother's, and my father's family came from the same place—high in the mountains in a small village called Piandelagotti. They both arrived in Australia at different times; my mother in 1928 as a six-year-old and my father as a 17-year-old young man in 1940. However, their story is not unique amongst migrants but still cherished. Amidst the decade that was ravaged by World War II—these two souls, originally from the same village but living worlds apart, met and fell in love. From what I understand, they met at a Christmas party in Perth around 1948. Remarkably, the gathering was hosted by one of our own—Innes Palandri, a relative also from Piandelagotti. daughter of Amadio and Annunziata, who ran the Ship Hotel (Inn) in Busselton.

**The Original Ship Hotel (Inn), Busselton, Circa Early 1900s**

Their lives intersected with both Nonnine's and Nonno's migration stories, playing a part in the family's early settlement in Western Australia's Southwest. It's to think that, despite coming from the same small mountain village, the families hadn't known each other back in Italy. Piandelagotti wasn't but it was a spread-out farming community, separated by forests, fields, and rhythms of rural life. Their meeting here, so far from home, feels like fate working quietly in the background. The amazing thing about this love story is the existence of hundreds of letters written to each other from as early as 1948 through to 1950.

**My Fathers Beautiful Handwriting.**

**My Mothers Equally Beautiful Handwriting**

From these letters, I was able to piece together and decipher the nature of their relationship—it was far from easy. Traditional Italian parents, the tyranny of distance, and the love and trust they shared, made it a bond that perhaps wouldn't exist readily in modern times. I've translated some of the excerpts from what I believe are the first letters sent by Carlo and Angelina, and the last letters before they were married. These excerpts demonstrate the difficulty in sustaining such a loving relationship during this time. On 10 April 1950, my parents were married in a service at Saint.

**My Parents Start Their Journey.**

Michael's Church in Canning—possibly my mother's family's local parish. After the wedding, Angelina moved to the stone house and farm on Caves Road, Margaret River. Up until the wedding, she had been living on the family plot of land in Canning. My father, at this stage, was working at the Cowaramup Mill as the number one bench man, cutting timber from trees that were taken from the virgin bushland surrounding Margaret River. For Angelina, this life was by no means easy. She had moved from a house in Perth to a half-built granite home surrounded by dense bush, 10 km from the nearest town. They had horses and a truck, but it was still difficult for a young wife to travel into town and connect with people.

**Dad with One of the Horse Teams on the Farm in 1950**

She was also living with her in-laws—my father's parents—and Giuseppe, my father's brother. Private time for Mum and Dad was at a premium, and work for her during the day was a mix of home and farm duties.

In 1951, they celebrated the birth of their first child, a boy: Ricardo. Around this time, my mother's family would visit the Margaret River house. During one of these visits, Giuseppe, my father's brother, was introduced to Atilia, my mother 's sister, who would eventually marry Giuseppe and start their family—my extended family. I have included an excerpt in Chapter 3 from another letter between my father and mother that at this meeting and the budding relationship.

In 1952, the second of our clan arrived—this time, a beautiful little girl: Carla. The stone house was starting to get small. With two young children, daily work for both Mum and Dad, being parents, clearing a farm, gardening, cooking, cleaning, and looking after ageing elderly in-law.

By 1952, much of the original 300 acres purchased by Nonno was cleared, and both Carlo and Giuseppe were running dairy cattle, which brought in a little money. Both brothers decided that they would partner in the farm, later to evolve into sharing machinery, labour, and skills across two properties, roughly 650 acres. By this stage, Giuseppe had minimised his outside work and was working on the farm, whilst my father was full-time at the timber mill.

**Dad with Ricardo and Carla in Front of the Stone House.**

In 1952, my mother's family—the Fontanas—moved from Perth to Rosa Glen, southeast of Margaret River. Nonnine purchased a farm and moved the family south to work the land. This was a great relief to my mother, as her family was no longer living five hours away in Perth.

In 1954, with money earned from his work at the mill, my father leased a block of land—Sussex Location 1199—adjacent and west of the original property purchased by Nonno. This property bordered a stretch of coastline that had the Ellensbrook house on it. This is the historical homestead of Ellen and Alfred Bussell, who were the founders of the Augusta–Margaret River–Busselton region. Today, this stretch of land is prized and highly valuable. However, at that time, it was virgin bushland, almost impossible for people to walk through, let alone live on.

This did not deter my parents. They were born to hard work and expect nothing less. They toiled—working their jobs, raising children, and then clearing their new land by hand with hand saw and axe. Some of the wood removed was purchased by the Cowaramup Mill, and some of it was milled by my father and used to build the house that would become my family home.

**The Wooden House—Notice Two Original Chimneys**

I'm still amazed by the ingenuity of people like my father who, with their family, were able to build houses and dwellings with no plans or fancy engineering or architecture—and yet those homes stand the test of time. This weatherboard house made of old jarrah is still standing in its original condition after 70 years. I doubt many houses built today could boast the same endurance.

Well, the rest of the story has already been mentioned. As the farm was cleared and the house expanded, so did our Italian version of the Brady Bunch. Although Ricardo and Carla lived their early adolescence in the stone house with our grandparents, the next run of children got to live in the new house, on the new farm. In 1955, we celebrated the birth of Lina, followed by Annunziata in 57, Francesco in 1960, and then finally me—Stephen.

**L. Annunziata and Lina – R. Me (Stephen) and Francesco.**

A lot of water from 1955 to 1966, when I was born, went under the bridge on the family farm (fattoria di famiglia). I will attempt to fill in as many blanks in the coming chapter titled *Nella fattoria* or *On the Farm*. Our family's story—from Piandelagotti to Perth and from Busselton to the loam soils of Margaret River—, is one of quiet strength. The early years of marriage, the merging of two Italian lineages, the expansion of the farm, and the building of homes by hand… all of it laid the foundation for what we became. As you turn the page, you'll meet the land that shaped us—the farm that fed our bodies, our dreams, and our legacy.

# Chapter 3
# Love Letters (Lettere d'Amore)

*"Le lettere d'amore non si scrivono: si vivono."*

– Jacques Prévert

### "Ti penso ogni giorno..." — I think of you every day...

They weren't just letters. They were lifelines—thin, folded threads that stitched two hearts together across distance, uncertainty, and time. Between 1948 and 1950, as Australia recovered from war and Italian families worked to build new lives, my parents fell in love the only way they could—through words. Carlo was in Margaret River, Angelina in Perth. They wrote in ink what couldn't be spoken in person: love, longing, frustration, humour, respect. And always, hope. These letters are more than memories. They are the foundation stones of our family's story.

### A Long-Distance Beginning (A coincidental beginning)

In the 1920s, both Giuseppe Fontana (Angelina's father) and Giacomo Palandri (Carlo's father) found themselves travelling to Australia in search of work and a better life. After docking in Fremantle, each man, at different times, was given a contact in Busselton, in Western Australia's southwest. There, both were introduced to Amadio Palandri and his wife, Annunziata. Amadio was a cousin to Giacomo, Nonno (my dad's father) and was also born in Piandelagotti, and was the proprietor to the Ship Hotel in Busselton. By coincidence—or perhaps fate —Amadio drew several families from Piandelagotti and Emilio-Romaglia to the Busselton and Margaret River. Among them were three Palandri families, as well as the Zanotti, Piancientini, Zani, Fiori, Fontana and Meleri families. Long before my father met my mother, the ground was being tilled, and the stars were aligning for the eventual introduction.

Theirs was not a love born of convenience or proximity. After meeting at a Christmas party in 1948, hosted by Innes Palandri (daughter of Amadio) in Perth—one of the many unofficial matchmakers of the Italian Australian community—Carlo was invited to attend with his family. A he sparks between Carlo and Angelina ignited slowly, then all at once. Yet there were 270 kilometres between them and no telephone. The only way to nurture that spark was through letters. Travel was difficult; the Palandri family owned only a truck, and the roads between Margaret River and Perth were nearly non-existent, carved through dense bush. After that Christmas party, the chances of Carlo and Angelina meeting again were slim.

The earliest letters, dated early 1949, were careful and formal. My father wrote with a blend of respectful admiration and shy affection:

**"Gentilissima Angelina, ricevo con piacere la tua lettera. Le tue parole mi colpito il cuore…"**

**"Dearest Angelina, I was pleased to receive your letter. Your words touched my heart…"**

Angelina replied in the same reserved, almost poetic tone, always addressing him as, **"Caro Carlo," and often ending with "Con affetto sincero,"**—with sincere affection. Yet beneath the formalities, there was a warmth blooming unmistakably.

### Across the Miles, a Romance Grows

By 1949, their letters revealed growing impatience with the distance. From the initial meeting at the Christmas party in 1948, their relationship deepened through constant correspondence. My father worked long hours at Cowaramup Mill. Angelina balanced factory work with family obligations in Perth. Their lives were busy, but their pens never rested. Angelina wrote about her family in Perth, and their hopes of finding land and work in the Southwest. Letters are referencing Ricardo Angelina's younger brother, and my mother's request for Dad to look after him. My father replied that he was indeed watching over Ricardo, confirming his wellbeing and mentioning frequent meetings. The letters also reference Atilia, my mother's sister, who eventually married Giuseppe—my Uncle Joe and dad's brother. Auntie Rene

(Renata) and Auntie Olga are also mentioned in terms of Olga having a Fiancée and Rene getting married. Some days, Carlo wrote two letters before receiving single reply. Letters alluded to reunite after Easter. Dad talking about repairs on the truck that would allow travel soon after the holiday. In one note from January 1949, he writes:

*"Vorrei che fossi qui, seduta accanto a me.*
*Ogni giorno senza te mi pesa come un anno.*
*Spero che il vento porti presto buone notizie."*

\*"**I wish you were here, sitting beside me. Each day without you feels like a year. I hope the wind brings good news soon.**"

They teased each other gently, too. One letter includes Angelina's complaint that he had forgotten to ask about her sister Atilia—perhaps the first hint of another family story in the making.

— ◆ —

### Letters of Promise and Future

Letters indicate that my father was able to visit Perth just after Easter 1949—a turning point in their relationship. I believe it was the first kiss shared between Carlo and Angelina. I believe it was because Carlo proposed to Angelina in this meeting. I imagine my father dropping to one knee, holding up a ring, and asking for permission to marry my mother.

The language in the letters exude this kind of demonstrative action, they truly loved each other even though they had shared so little time physically together. It is poignant to note that they were married in the Easter of 1950, very close to a year after they were engaged.

This poignant letter dated 26 April 1949, just after the Easter visit marks a milestone in their relationship—the first time Carlo refers to himself as Angelina's fiancé:

"Mi hai dato la risposta più bella del mondo, e posso finalmente chiamarti la mia fidanzata. Ogni giorno sento il nostro legame crescere, anche se la distanza ci separa. Un giorno, tutto questo sarà solo un ricordo dolce."

"You gave me the most beautiful answer in the world, and I can finally call you, my fiancée. Every day I feel our bond growing, even if distance still separates us. One day, all of this will be just a sweet memory."

The letters also hint at my mother getting permission from her father and her brother who was a lot younger than my father. This obviously is a traditional aspect of marriages during this time. Nonnine Giuseppe, my mother's, Father went as far to say that if Carlo is committing then that is good enough for him, a testament to my father's loyalty and integrity. One of the letters also alludes to the fact that they would be unable to see each other for 8 months, meaning Christmas of 1949. Throughout the year 1949, the tone of their correspondence shifts. They begin discussing dreams: building a home, raising children, planting vines, raising animals. In December of that year, Carlo writes:

"Il terreno è duro, ma con te al mio fianco, posso renderlo un giardino."

"The ground is hard, but with you by my side, I can make it a garden."

It's no longer just affection—it's commitment. Plans are being made. Their families were consulted, dates whispered.

### The Final Letter (The Culmination of Love)

From the initial meeting over Christmas in 1948, and many letters numbering over 100 the final letters are the culmination of a true love story. Two souls from the same region and the same town in Italy, manage to meet thousands of miles away from home where they moved to the same State only hundreds of kilometres away from each other. The odds against such a union are unbelievable, yet it happened. This was not an organised marriage that occurred so frequently during this time, this was born from smouldering desire and love everlasting. Carlo quotes in his last letter before they were married "all it took was one smile and one kiss and he was Angelina's." Researching this it was much more amazing: Carlo went to school in Italy until grade 5 and then was required to work on the family property for survival, but the evidence of his writing is amazing, he is quite literate and extremely neat. However, his letters indicate that he could only write in Italian, not English and none of his letters are in English. The first letter shared by Angelina apologises for any mistakes, indicating and stating that she has not written in Italian for quite a while. My father arriving in 1940, by 1950 shows he is still struggling with learning the English language. Despite this he can write hundreds of letters to grow and strengthen this relationship. Throughout the year of writing, we witness traditional and cultural expectations coming through, the need for Father and brother approval, the sharing of photos and fostering the protective, big brother relationship between Ricardo (Moms Brother) and Carlo and the letters to siblings and cousins in Italy. My mother outlines what she describes as getting through the bombardments or temptations away from their relationship, in the long months apart. There is also evidence of gifts being shared between families as a type of dowry for the upcoming nuptials. Overall, the love letters provide the detail to the journey of love that became the origin story of my family. My mother would often say that every night, after all the kids were in bed, that she and dad would hold each other and just dance, reading the letters tells me this was true love and this little story was how it was, a true love for the ages.

One of the last known letters before the wedding, dated late March 1950, is from Angelina:

"Tra poco, tutto cambierà. Non sarò più solo tua corrispondente, ma tua moglie. Ogni parola scritta finora sarà con-
servata nel mio cuore."

**\*"Soon, everything will change. I will no longer be just your correspondent, but your wife. Every word written so far will be kept in my heart."**

Below are excerpts from the final letters exchanged between Angelina and Carlo in the days leading up to their wedding. Each letter stretched over five handwritten pages, filled with heartfelt expressions of longing, love, and hope. After the year began, life together, side by side.

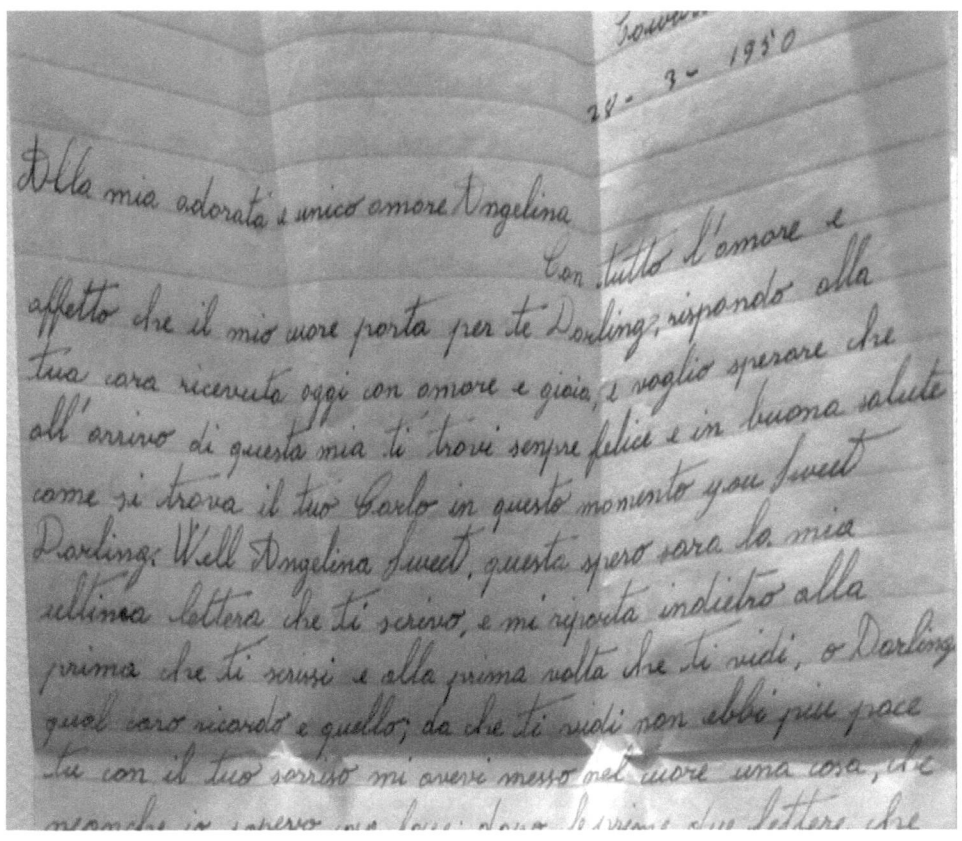

**To My Beloved and Only Love, Angelina,**

With all the love and affection my heart holds for you, Darling, I respond to your dear letter, received today with love and joy. I hope that when this letter reaches you, it finds you happy and in good health, as your Carlo is right now.

Well, Darling, sweet Angelina, this—I hope—will be my last letter I write to you, and I hope to see you before Easter and at the first kiss you give me.

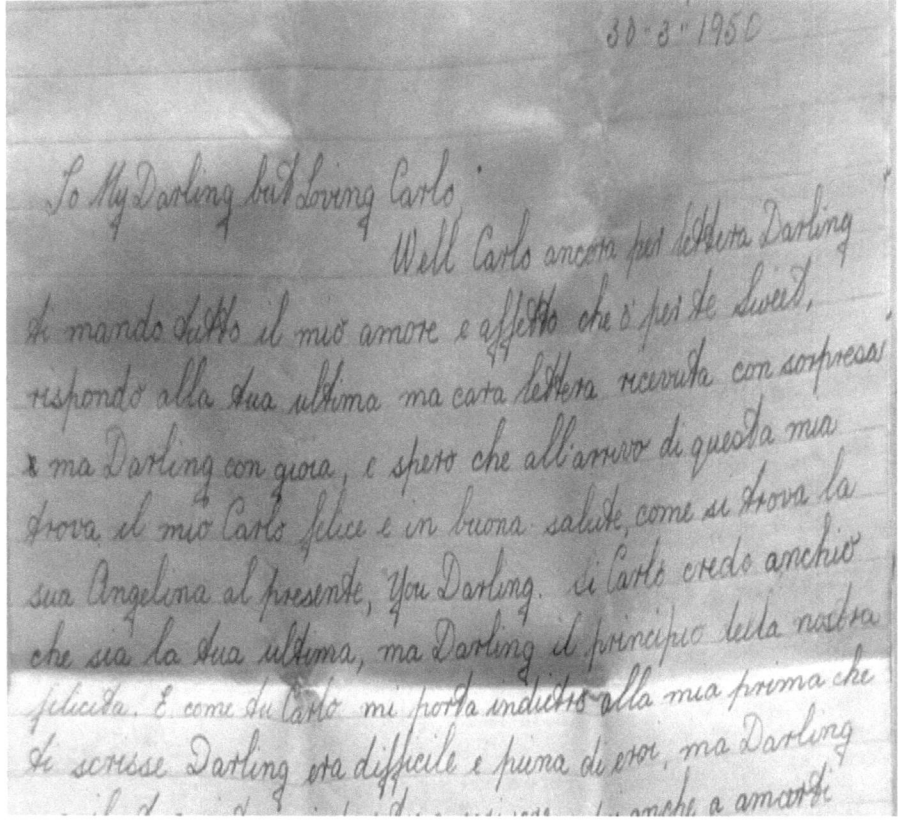

**To My Darling, Kind Loving Carlo**

Well Carlo, once again your fiancée Darling sends you all my love and affection, which is always yours. I'm replying to your last letter, which I received with surprise but joy. I hope that when this letter arrives, my Carlo will be happy and in good health, as I am now, your Angelina. You, Darling, say this will be your last letter, but to me it's the first of the most beautiful. It's as if your letter pushed me back to the moment, I first wrote to you. Darling, it was hard at first, but with your help I learned to write and love you. What you gave me was so difficult—so much love.

# Chapter 4
# Nella fattoria (On the Farm)

*"Chi semina raccoglie."*
*(Who sows, reaps.)*

The land in Margaret River was thick with dark loam and possibility. It didn't greet my parents with softness—it tested them. Beneath towering karri and marri trees, they carved a life from the earth, coaxing a future out of soil that clung to boots and burned in the sun. Carlo and Angelina built their farm with bare hands, borrowed tools, and unwavering hope. There were no instructions, just instinct. No comfort, just commitment. Before the vines, before the fences, before the laughter of six children, there was only hard ground, harder work, and the quiet courage to believe this place could become home.

### Beginnings and Bushland

In my lifetime, the farm wore many faces. When I was little, it was still transforming—shaped by axes, sweat, and stubborn hope. The bush had been cleared of towering jarrah and karri trees, the kind that once shaded this region long before fences arrived. Those trees came down one by one, their absence leaving tracks and roads through what remained of the forest. It was a place constantly evolving: first a dairy, then beef cattle, then sheep, then goats—and then sheep again. Somewhere in between, we even tried a vineyard.

**Early Clearing of Jarrah**

To my siblings and me, this rotation of animals and crops felt like adventure. We didn't see the hardship our parents bore behind it. We knew the mud and the fun of chasing cows and sheep or balancing on fences; we didn't know the weight of failed seasons or leaky roofs.

When Dad passed, we leased the property to another Italian man. He didn't love the land like we did. Over time, it slipped into disrepair, and I could hardly bear to watch.

The sheds crumbled. The fences sagged. Our once-beautiful farm was falling apart, and with it, a piece of our story. That broke my heart.

Eventually, we ended the lease. In the years before the final sale, we allowed an earthmover to mine yellow building sand from the back paddocks. Those same paddocks where we had once buried dead animals—our sheep, cows, a dog or two—also provided us with the clean sand for Christmas trees we'd set up each year, a tradition strangely rooted in loss and renewal.

And sometime during those years, I built a small campsite in the bush. We hardly used it, but I enjoyed the process. It gave me a glimpse—just a glimpse—into how my parents must have felt building everything from nothing.

When the Palandri family arrived in 1940, the land they had bought—along with the second block Carlo leased in the 1950s—was, quite simply, untouched bush: virgin country. There were natural springs scattered across the property and a brook that ran gently through it, named Ellensbrook. It was wild, fertile, and unforgiving.

Clearing the land was gruelling work. There were no tractors or chainsaws then—only crosscut saws and axes. My grandfather (Nonno), my father Carlo, and his brother Giuseppe laboured for years just to clear the original block. Fortunately, Nonno had timber experience. The boys quickly learned sleeper cutting with a broad axe—dangerous, deliberate work. They sold timber to local mills, cutting sleepers directly from the felled trees. Timber came first; farming followed.

Bit by bit, the land began to open. Enough was cleared to build a modest house and plant the first crops. As I've described elsewhere, this was a far cry from their lives in Piandelagotti.

**Dad and Mum in Front of a Big Tree to be Cleared Off the New Block**

There, farming the rocky mountain soil was an act of desperation. Here, in the southwest corner of Western Australia, the land was rich by comparison.

My father told me stories of life back in Italy. There were stretches where they went without meat or any real protein for weeks, sometimes months. They owned just one cow, and she wasn't for eating—she gave them milk, cream, and cheese, and was too valuable to butcher. To survive, they would steal eggs from wild birds' nests. That was protein, resourcefulness born of poverty.

In contrast, here they could raise animals, harvest timber, and make a living. My father excelled in timber milling. He became a highly skilled worker and eventually took a job at the Cowaramup Mill as the lead benchman. But always, the land called him back.

## Milking Time and Mishap

By the early 1950s, the Palandri farm had entered its first true working phase—as a small dairy. A herd of about fifty milking cows grazed the newly cleared land, and it was my uncle and Nonno who managed the dairy side, while my father, Carlo, worked long hours at the mill. With every year, the farm grew: new livestock were introduced—pigs, chickens—and second-hand machinery slowly arrived, but milking was still the central rhythm of the farm.

It was a busy time in my parents' lives. They were newly married, and children were arriving—my older brothers and sisters, one after the other. With funds from Dad's mill job, he was able to lease another 300 acres of untouched land, adjoining the original property and stretching towards what was then called Ellensbrook Beach, now known as Mokidup. And so, the process began again: clearing, fencing, building, and carving a life from the wild.

## Working the Dairy Every Morning at 4 am

That second block was no easier than the first. Jarrah, karri, and marri trees loomed thick and defiant. With no modern bulldozers or chainsaws, my father, mother and uncle once again relied on crosscut saws and axes. It was hard, raw workhands blistered, shirts soaked, days blurred together with the sound of steel meeting wood. But there was pride in it. There always was.

Eventually, my father would cut and mill the timber from that land and build a second Palandri house with his own hands—crafted from thick, aged jarrah. That story, like so many in this chapter, deserves its own telling one day.

To keep both blocks running, my father and uncle formally partnered. They shared machinery, pooled resources, and worked side by side through breakdowns, births, floods, and bad seasons. The dairy remained on the original stone house block for many years, even as the new land began to take shape. Each morning, well before dawn, the whir of engines and the lowing of cows signalled the start of another day. At 4 a.m., the dairy came to life.

On one of those mornings—long before I was even a thought in my parents' mind—something happened that still echoes through family conversations. My eldest brother, Ricardo, was just a boy. The dairy was powered by a sturdy old Briggs & Stratton diesel engine—uncovered, unguarded, and as loud as it was dangerous. There were no safety protocols in those days, certainly no occupational health inspections. Everything ran on common sense, muscle, and routine.

That morning, Ric got too close to the flywheel. In a blur, he was flung hard across the concrete floor and knocked unconscious. Panic followed. In the 1950s, medical care was basic, and distances were great. For days, Ric lay in bed, tended lovingly by our grandparents. By some miracle, he recovered fully—but the story became legend.

According to my siblings, our grandparents never let go of that fear. Ric was the first grandson, the first Palandri child born on Australian soil. From that day on, they doted on him. Some say he got away with murder after that—and maybe he did. What's certain is that the Briggs & Stratton engine became strictly off-limits to everyone who followed. It remained the heartbeat of the dairy, but to us younger siblings, it was more than machinery—it was a reminder.

Of how close everything was to breaking.

**Nonna Always Doted on Ricardo 'The First-Born'**

**The Vege Patch and the Vines**

My father used to speak often—almost wistfully—of how generous the land in Margaret River had been to him. The contrast to his youth in the Apennines could not have been starker. Back in Italy, farming was a brutal endurance. In the 1920s and 30s, the mountainous soil of Piandelagotti yielded little but rock and hardship. The fields were steep, the earth thin and reluctant. There were few machines and even fewer opportunities. Industry had not yet touched those parts, and without capital to invest in livestock or equipment, farming remained a grinding, hand-to-mouth existence.

But here in Australia—this land was different. My father never forgot his awe at how it responded to care. Rich in nutrients, the soil didn't fight him the way the Italian ground once had. And before there were pastures or paddocks, before milking sheds or sheep pens, there was the vegetable patch.

They carved it out early, long before I was born. By the time I came along, the garden was already thriving—sprawling, bountiful, almost a full acre in size. It was the heart of the homestead, a living emblem of independence and survival. Rows of beans, zucchinis, pumpkins, tomatoes, lettuces, potatoes, onions, and carrots—all bursting from the ground with colour and promise. From this single space, the family fed itself, traded with neighbours, and stocked the pantry with jars and preserves to last through winter.

Flanking the patch was a small but diverse orchard. My father and grandfather planted it with care: apricot, pear, and apple trees, alongside fig, peach, and plum. A single almond tree stood like a curiosity—fragile in its early years, but eventually generous. My father even grafted a lemon branch onto an orange tree. Remarkably, it took—and for decades afterwards, we harvested the most curious tart-flavoured oranges from that hybrid. Even after my mother passed and the land was eventually sold, those oranges remained one of the most potent living memories of our family's ingenuity. But the real legend of the garden was the grapevine. It was said that Nonno, on one of his early visits to Australia, smuggled in a cane from a red grape variety used in Italy both for wine and for the table. It wasn't just any grape—it was *Black Russian*.

To this day, I have never encountered its equal in Western Australia. Dark-skinned, full-bodied, sweet and complex, the grapes seemed to hold a flavour of the old world and the new. When I look at the vines I've since propagated at my own home, I feel a direct thread linking back not just to our family but to our ancestral home. Food wasn't only grown; it was gathered. The surrounding bush teemed with wild game—rabbits, kangaroos, and ducks—plentiful and accessible. With a steady hand and a little time, a meal could be taken from the land with a rifle or trap.

Marron swam in the creeks, and fish could be caught with a simple line. For a family that had once resorted to stealing eggs from wild bird nests in Italy, this abundance bordered on miraculous. And with the added income from Dad's job at the mill, they were able to buy more than one cow, giving the household ready access to milk, cream, butter, and—luxury of luxuries—meat. They began to live not just to survive, but to flourish. The farm provided. This patch of earth did more than nourish us. It rooted us. It was proof that life here, however foreign it first seemed, could be cultivated with patience, sweat, and a stubborn belief in tomorrow.

## Wild Meat and Stray Bullets

In the years after the war, Margaret River offered a different kind of abundance. The land gave what it could—if you knew where to look, and how to aim. Kangaroos, wild pigs, rabbits, and bush birds weren't just wildlife—they were food. Hunting was part of life, not sport. For many farming families, it supplemented the larder and, in hard times, ensured there was something on the plate besides bread and preserves.

My father, however, would have been the first to admit that he was a terrible shot.

There's a family story—often retold with chuckles around the table—about one of Dad's early attempts at hunting. It was a rabbit. Not running. Not hiding. Just sitting there, as if offering itself up. He lined it up with his old bolt-action .22 rifle. The first shot missed. So did the second. And the third. Each bullet kicked up a puff of dirt near the rabbit's feet, but the creature didn't budge. Whether it was confused or simply unimpressed by Dad's marksmanship, no one knows. Finally, with the last bullet in the magazine, Dad aimed once more. The shot missed again—this time ricocheting off a stone and straight into the window of a nearby shed, shattering the glass.

My mother was watching. So were my grandfather and Uncle Giuseppe. Laughter echoed through the paddocks. After that, Dad retired the .22 for a

**Zio Giuseppe with Some Rabbits.**

small shotgun—something with a bit more spread and a slightly better chance of hitting something edible.

There's another tale, grimmer but no less legendary. During the early days of building the new house on the second block, a large kangaroo bounded too close to the site. With nothing in his hands but a broad axe and perhaps a misplaced sense of confidence, Dad hurled it at the animal. It struck hard, dropping the kangaroo. He followed quickly to finish what the axe had begun. That night, they ate kangaroo stew—proof that even mistakes could be made useful.

Ricardo, my eldest brother, was more successful with a rifle than our father. As a boy, he took to hunting and fishing with skill and a touch of pride. The stories of his catches—massive fish, rabbits, pigs, and wild fowl—became whispered fables passed between us at birthdays and barbecues. One hunting tale, however, took an unexpected turn.

Ric was targeting practising with the .22, aiming at a makeshift bullseye propped against the old chicken coop. A shot went astray, ricocheted, and hit my sister Carla square in the forehead.

Thankfully, it wasn't a serious wound—more shock than blood—but the event quickly joined the family's list of infamous mishaps. To this day, we joke that Ric was the first (and hopefully only) Palandri sibling to shoot another.

By the time I was old enough to shoulder a rifle, Ricardo had left home. But Francesco, my other brother, often let me tag along on evening hunts. He carried the real rifle. I had a pitiful little air gun—better suited to frightening off birds than taking down game. Still, I treasured those outings. They were part initiation, part education, and completely tied to our identity as bush kids.

Not all our companions were siblings. Just a mile or so down the road lived my cousins—the children of Giuseppe and Atilia. Nine of them in total: Rosa, Lucia, Luigi, Natalia, Elizabetha, Giuseppe, Giacomo, Maria, and Domenico They were our constant playmates and occasional co-conspirators. We didn't think of ourselves as extended family. We were just *family*. The same blood, the same farm dust in our hair, the same scraped knees and shared adventures.

Together, we roamed the bush with reckless enthusiasm. We set traps, followed tracks, argued over who spotted what first. If we returned empty-handed, it didn't matter. The real prize was in the telling—the stories, the laughter, the memory of chasing something wild under the canopy of a karri sky.

And in the middle of it all—me. Stephen. Among the Giuseppes and Giacomos and Domenicos, my name stood out like a misplaced accent. Another quiet marker that something in our migration had shifted. Not just in geography, but in identity. They remained the names of the old country. I was something new. And somehow, that difference—small as it seemed—stayed with me.

— ◆ —

## Hay Season and Flying Bales

The farm brings back so many memories—most of them good, some of them painful, all of them honest. I loved working the land, even when it was hard, even when it left your back sore and your hands raw. What we didn't have in equipment, we made up for in sheer grit. Ours wasn't a polished, modern setup like some of the neighbours had. There were no big shiny machines, no hydraulics to speak of. Just muscle, sun, and steel.

And when it came to hay season, that trio was put to the test.

Hay season always rolled around at the end of spring, when the grass had grown tall and started to grey under the warm sun. Around this time, the first sounds of cricket would begin trickling from the television—a signal of summer's approach. That was my cue. I'd sneak the old hand-push lawn mower out into the paddock behind the house and pace out a pitch, rolling it with hopeful dreams of long summer matches. But that's a story for another chapter.

**Collecting Hay before Machinery.**

Before any of the cutting could begin, there was prep. I'd watch Dad as he worked meticulously on the machinery. The hay mower fascinated me. When parked, its long blade stood upright at the back of the tractor like a scorpion's tail. Once lowered to the ground, it dragged across the paddock like something half-animal, half-machine. Its teeth needed sharpening—one at a time—with a hardened metal file. A slow, deliberate task that required patience and rhythm.

While Dad filed each tooth, we kids were sent off on "stick and rock patrol"—a game with real consequences. If a blade hit a stray branch or hidden stone, it could shear off or bend. So, out we went, six of us, scrambling through the grass, tossing sticks into little piles and hurling rocks as far as we could. We made a game of it, of course competing to see who could throw the furthest, or who could craft the best nickname for their siblings. And yes, sometimes we got hit by flying debris. That was part of it.

Once the field was clear, the mower began its slow dance—up and down, back and forth—until all the grass lay flat, drying in the sun. Then came the rake. This machine had its own magic. Its belts were tightened, its wheels greased, and with every pass, it pulled the cut grass into tidy rows like the lines of a poem waiting to be bound.

And then came the baler. I loved the baler. To me, it was a monster—a glorious, mechanical creature with spiny tines that scooped up the hay and fed it into a chute. Inside, it compressed the dry grass into tight, rectangular bales, then sealed them with twine before spitting them out the back like stubborn parcels. That sliding door on the chute always reminded me of a guillotine. I had visions of being caught in the rollers and vanishing into the machine, never to return. But no one ever did. The baler, for all its menace, did its job well.

Then came the hardest part: collection.

There was no fancy auto-loading mechanism. This was old-school. We walked beside the trailer as Dad drove slowly through the rows, tossing bales up one by one. Sometimes we had enough hands to form a rhythm—one throwing, one stacking, one steering. But often, it was just one or two of us—and in those moments, the tractor would move forward on its own, chugging along in low gear like a sleepy ox.

We built towers—wobbly, leaning stacks of bales ten or twelve high. The goal was always to get as many as possible in one trip. And inevitably, the stack would sway, teeter, and topple. I still remember one spectacular fall—thirty bales hitting the ground like a soft explosion. We laughed; Dad didn't. We had to load them all over again.

At the hayshed, a new ritual began. Stacking became a game of giant Jenga, angled to reduce the risk of spontaneous combustion from trapped moisture. Some of the previous season's bales had rotted, and rats had made homes inside them. Dodging them became part of the fun. But the shed was also a playground. Between real work, we built forts and imagined battles, the bales our castle walls and shields.

Our uncles were always nearby encouraging us with clipped phrases, some in Italian, others in stern glances. Even when the work was heavy, they had a way of nudging us forward without saying much. We got the job done. And, if everything went well, it was always done just in time for the Margaret River Show. That was the real milestone. If the hay was stacked before the fair, we knew we had earned the chance to celebrate.

### Fencing and Flying Steel

Fencing wasn't just a job—it was a never-ending part of life on the farm. Storms would bring down trees across the wire, cattle would lean or break through weak spots, and rooms and rabbits did their share of damage too. Whether it was fixing a collapsed section or building a new run from scratch, fencing was a constant. The cycle never stopped.

Before copper logs came into use, making fence posts meant harvesting our own jarrah. It was laborious, dangerous, and exhausting—but oddly satisfying.

My brother and I would head out with the chainsaw in tow and find a jarrah tree with a clean, straight trunk. Once selected, we'd debranch and bark the tree, using the squared edge of an axe to strike at the bark, then the sharp side to peel it away.

With the trunk cleaned, we'd measure and cut the lengths needed for posts. Splitting was done the old way—with steel splitting wedges, or "billits". We'd find a natural crack and set a wedge at each end, driving them in with sledgehammers until the timber split along its grain. It took strength, rhythm, and a bit of luck. On a good day, we might split up to a hundred posts—though that was rare. The work was hot, hard, and full of risk. Snakes in the undergrowth, sharp tools, unpredictable terrain, and machinery that could turn on you in an instant.

One day, while my brother was felling a tree, the chainsaw blade snapped mid-cut. It whipped around, slicing into his leg just above the knee. It was a deep gash—nasty and bleeding—but he managed to climb onto the tractor and get himself home. He refused stitches, of course. Just bandaged it up, muttered something about being fine, and got on with it. That was the way things were.

Years later, when our jarrah supply was all but gone—thanks in part to the nearby timber mills and our own post-splitting efforts—we had to look elsewhere. Rosa Brook, to be exact. That's where one of our uncles lived, a man famous in the family for his string of farm accidents. But it was also where we learned a new way of making posts—one that felt part invention, part insanity.

When we arrived, the logs were already cut and barked, stacked neatly in a pile. My uncle stood over them with a glint in his eye and what looked like a metal cylinder in his hand—a kind of giant bullet, with a fuse sticking out the end. It turned out to be a homemade blasting device.

He carefully measured out gunpowder, packed the explosive, and hammered it into the centre of a log. We watched, barely breathing. Then he lit the fuse—and everyone ran. The explosion echoed through the bush, splinters raining down like wooden confetti. The first attempt? Too much powder. The log was obliterated.

But after a few more trials—and slightly less dramatic blasts—we found the right measure. It wasn't as neat or satisfying as hand-splitting, but it worked. The posts were rough, sure, but a fencepost's a fencepost.

Whether it was axe, wedge, chainsaw, or gunpowder, fencing was a rite of passage. It wasn't just about holding in stock—it held together the rhythm of life on the farm. We sweated, bled, and laughed through it all.

## Vehicles

On the farm, learning to drive didn't begin with cars—it began with tractors. Like so many farm kids, our first experience behind the wheel wasn't on asphalt, but bouncing along paddocks with the roar of a diesel engine in our ears and our father's arms around us.

Our tractors were old and unforgiving—no power steering, no padded seats, just steel, rubber, and a gear system arranged in a basic "H" formation: three forward gears, one reverse. The clutch was on the left, the brake on the right. The brake pedals were split into two—joined by a lever most of the time—so you could lock one rear wheel to pivot sharply if needed. These were not forgiving machines, but they taught us resilience.

We all learned the same way—sitting on Dad's lap as he guided the steering wheel, his rough hands over ours. He'd talk us through the gear changes, the clutch control, and how to feather the brake without stalling. It was overwhelming at first. At five years old, the driver's seat felt like the command chair of the Starship Enterprise, surrounded by levers, gears, and mysteries. But slowly, the mystery turned into muscle memory.

As we grew more confident, Dad would step back, letting us steer unassisted across open paddocks, usually while feeding out hay to the cows. There were no second chances when it came to precision: he'd bark instructions like, "Back it up to the slasher!" or "Line it up with the trailer!" That meant reversing with exact accuracy, lining up the tractor's tow bar with the hitch—two holes, no more than fifty millimetres apart—so a steel pin could drop through. We had to nail it or try again, and again.

Eventually, we graduated to handling it on our own. Hook up the ploughing discs. Feed the cows. Chain the harrows. Each task layered responsibility on top of experience.

**Francesco Driving the Old Fiat Tractor**

Of course, there were mishaps. One day, my older brother was told to park the tractor in the shed. He underestimated the turning radius, slammed into a support beam, and brought the entire shed down—right on top of the tractor. I laughed until my sides ached. Dad didn't laugh. What came out of his mouth was all in Italian, and not the kind you'd learn in school. That accident cost us a week of repair work.

When hay season arrived, reversing a trailer loaded with bales into the hayshed became a rite of passage. My sisters often had this duty, though they weren't thrilled about it. Reversing a long trailer into a narrow paddock isn't easy at the best of times, let alone with Dad yelling from a distance, his hands flying in the air. When a bale stack was knocked over, the shouting got louder. But those moments—all tension and comedy—became part of the lore.

I passed these lessons on to my own children. One day, I sat my son on my lap and let him steer the tractor over a line of small trees we were clearing. To his delight, we flattened them. It was exactly what we'd intended, but the thrill in his eyes told me everything. He still talks about it—the day he drove the old Fiat tractor for the first time. The same way I still remember mine.

Eventually, we moved on to driving cars, graduating from tractor seats to rusted-out utility vehicles. Our first car was a relic—a 1940s Hillman Hunter ute we called *Cuppatanni*, named after the old man who gave it to us. It looked and felt like a Sherman tank: steel everything, razor-thin tyres, and a stubborn engine that rarely started. We had to leave it parked on a slope just to roll-start it. When even that failed, we used the tractor to tow it back uphill.

The Hillman got worse over time. At one point, the brakes completely gave out. Our solution? We'd coast it to a stop by bumping into a tree or a fence post. Once, a girlfriend of mine was behind the wheel. When the brakes failed, she simply steered it gently into a tree. No damage—the car never got up enough speed to make a dent—and the bumper, made of solid chrome steel, didn't even flinch. She was shaken. I was amused. It became one of those "welcome to farm life" moments that neither of us ever forgot.

Learning to drive this way wasn't just about machinery. It was about learning judgement, patience, improvisation, and resilience. We weren't handed the keys; we earned them—with diesel on our hands, sunburn on our arms, and a few bruises for good measure.

## **Clearing**

Farm life was never just endless work—though there was certainly plenty of it. Amid the routine and responsibility, we often found ways to turn even the toughest jobs into something fun, something shared. Clearing the land was one of those jobs. It had started decades earlier with my parents, grandparents, Zio Giuseppe and Zia Atilia, when they first turned the virgin bush into arable farmland. But that transformation was never final. The land had a way of creeping back—regenerating, reclaiming—and so, the battle to keep it clear became ongoing.

Fortunately, we had the manpower. With so many siblings and cousins, the job of tidying the paddocks—especially after slashing or bulldozing—often turned into a group effort. We'd scatter across the fields, picking up sticks and stones the machines had missed. Larger trees, once pushed over, were piled high for burning. The rest—branches, roots, stray rocks—were gathered by hand. Naturally, the work sparked a bit of competition. Banter flew freely, as did the occasional stick or small stone.

One day, I remember Francesco trading jabs with Lina in the paddock. It was a hot, dusty afternoon. We were all dragging ourselves through the field, half working, half arguing. In the midst of it, Francesco tossed a stick with more force than necessary. It struck Lina squarely. He's always claimed it was an accident—just poor aim—but Lina never let him forget it. To this day, she swears he threw it in anger. Whether it was clumsy or calculated didn't really matter. It became part of family folklore.

Clearing wasn't limited to paddocks. One of the biggest battles was with the grass trees—thousands of them—sprawling across a large section of our property. They were beautiful in their own way, but for farming, they were a nightmare. Hiring a bulldozer was too expensive, so we did what we always did—we used what we had: ourselves.

This campaign, oddly enough, was led by Mum. She had what can only be described as a vendetta against those trees. She approached the job with a relentless determination that was both inspiring and slightly alarming. Day after day, she'd go out with a steel bar and a can of diesel. The method was unconventional but effective—she'd pierce the heart of the grass tree and pour diesel into the opening. It sounded like nonsense, but somehow it worked. The trees would die off slowly, one by one.

When we were around, Mum would rope us in. Together, we cleared acre after acre. In the end, she managed to wipe out nearly 50 acres' worth of grass trees—an incredible feat, especially given the crude method and sheer number of them. Sometimes, I think about how much those grass trees would fetch today at nurseries—thousands of dollars apiece. We could have been millionaires if we'd only thought to dig them up and sell them. But hindsight doesn't build a farm.

As the cooler months approached, another seasonal task took priority: preparing the property against fire. We all feared the bushfires that could erupt with a single spark—lightning, a cigarette tossed from a car, or a careless match. Every year, both our families—Palandri and Fontana—armed themselves with lengths of pipe filled with diesel and a wick tucked into one end. We'd walk the boundary lines of the farm, lighting controlled burns along the roadside and fence lines. The aim was simple: eliminate the fuel before summer could.

It was dangerous work, but also exciting. The tractors stood ready, each fitted with makeshift firefighting units—usually a water tank and pump. Everyone had a job. The neighbours knew the routine too, often coordinating their burns with ours. We watched the flames closely, alert for signs of trouble. Sometimes, we'd gather to burn off noxious weeds or bushes that cattle wouldn't touch. The smoke hung thick in the air, and our faces were streaked with soot. But it was a rite of passage. We were protecting the land.

For young boys, the thrill of wielding fire—even in a controlled way—was hard to resist. We lit up patches like little gods, walking the edge between danger and duty. Remarkably, none of us grew up to be arsonists. Fire, for us, was never about destruction. It was about stewardship—managing the land, guarding it against worse flames.

Clearing, burning, and battling grass trees— these weren't just chores. They were how we came to know the land. Every stick we gathered, every firebreak we lit, every stubborn grass tree we killed—it all built a deeper bond. We weren't just kids on a farm. We were part of the farm. The land shaped us, just as surely as we tried to shape it.

### Cattle, Castration, and Sibling Scraps

Certain times of the year brought with them jobs that were both essential and unforgettable. One of the most memorable—and brutal—was cattle sorting. Shortly after calving season, we'd have to separate the young calves into bullies (young males) and heifers (young females). Because we were raising beef cattle, we didn't want too many uncastrated bullies growing up and impregnating the heifers, which would disrupt our carefully timed breeding cycles and the herd's overall health.

So, we sorted, and we castrated. The method was called elastration—a simple but harsh process that involved wrapping a tight rubber ring around the scrotum of each young male calf. This cut off the blood supply, and within weeks, the scrotum would drop off. The testicles died and the calf became a steer. It sounds cruel, but it was common practice at the time.

Once we had herded the calves into the stockyards, we'd begin the selection. Bullies on one side, heifers on the other. Then came the wrestling match. My brothers and I—brimming with energy and pride—would throw we into the pen, tackling the young bullies to the ground, holding them firmly in place until Dad arrived with the elastrator. It was dangerous, sweaty work, but we loved it.

It was one of the few times we got to show off our strength and coordination in front of the grown-ups. In fact, we often joked that our toughness on the football field was forged right there in the cattle yards, face-down in manure, grappling with calves. Sheep work brought similar challenges, if not the same glory. We weren't shearers—none of us had that skill—but we could still chase, catch, and corral them. The sheep were slower than calves but twice as stubborn. They never went where you wanted them to, so it became a game of speed and cunning to outwit them and steer them into place.

We also kept a single dairy cow for household milk, cream, cheese, and butter. That cow fell under the care of my sister Annunziata, who, to this day, tells the story of how she became a track athlete thanks to that very cow. This was no docile house cow—she had a horn that curled forward into her own forehead and a wild streak to match. More than once, Annunziata was seen sprinting across the paddocks, the angry cow hot on her heels. She would later credit those sprints for her prowess on the netball court and in school athletics. "It was either run fast or get gored," she'd laugh. Every animal on that farm had its story. And every story added a bit more grit—and a few more scars—to our lives.

**Cows in the Yard Ready for Some Work**

## The Mill and the Magnificence of Timber

Tucked away on the farm was a relic of our family's early days—a small spot mill built long before I was born. It was never used commercially like the Ryan Mill where Dad worked, but it was there for when we needed to mill our own timber be it for sheds, fences, or the extensions to our home.

Whenever we fired it up, it became a full family affair.

The mill was powered by the tractor's PTO drive. A massive 30-metre-long belt connected the tractor's flywheel to the mill's own pulley system, driving the enormous 62-inch saw blade. It wasn't a machine you used lightly. That blade was terrifying—razor sharp and loud as thunder. In all my years on the farm, I only saw the mill run once or twice, but each time was unforgettable.

Dad and Uncle Giuseppe would take the lead, benching and tailing out the sawn timber. The older kids had their own jobs—stripping bark from the logs, positioning timber on the sleds, or stacking the final cuts. The scrap wood was set aside, destined for firewood piles. As the youngest, I had one of the most tedious—and fascinating—jobs: cleaning out underneath the mill, where sawdust clogged the workings.

I'd crawl beneath the structure when the saw was quiet, scooping out wet, matted piles of fine dust. It wasn't glamorous, but I didn't mind. The cool dampness under the mill was a world of its own. Frogs lived in the sawdust piles, and I'd often pause my work to play with them—mud-covered hands exchanging scoops of sawdust for amphibious amusement.

But even in rest, the mill was dangerous. The teeth of that blade, freshly sharpened, could tear flesh from bone with the lightest graze. I learned this the hard way—bumping into one of the teeth and slicing my hand open. There were no stitches, just a bandage and the kind of silence that comes from knowing you should have been more careful.

Despite the risks, the mill held a certain magic. Watching my father wrestle giant logs into place, hearing the thunder of wood meeting steel, seeing rough bark transformed into perfect planks—it was awe-inspiring. It showed us just how skilled he truly was. His strength and mastery of timber were renowned throughout the Southwest. But to me, it was more than a trade. It was a legacy—a craft handed down from his own father, born in the Apennines, refined in the forests of Western Australia. And on those rare days when the spot mill roared to life, that legacy echoed loud and proud across the farm.

## The Vineyard Dreams

From as early as I can remember, there was always wine on the table. Not in a ceremonial sense or just for special occasions—wine was part of life, as ordinary as bread and water. My father, Carlo, would pour it into a tumbler without thought, drinking it as others might sip water or tea. Rough red, Chianti in the straw-covered bottle, or even the odd flagon of local brew—it didn't matter much. There was always a bottle within reach, and always a story swirling inside the glass.

He had learned to love wine back in Italy, where times were often hard, but the family always managed a few rows of grapes. He and his brother, Giuseppe—my Zio—used to laugh when they recalled their first attempt at making wine as teenagers, claiming it was better than anything they could buy in Australia. It was probably bravado, but there was truth behind the jest. They knew how to coax something meaningful from the earth.

There was, of course, a darker side. I believe my father's attachment to wine—and to cigarettes—was rooted in the scarcities of wartime. When luxuries were rare, anything that gave comfort became precious.

It's likely that these habits, formed in youth and carried across oceans, contributed to his health declining later in life. Still, for him, wine wasn't just a drink—it was tradition, survival, and memory in liquid form. He even had the peculiar custom of pouring a splash of wine into his morning coffee, substituting it for milk. Strong stuff too closer to moonshine than table wine.

He would sometimes order Chianti from The Re Store in Perth, delivered by train to Margaret River. I still recall the excitement of driving to the railway shed to collect the wooden box. At other times, he sourced wine locally rough reds sold in flagons by backyard winemakers, often other Italians. But my father didn't just want to drink wine. He wanted to make it. Properly. Proudly. It was a dream he nurtured over decades. Even while working long hours in the timber industry, he never let go of that vision.

He and Zio Giuseppe dabbled—brewing ginger beer, hop beer, even trying their hand at spirits. The old stone house we lived in had a vast underground cellar, and we later learned it had been used during the war years for clandestine alcohol production, likely when such things were frowned upon—or banned outright.

By the mid-1970s, things began to shift. Uncle Giuseppe left the timber industry and began working casually at vineyards like Vasse Felix. The cellar stonework at Vasse Felix, in fact, is still whispered to be Palandri handiwork. Zio picked up vineyard work, and his interest in wine deepened alongside the vines.

Meanwhile, my father took on occasional tasks with the early Cape Mentelle vineyard and got to know the owners. I remember him taking Frank and me there to clear Double Gs'—those wicked, spiked weeds—from the soil before the first vines were planted. It wasn't glamorous work, but we were preparing the land, unknowingly laying the groundwork for one of the great vineyards of the region.

Before Vasse Felix or Cape Mentelle hit their stride, Dad and Zio even worked with another Italian, Mr Meleri, to produce a rough wine that was commercially sold.

It didn't have the refinement of Margaret River's future icons, but it was wine nonetheless—and theirs.

Before Vasse Felix or Cape Mentelle hit their stride, Dad and Zio even worked with another Italian, Mr Meleri, to produce a rough wine that was commercially sold. It didn't have the refinement of Margaret River's future icons, but it was wine nonetheless—and theirs.

Eventually, they decided to plant their own acre of vines, just beside the stone house. An acre doesn't sound like much until you realise it requires 500 posts—and back then, there were no treated copper logs or pre-cut timber.

So, we did it the old-fashioned way. We found Jarrah, we split the logs ourselves, and we shaped every single post. The land provided the material, and we provided the sweat.

Post holes were dug with a second-hand auger bolted to the tractor. It struggled against rocks and stubborn soil, but it got the job done. We planted the posts by hand, one by one—backbreaking work, made lighter by the number of hands.

With ten to fifteen of us—cousins, siblings, friends—it didn't take long. We strung wire, set up rows, and planted the canes. For two years, the vines did little more than stretch toward the sky. But by the third year, tight, black clusters of Cabernet Sauvignon grapes began to appear.

Our first vintage was a joyous mess. We harvested with secateurs and buckets, trudging through the rows, cutting and collecting. Uncle Giuseppe drove the tractor. Dad and the older boys heaved the buckets into the vats. And when it came time to crush the grapes, there were no machines—just our feet.

We rolled up our pants, climbed in, and stomped with laughter until our legs were stained purple and the juice frothed around our ankles. The must—juice and skins—went into an old concrete tank for fermentation. It wasn't elegant, but it worked. I remember someone warning us about the toxic gases in the tank, how a single slip into the fermenting vat could be fatal.

We didn't take it too seriously. We were kids. We were too busy trying to catch the steady drip from the tank's underside—sitting there for hours, mouths open. One day, Zio caught us half-drunk, wide-eyed and wobbly. We didn't try that again.

The wine was rough, sure, but it was ours. That single acre produced up to four tonnes of grapes annually—around 2,500 bottles. As time passed, we upgraded: a proper grape press, a rudimentary filtration system, small modern touches to an otherwise rustic operation. The concrete tank remained—it was part of our story.

My father had planned to expand the vineyard to a second property. But he passed before that dream became real. After Mum died, we eventually sold the farm. Today, 60% of that land is under vines, with a sleek wine facility rising beside the old wooden house, built from the granite beneath our feet.

That land never stopped giving. Grapes, timber, shelter, and hope. It gave us wine. It gave us each other. And in its way, it gave us everything.

# Chapter 5
# Festa e Fede (Feast and Faith)

*"A tavola non si invecchia mai."*
*(At the table, one never grows old.)*

Before there were calendars or clocks to guide our days, there were feasts and faith. The rhythm of our family life beat in time with the church bells of Margaret River and the scent of simmering sauce in the kitchen. Every sacred ritual had its secular twin: baptism followed by biscotti, Easter mass followed by lamb on the spit, rosary beads beside ricotta. For us, food and faith weren't separate—they were braided into one another, as tightly woven as the strands of Mum's fresh pasta. To be Italian was to eat with devotion and pray with appetite. And in the heart of our home, both were done with joy, reverence, and the occasional splash of wine.

## Mangiare (Eating)

They say that love is best served warm—and in our family, it was almost always served with fresh bread, pasta, or polenta. The kitchen was the heart of our home, and my mother, Angelina, was its beating pulse. Long before I knew words like "umami" or "al dente," I knew the smell of her ragù simmering on the stove, the crackle of hot oil in the pan, and the unmistakable comfort of walking through the door after school to the scent of bread just pulled from the oven. That smell didn't just mean food—it meant we were home.

As mentioned in earlier chapters, my mother was a remarkable cook. She didn't rely on recipes or precision; she relied on heart, instinct, and memory—particularly the memory of Emilia-Romagna, the region of her birth. Though she only spent the first five years of her life in Piandelagotti, a tiny mountain hamlet, those years shaped a culinary foundation that would last her a lifetime. I can imagine her as a little girl, following closely behind her mother, Maria Fontana (née Lunardi), as they moved through the kitchen of the Albergo Alpino guesthouse. Watching, listening, absorbing. It was there that Mum must have inherited the essence of her region's cuisine—a rich, earthy, deeply Italian way of cooking.

Emilia-Romagna is a food-lover's paradise. Its legacy is written in meats—prosciutto, pancetta, coppa, mortadella, salami. It's the birthplace of iconic pasta: lasagne, tortellini, tagliatelle—all made with eggs and flour, hand-rolled to perfection. It reveres its grains too—risotto and polenta are staples. And of course, no food from the region would be complete without a generous grating of Parmigiano Reggiano—the king of cheeses, aged and sharp, a crown jewel on any dish. Even the breads—gnocco fritto, crescentina—held stories, as did the desserts, like zuppa inglese, that curious Italian cousin of the English trifle, rich with custard, cake, and a good splash of Marsala wine.

Despite all this richness, my father ate like a bird. His favourite meal? Aglio e olio—simple spaghetti tossed in olive oil, garlic, a sprinkle of parsley and pepper, and a final flourish of Parmigiano. That was it. He was not one for fuss. But Mum, never disheartened by his simplicity, continued to cook with heart. Her spaghetti Bolognese, carbonara, and pasta e fagioli were each a triumph of flavour, texture, and tradition. Her Bolognese ragù was classic provincial fare—slow-cooked meat, tomatoes, rosemary, garlic, and parmesan—heart and soul-warming.

If there was a signature to my mother's cooking, it was her bread. She baked crusty loaves twice a week, and we children could set our clocks by the scent wafting from the oven. That smell was magnetic. It drew us in from the schoolyard, drew in neighbours and extended family too. Without fail, people would "just happen" to drop in as the bread came out of the oven. Mum would act surprised—maybe even a bit annoyed—but I suspect she secretly loved it. She thrived on the joy of others. Soon she began making extra loaves on baking days—four or five at a time—to account for the unofficial visitors.

Dinner in our household was something to behold. Mum would set the table with pasta, lasagne, risotto, and one of my favourites—polenta. There was nothing fancy about it. She made it the traditional way, slowly stirred, thickened just right, and stirred through with Parmigiano. She would then spread it out over a large cutting board, ladle on a beef and tomato sauce infused with herbs and top it with another layer of cheese. Then came the real fun—forks in hand, we children would gather around the board, each with our own technique. Some carved out tidy squares, others launched chaotic trails into the golden field. I was the youngest, so I was usually outpaced by my older siblings, but it didn't matter.

The experience—the noise, the clatter, the laughter—was nourishment of its own. Mum's food did more than fill our stomachs; it bound us together. During Lent, particularly on Fridays, our meals took a more austere turn. No meat. If there wasn't fish, there was riso al latte—a soup of milk and rice, warm and creamy like a savoury porridge. I hated it.

Still do, truth be told. But tradition was tradition, and Mum was firm—we had to finish our soup before we earned dessert. Annunziata, my older sister, often accuses me of being spoiled as the youngest, yet somehow, she always ended up with fried chips while the rest of us choked down the rice soup. Go figure.

On other Fridays, we were treated to crescentina—small puffs of fried dough, golden and hollow. We'd fill them with whatever we had: jam, cheese, or even a swipe of Vegemite. These weren't confined to Fridays either. We'd have them for breakfast, lunch, or snacks. Sometimes we'd eat them plain. They were quick, satisfying, and stretched the family budget without sacrificing taste.

Then there were the tortellini in brodo—a dish that defines love and labour in our family. Tiny parcels filled with meat, cheese, herbs—folded one by one by Mum's strong hands. Making them was an epic event, reserved for holidays or extended family gatherings. For my 21st birthday, Mum spent the entire day preparing them. She rolled the pasta until it was nearly translucent, cooked and seasoned the filling, then folded hundreds—perhaps thousands—of tortellini with the precision of a jeweller. It was a gift, not just of food, but of time and care and tradition passed on.

Another favourite was cotoletta di manzo—beef cutlets pounded thin, dipped in flour, then egg, then breadcrumbs mixed with parmesan and parsley, and fried in olive oil until golden. They were a crowd-pleaser, appearing at nearly every celebration. Crunchy, savoury, and gone in seconds.

While Italian food was our foundation, we were also farmers in Western Australia, raising beef cattle on our land. Every few months, we'd slaughter a cow, and the meat would be divided into steaks, sausages, roasts—and offal. Liver, kidneys, tripe, brains—Dad loved it all. The rest of us, not so much. While we tucked into barbecued sausages or steak with chips and salad, he'd eat lamb's fry or calves' brains with relish. I never understood the appeal, but it was one of his few indulgences, so we let him enjoy it in peace.

Mum wasn't rigid. She adapted to our Australian surroundings. One of her "fusion" dishes was a beef curry—not an Indian curry, but a stew flavoured with Keen's Curry Powder, full of potatoes, carrots, and onions. It became a regular part of our table, a symbol of how Mum allowed her traditional Italian roots to evolve in this new land.

Fish was another pillar of our diet. In a later chapter, I'll tell the stories of our wild fishing trips but suffice it to say our catches became regular meals. Herring and skipjack trevally were the usual bounty. Mum would clean and scale them, flour and season them with salt and pepper, then fry them in olive oil until crisp. When we brought home larger prizes—shark, blue groper, or the occasional octopus—Mum treated them like royalty. She'd stuff the fish with tomato, rosemary, and seasonings, bake them until flaky and golden. These meals felt like events.

Mum's food was never just about sustenance. It was a living bridge between two worlds—Italy and Australia, past and present. Each dish told a story: of her childhood, of our family, of the journey from hardship to abundance. Her cooking taught us not just how to eat, but how to live with generosity, with warmth, and with pride in who we were.

In our home, mangiare—eating—wasn't a routine. It was a ritual. It was faith, love, identity, and connection, served fresh every day, and always warm.

## Colazione (Breakfast)

If dinner was where our family came together in joy, then breakfast was where the day began—with fire, ritual, and the smell of toast thick with butter. In the last chapter, I wrote of Mum's unmatched gift for feeding not just our stomachs, but our souls. But it was in the earliest hours of the day—when the sun had yet to rise, and the farm was still cloaked in dew—that her quiet magic truly came alive.

Breakfast in our home was never a rushed affair, even when the world outside was already stirring with cows to be milked and children to be readied for school. Somehow, no matter how early we rose or how cold the air bit at our feet, the kitchen was always warm. The heart of that warmth was the hulking Metters No. 3 stove, standing like a black-iron sentinel in the corner of the room, fed by fire and love.

**The Metters No 3 in the Farmhouse**

Mum would wake before first light, often moving like a ghost in the half-dark, her slippers padding across the lino floor. She'd prepare the firewood the night before—split with care, chosen not just for heat but for burn time—and start the morning by splashing a bit of diesel onto the kindling before tossing in a match from a safe distance. Most days, it caught with a satisfying whoompf. Other times, it erupted like thunder, shaking the walls and leaving a cloud of soot on the ceiling. We'd come running to find Mum casually wiping her hands on her apron, utterly unbothered. That was her way. Practical. Unflinching. Unshakable.

By the time we dragged ourselves from our beds, the kitchen was already glowing with golden heat. My cup of milky sweet coffee—rich, creamy, comforting—waited for me on the stove's ledge. But the real magic was in the toast. This wasn't store-bought sliced bread charred in a pop-up toaster. This was homemade Italian bread, cut thick with a knife, then placed directly into the open oven or laid across the hot stovetop until the lard or butter soaked through and crisped the surface into something between a toast and a shallow fry. The smell alone could drag you from sleep.

I'd sit down, plant my feet on the open oven door, and begin my morning ritual: coffee, toast, fire, and Mum—the four elements of a childhood breakfast.

Mum baked bread every second day, never failing. She worked without a timer or recipe book, just instinct and memory. She'd knead the dough with both hands, folding it with strength and grace, then let it rise in large bowls covered with clean tea towels. When the loaves came out of the oven, crusty and steaming, we'd tear into one before it had a chance to cool—scalding our fingers, smearing them with melting butter, devouring it like a feast.

By then, the smell had drifted beyond our walls. Brothers, neighbours, cousins—anyone within a whiff of the rising steam—seemed to appear. Mum would sigh and shake her head, but the glint in her eye gave her away. She lived for this. Feeding people was her way of loving them.

In the early years, Mum churned butter by hand from our own cows' cream, adding just enough salt. Spread over hot bread, it needed no accompaniment. That alone could be breakfast, lunch, or dinner.

Our dairy farm was modest—about sixty cows—but to us, it was a kingdom. Every morning, before school or church or chores, the cows had to be milked. We used an early automated system powered by a Briggs and Stratton diesel engine, which clattered and hummed with a life of its own. But behind that sound lived a darker memory—one that became part of our family's folklore.

Before I was born, my older brother Ricardo had gotten too close to the spinning belt wheel. His clothes caught, and he was thrown hard against the stone floor. He was unconscious for days. It was a terrifying time, and it changed the way we viewed the machine. From then on, there was one unbreakable rule: no child near the engine while it was running. These were the days before workplace safety regulations—we learned by consequence.

But even with its risks, the dairy gave us the most incredible ingredients: fresh milk, thick cream, hand-churned butter, soft cheese. The food that came from our cows felt alive, and it fed us in ways supermarkets never could.

Sometimes, after the early morning milking, we'd stay out at the mungitura capannone—the old milking shed—for breakfast. There, we turned work into celebration. An old copper fireplace, usually reserved for sauces or passata, became our breakfast stove. We'd remove the copper pot and replace it with a massive 60-inch toothless saw blade that sat perfectly over the fire.

It became our grill.

## Coffee and Colazione at the Dairy

We'd cook eggs in foil, thrown right into the flames. Coffee was brewed in an ancient moka pot, its black handle singed from years of use. Cream was warmed in jugs, and bread, again slathered in lard or butter, was toasted until golden and crisp. Bacon, cut thick from the slab hanging in our curing shed, sizzled until its fat danced. Cheese, still aging in the pantry, was sliced and served with everything. That breakfast, shared among brothers and neighbours before dawn, felt like a feast stolen from kings. Back inside, there were days when breakfast looked more "normal"—Weet-Bix, cornflakes, porridge—but never dull. Even those were transformed by the presence of cream from our cows or jam from our own preserves. On special mornings, Mum would fry homemade sausages, made using a recipe from our ancestral home in Emilia-Romagna, flavoured with garlic, rosemary, and a hint of spice. These sausages weren't just food—they were heirlooms.

That same day, she would salt and cure bacon, stacking it in the cool room, ready for future breakfasts. It was never wasteful, always intentional.

Now, there are those who say Ricardo, after his accident, was the most spoiled of all the siblings—even more than me, the youngest. And they may be right. I still remember waking up late one morning, still in my pyjamas, and finding that Mum had cooked him a full steak and two eggs for breakfast. No one else got that kind of royal treatment—not even Dad. Maybe it was pity. Maybe it was love. Or maybe it was just Mum's way of quietly making things right.

Then came the treats—the bombolini, small fried doughnuts rolled in sugar while still hot. We'd queue like beggars in our own kitchen, hoping for seconds. On other days, she made crescentina, a kind of fried provincial bread that puffed like an Indian poori. We'd fill it with jam, drizzle it with syrup, or—sacrilege to some—spread it with vegemite. It was humble, yet it felt like a holiday.

Modern nutritionists might faint at the idea of our breakfasts—fried lard toast, thick bacon, sweet doughnuts—but we were farm kids. We ran, lifted, chased, hauled, and climbed all day. Calories weren't a problem. And nothing we ate came from a packet. Nothing was wasted. Everything was made by hand.

If I had to name a single breakfast moment that stayed with me forever, it would be this: one day, my father quietly offered me cipollotto e aceto d'olio—a spring onion, dipped into olive oil and balsamic vinegar. That was it. No toast. No eggs. Just that. It was sharp and earthy, vibrant and old. A peasant's breakfast. A memory from his boyhood in Italy. That bite of onion was more than food. It was a tradition, a story, and a gesture of quiet heritage. My father wasn't just feeding me—he was reminding me where we came from.

## Pranzo (Lunch)

Lunch was never a grand event in our household—at least not on ordinary days. It lacked the ceremony of dinner or the quiet ritual of breakfast. Instead, it was a functional pause in a day that was already thick with work, chores, and movement. During the week, school or farm duties dictated our routines. For Mum and Dad, there was no long siesta, no tablecloth spread with indulgence—just a few precious minutes to eat before diving back into labour.

On weekends, it was a different kind of busy. There were jobs on the farm, shopping runs to town, or sporting matches to get to. Church, of course, punctuated our Sundays. Mum and Dad might take us along on errands, and we kids would scatter afterward into our own rhythms of games and responsibility. Amidst that hum of activity, lunch was usually fast, simple, and unfussy.

Dad, ever the minimalist when it came to food, was content with the basics. He took pleasure in a slice or two of homemade Italian sausage, some crusty bread, and a tomato or cucumber straight from the garden. Occasionally, he'd treat himself to a can of tuna or, on special days, braised steak and onions from a tin. He'd eat this with the quiet satisfaction of a man who'd known hunger and was grateful for whatever lay before him.

We never lacked for the staples: there was always bread—Mum's crusty loaves, baked fresh every couple of days—alongside cheeses, fruit, and vegetables from the garden. For us kids, lunch meant assembling what was available. A slice of cheese, some tomato, maybe a sausage. It was informal and varied, but it always tasted of home.

School lunches were another matter. Mum would wake before dawn to light the stove and prepare food for whoever was at home, and for Ricardo—always the eldest and perhaps the most indulged—she packed something extra special. Each lunchbox held thick-cut sandwiches made with her homemade bread, filled with slices of mortadella, salami, or sausage, and real cheese cut from the wheel. These weren't the plastic-wrapped slices or bland cold meats you'd find in shops today. These were robust, flavourful, and proudly different.

Our lunches stood out in the schoolyard. Each one was a miniature feast: two hefty sandwiches, a garden vegetable—usually a whole cucumber or tomato—and seasonal fruit. The Aussie kids would look on in astonishment. While they gnawed at Vegemite sandwiches or unremarkable white bread triangles, we bit into layers of cured meats and homegrown produce. Some stared. Others made jokes. A cucumber at recess drew strange looks, and our sandwiches were often twice the size of theirs.

This difference, innocent though it was, became the seedbed of the racism we all came to know. The taunts started subtly and grew more pointed over time: *salami muncher, wog, dago, greaseball.* We didn't understand it. We were just kids eating lunch. Yet somehow our food, our names, our appearance, and our closeness as a family made us targets. Within four grade levels at our school, there were four Palandri's. We stuck out, even when we tried not to.

I sometimes wonder what lay behind the jeers—envy, ignorance, fear, or just cruelty. Maybe it was because we did things differently. Maybe because we did them well. Either way, it toughened us. We learned to take pride in what set us apart, even when others tried to make us ashamed.

One memory still makes me laugh. I had stayed the night at my cousin's house and for some reason, Zia Tilly wasn't home. Uncle Giuseppe—Zero—was left in charge of getting us boys ready for school. There was no lunch prepared, so he marched straight into the garden and returned with four hefty watermelons. That was our lunch—one melon each. But he wasn't done. He also placed a large cutting knife in each of our schoolbags so we could carve them up. At recess, we plopped down and pulled out our fruit and blades like it was the most natural thing in the world. You can imagine the look on the other kids' faces—shock, envy, maybe a little fear. We just grinned and dug in.

While many kids were buying sausage rolls or meat pies from the canteen, we were carving watermelon with hunting knives. And you know what? I wouldn't trade it for anything. Occasionally, there were big lunches—real celebrations where the whole extended family gathered. These were rare but unforgettable. The Palandri's alone brought fifteen children and four adults, and with Mum's side—the Fontana's—another six kids. There would be a blur of cousins playing cricket, chasing each other through the orchard, barefoot and wild with joy. The adults, meanwhile, cooked and talked and laughed under the apricot trees.

One particular day stays vivid in my memory. It was warm and clear. Trestle tables were set up on the lawn of the timber house, beneath the apple trees and next to the towering apricot that shaded much of the yard. Every uncle, aunt, cousin, and grandparent seemed to be there. The long table groaned with food: bruschetta piled with chopped tomatoes and basil, crusty bread, bowls of olives, and dishes of salami, mortadella, and cheese.

There was *giardiniera*—pickled vegetables from our own garden. Dad's specialty. Cauliflower, carrots, onions, broccoli, all swimming in salty, briny, sometimes chilli-spiked vinegar. Salads came in every form: cabbage and apple, tomato and basil, potato and parsley. Everything was fresh, dressed in olive oil and balsamic, served simply but beautifully.

The meats were either cured by us or bought from an Italian butcher. They were laid out on large plates, sometimes interspersed with olives or pickled peppers. Cheese came from our own cows, aged just right and sharp with flavour. Wine flowed freely, poured from reused bottles and jugs, always homemade.

I can still picture the old men lined up on the bench: Dad, Uncle Giuseppe, and a few of the Fontana uncles. Each one held a glass of wine, a pipe or a hand-rolled cigarette, and a satisfied smile. One of them—my father, I believe—had an accordion in his lap and was playing it softly. A few sang along in low, nostalgic voices, their heads nodding in time to tunes from the old country. It was beautiful, unfiltered, real. A moment of joy carved from the hard wood of everyday life.

Those family lunches, though simple, were steeped in tradition. We didn't need fancy food or formal settings. The joy came from the laughter, the togetherness, the sharing of stories and meals and history. It was like those scenes from Mediterranean villages you sometimes see on cooking shows—long tables in cobbled streets, families bringing dishes from their kitchens, children darting between chairs, and wine being poured from unlabelled bottles. But ours wasn't a romanticised imitation. It was real. It was ours. Lunch, while not always ceremonious, was never insignificant. It reflected who we were—busy, humble, connected. Whether it was watermelon and a knife on a schoolyard bench, or a trestle table groaning with olives and cheese beneath the trees, *pranzo* was where we stopped, gathered, and reminded ourselves that we belonged to something bigger than ourselves.

Even now, when I sit down for lunch—just a sandwich or a plate of leftovers—I remember. I remember Mum's quiet efficiency, Dad's simple pleasures, and the chaos of fifteen cousins running barefoot through the orchard. And I know that those meals, those moments, helped shape the person I became.

## Compleanni (Birthdays)

They say the youngest always has it easiest. In a family like ours—six siblings, plus fifteen first cousins, all raised in the tangled web of tradition, resilience, and post-war reinvention—the youngest is bound to be spoiled or at least teased for it. And I was. Even now, my brothers and sisters' joke that I was a "mistake", a late arrival after Mum and Dad had run out of both energy and

Italian names. I got the name Stephen, not Stefano. By the time I came along, our family had already begun shifting from being newly arrived Italian migrants to becoming something new—Australian, but with Italian roots dug in deep. That shift showed up clearly in how we celebrated birthdays.

When Ricardo and the older siblings were young in the 1950s, birthday parties were modest affairs. Resources were tight, and so were the hours in the day. Celebrations would be small, practical, and based around family. Gifts were often handmade or modest: a book, a new shirt, perhaps a wooden toy.

There might be a small cake if eggs and butter were available. But more than anything, there was food and family, gathered around a long table, the clatter of forks mixing with conversation in fast Italian, hands flying as much as voices.

The cakes in those early years weren't store-bought or lavish. They were simple sponge cakes, sometimes flavoured with lemon zest or a splash of amaretto. Decorated with love, not precision. They didn't need to be perfect—they needed to be shared. By the time the 1980s rolled around and it was my turn, the game had changed.

My birthday parties were anglicised affairs, shaped not only by Mum and Dad's traditions but also by the shifting culture around us. I invited kids from school—mostly Australians from a range of backgrounds.

Our food was a mix of old-world and new: fairy bread on crescentina (our pillowy fried dough), sprinkled with 100s and 1000s; jars of lollies; paper party hats and buttered popcorn. It was a hybrid of cultures, and I barely noticed.

That was just the world I knew—a blend of Italian heart and Aussie childhood. We still had lasagna and cotoletta on the table, but it sat next to sausage rolls and fizzy orange drink.

But Mum never let a birthday pass without a table groaning with food. She was no ordinary cook. We've already spoken about her skills in the kitchen,

**Notice the Table Full of Cake**

but birthdays were when she turned it up a notch. If apples were in season, there was her famous apple pie—so good my older brother later turned the recipe into a commercial success, selling them at markets and eventually at our vineyard café. She had a sense for fruit—when the apples were just tart enough to hold their shape and still sweet enough to caramelise.

Then there were the cakes: torta al cioccolato, her go-to chocolate birthday cake, rich and moist and iced with thick ganache that left your fingers sticky and your heart full; tiramisu with layers of espresso-soaked savoiardi and mascarpone; and zuppa inglese, a boozy, layered trifle-like dessert that always felt slightly forbidden. We loved that one especially—it made us feel grown up, like we were in on a family secret. Breakfast on your birthday was special too.

If it was a weekday, you'd wake up to toast and milky coffee, served on a warm plate next to the fire. But if it was a weekend? That was something else entirely: bomboloni (doughnuts) rolled in sugar; frittelle (pancakes) drizzled with syrup; or even a full fry-up with bacon and eggs, served with slow-fried potatoes, tomato slices seasoned with salt and oregano, and thick slices of crusty bread.

Mum made it feel like you were royalty, just for that one day. You knew she'd woken early and planned everything. Even the table setting changed. A birthday was never treated as "just another day."

The biggest birthdays, like 21sts, were landmark events, and each one reflected the changing nature of our family and our place in Australia. Annunziata's 21st birthday was in the late 1970s. By then, Margaret River was still a quiet, sleepy town, its identity not yet defined by wine or tourism. The dairy and timber industries ruled, and surf culture was only just beginning to show its influence.

Her party brought with it an entirely new world for me. She had friends down from university in Perth—long-haired, artistic types, some playing music, others carrying guitars or sketchbooks. They descended on the farm like a caravan of colour and energy. To me, barely ten years old and still very much a wide-eyed country kid, they were the most exciting people I'd ever seen.

They were lovely—open, kind, free-spirited—but also completely different to anything I'd known. For example, one morning they watched my father Carlo pour a little red wine into his strong morning coffee, a nod to an old Italian peasant habit. They were shocked, amused, and being young men eager for new experiences, asked if they could try it too. My father, ever patient, gave them a quiet warning: "Un po', ragazzi... solo un po'." ("Just a little, boys...") They laughed, took their sips, and within the hour, were slurring their words and sliding off their chairs. Dad's quiet chuckle echoed across the kitchen.

The party itself was a classic 1970s Australian barbecue, with a distinctly Italian twist. Our grill was a converted 44-gallon drum, braced on bricks with a massive 60-inch toothless saw blade laid across the top. After the meat was cooked—usually sausages, marinated steaks, and skewers—the blade was removed, and the fire was kept burning low into the evening. Guests sat around telling stories, sipping wine, and devouring Mum's desserts by the flickering firelight.

My own 21st birthday, almost a decade later, bore the marks of both tradition and change. Margaret River had started to grow up. The vineyards were thriving, tourism was gaining momentum, and the social fabric of the town had begun to stretch and diversify. Fewer people drank heavily, and parties became more about the experience than the beer count.

I didn't have a huge guest list—many of my cousins had moved away, and I was no longer in daily contact with as many local kids. But the family was there, and that was enough. Mum, perhaps sensing how things were changing, decided this party should echo the past. She made over 5,000 tortellini by hand for the soup course. Five thousand. I watched her roll, stuff, fold, and pinch each one with the same care she'd shown for decades. It was her gift to me—and to tradition.

She also prepared over 60 cotoletta—crumbed and fried beef cutlets, crispy on the outside, tender on the inside. There was antipasto: olives, salami, giardiniera. Salads made with tomatoes still warm from the garden, basil torn and scattered by hand. Everything was made from scratch. No store-bought shortcuts. It was Mum's way of holding onto something precious, even as the world around us changed.

My father had passed away by then, and though the party was full of joy, his absence was felt deeply. I looked around and realised just how much had changed since the early days. Our big extended family was now spread across the state. Some had started their own families; others had moved to the city. But around that table, with a bowl of tortellini e brodo in front of each of us, it was as if time had folded in on itself.

Those birthday parties told the story of our family's evolution. They began as humble gatherings of immigrants clinging to culture and grew into vibrant celebrations where old met new. They mirrored our journey from Piandelagotti to Margaret River—a migration not just across oceans but across generations and identities.

What stayed constant was the food and the love behind it.

Whether it was homemade chocolate cake or crescentina with Vegemite, whether it was an apple pie for a six-year-old or 5,000 tortellini for a 21-year-old, each birthday meal was an act of love. And Mum's kitchen, with its cracked tiles and warm chaos, was our family's cathedral.

We didn't always have balloons or party entertainers. We didn't need them. We had Mum. We had each other. And we had the food. And as the youngest—the so-called spoiled one, the mistake with the Anglo name—I carry these memories not just as nostalgia, but as a map. A way home. A reminder of who we are, and how we celebrated being alive, one birthday at a time.

## Pasqua (Easter)

The observance of Roman Catholic rituals, traditions, and ceremonies was an unmissable thread woven through the fabric of my childhood. It wasn't just religion—it was rhythm, the beat of our family life. From the sacraments to the seasons, the Church loomed large, especially in those early years. I've often thought that as time passed, some of the rigidity softened a little. My older brothers and sisters, born years before me, seem to have followed those rituals with a kind of solemn devotion that gradually gave way to more relaxed observance by the time I was growing up.

There were whole stretches of the year where it felt like the Church had us on a leash. So many feast days, saint days, processions, and services—they blurred together until the calendar seemed less like a timeline and more like an endless cycle of holy obligations. Easter was perhaps the best example: not just a day, not even a weekend, but an entire season—starting 46 days before Easter Sunday with the arrival of Lent. Just as we'd finished packing away the nativity set and recovering from the indulgences of Christmas and Epiphany, we were flung headfirst into the Passion, the suffering, and the resurrection.

It always began with Shrove Tuesday.

Shrove Tuesday was our last hurrah before the fast—a feast of meat, richness, and flavour. That dinner was something we all looked forward to. Mum might make lasagne layered with slow-cooked meat sauce, or a traditional osso buco so tender it fell off the bone. Sometimes it was roasted goat—capretto—rubbed with herbs and garlic and slow-roasted to perfection. In later years, as our diet modernised, it could be a juicy steak with potatoes or a full roast dinner. The meal wasn't just about food—it was about contrast. It was everything we were about to give up, served with the full awareness that it was temporary. My parents would always remind us—sometimes gently, sometimes with the full weight of Old Testament gravity—how lucky we were to have such food. We'd hear stories of Catholic endurance, of saints who lived on bread and water, or of children who fasted out of necessity rather than faith. The lesson was always clear: sacrifice builds character.

Then came Ash Wednesday. That night we'd go to Mass, the church dimly lit and solemn. At the centre of the ceremony was the ritual of the ashes. The priest would dip his thumb into the blackened remnants of the previous year's palm leaves, press it onto our foreheads, and murmur, "Remember that you are dust, and to dust you shall return." There was something haunting about that phrase, even as a child. The cool smear of ash on my skin felt like a mark of belonging—and of burden.

The next day at school, the ashes hadn't yet worn off, and you could spot the Catholic kids from across the oval. We wore our faith on our faces, and to the non-Catholic Aussie kids, it was open season for jokes. "Oi, what's that on your head?" "Did you get burned?" "Why are the wog kids marked like that?" It wasn't easy to explain Lent to a kid who didn't know the word, let alone the concept. So, we'd shrug, laugh, and find the first chance to 'accidentally' wipe our foreheads clean.

From that point, for the next six weeks, our Fridays took a turn. No meat, no indulgence, just simple food and the quiet understanding that this was how it had always been. Mum would do her best to keep meals meatless but still meaningful. There were traditional dishes she fell back on—rice soup being one of the most frequent. I've mentioned it elsewhere, and I'll say it again: it was like a watery rice pudding, made of milk and rice, with no protein and very little joy. Not a risotto. No cheese, no stock, just a bland white porridge masquerading as dinner.

I did my best to choke it down without complaint. Annunziata, however, was a different story. She hated that rice soup with a passion and let everyone know it. Arguments would flare across the table, voices raised, forks downed in protest. Eventually, to keep the peace—and likely to preserve her own sanity—Mum would fry her up a plate of chips. And they say I was the spoiled one.

Not every Friday was grim. Sometimes we had crescentina, our beloved fried bread, which could be topped with anything non-meat. Cheese, tomato, even just a smear of garlic oil—it felt like a treat. If we were lucky, we'd finish with bomboloni, sweet sugar-rolled doughnuts that made the sacrifice of the main meal feel somewhat worthwhile. On extra good Fridays, we'd get fish and chips—pan-fried herring with lemon and garlic, served alongside thick, hand-cut chips or crunchy polenta fries. Lent didn't always mean deprivation. Sometimes, it was just a different kind of nourishment.

As time went on, the idea of Lent began to shift. Fasting evolved from giving up meat to giving up vices. Mum would stop drinking wine for those six weeks, Dad might ease up on smoking his pipe, and some of us kids would try to give up things like chocolate or TV. We weren't always successful—but the intention mattered.

Lent always ended the same way, with a sense of mounting anticipation as Holy Week approached. It was the final stretch, the prelude to the resurrection, the moment when all that restraint made way for rejoicing. But even before the chocolate eggs and the roasted lamb of Easter Sunday, there was meaning in the waiting. Lent was about memory, about tradition, about the long arc of sacrifice that shaped who we were.

It wasn't always easy, and it certainly wasn't always enjoyable. But it grounded us. It gave shape to the year. And in its own quiet way, it taught us discipline—not just to follow rules, but to understand why they existed in the first place.

## Easter Week

The first Sunday of Easter week was always Palm Sunday, and it marked the true beginning of one of the holiest and most vibrant times of the year in our family calendar. As children, we would pile into the car for Sunday mass, where the church would be transformed with long fronds of fresh green palms woven into crosses and bundled along the aisles. The Saturday before, our family would head out across the farm, secateurs in hand, to cut bundles of palms for the church. It was our contribution, our way of honouring tradition and supporting the parish that had been so central to our lives.

Though there were masses held every day of Easter week, the next one we would attend was Maundy Thursday—an evening mass steeped in symbolism. This was the mass of humility and service, the one where the priest would wash the feet of twelve members of the congregation, in emulation of Christ. Often, my father Carlo was among those chosen. He had served the church with quiet dignity his whole life—doing maintenance, setting up for mass, tending to odd jobs without fanfare—and I felt proud, almost overwhelmed, seeing him take his seat among the twelve.

I, too, had served in the church as an altar boy for many years, and that Maundy Thursday ceremony always stirred something deep in me. It wasn't just ritual—it was recognition. A simple, solemn gesture that affirmed the worth of people like Dad, who didn't ask for attention, but earned respect through devotion and quiet work.

But of course, as kids, there was another layer of excitement surrounding Easter: the glorious five-day school holiday that stretched before us like a gift.

Chocolate was a given-on Easter Sunday, but those days off were more than sugar and sermons—they were a burst of freedom, possibility, and family.

Would we be kicking the football in the paddock? Heading over to a cousin's place for backyard cricket? Or just disappearing into the bush to play games we made up as we went along? The cousins from Perth were often down for the weekend, and the house was full of noise and energy. With fifteen first cousins in the extended Palandri family—plus their parents, partners, and assorted tag-alongs—the farm became a hub of organised chaos.

But the tradition that defined Easter for us—the one that eclipsed even the chocolate—was Good Friday fishing. That day was sacred. Not only because it commemorated the crucifixion of Christ, but because it brought the entire clan together in the spirit of camaraderie, laughter, and a shared love of the sea. I've detailed some of these fishing adventures in another chapter, but Good Friday stood apart. The herring would be running, sometimes so thick in the bay you could see the water shimmer. Skipjack and the occasional salmon would sweep through too, and with up to thirty people fishing, we'd often haul in fifteen to twenty dozen herring in one morning.

The clean-up was swift and communal. Scales flew, guts were discarded, and fillets stacked. Mum would then take over, frying the herring in shallow pans with butter, garlic, lemon juice, and a pinch of salt. Outside, long tables would be set up on the lawn or the verandah. The adults would gather inside at the dining table, seeking a bit of calm, while we kids chattered and elbowed each other outside, eagerly grabbing fish as fast as they were served. No one ever left hungry.

And then came the delicacy we waited for all year—*uova di pesce*, the fish roe. These precious sacs of herring eggs were scooped from the fish, washed, and fried until crisp. Pale and crunchy, they were served piled high on a plate like treasure. That taste, delicate and unmistakable, was part of the magic of Good Friday. You couldn't buy it. You had to be there.

Sometimes we'd attend the Stations of the Cross mass on Friday night or Saturday morning. Sometimes not. But Sunday was non-negotiable. Easter Sunday mass was a celebration, bright and hopeful, filled with music and families in their best clothes. Then we'd come home and resume our own traditions—more food, more chocolate, more family.

As the years passed, the religious observances softened. Fewer of us attended every mass, and the symbolic rituals faded. But the core of it—family, food, and fishing—remained. That, to us, was Easter. That was what anchored us.

Even now, my own children treat Good Friday as untouchable. They remind me every year that it's not just another public holiday. It's Good Friday. The fishing trip, the feast, the stories—they're still part of who we are.

Easter Monday and Tuesday were quieter. By then, the frenzy had passed, the guests trickled away, and the house slowly returned to its usual rhythm. These were days of rest, of gathering ourselves before the world started spinning again. But even in the quiet, there was a deep sense of contentment. We had honoured tradition, celebrated life, and gathered once more as a family.

That's what Easter meant to us—not just resurrection, but reconnection.

## Natale e Capodanno (Christmas and New Year)

### Holidays

Christmas was always more than just a day—it was a whole season. A stretch of time woven together by community, family, faith, food, and anticipation. But for me, as a young boy, it wasn't just Christmas Day that stood out—it was the build-up. The slow and delicious stretch of December as school ended, the weather heated up, and the long-awaited summer holidays finally arrived.

Back in the days of the three-term year, our Christmas break felt endless—

weeks and weeks of open skies, late sunsets, and the freedom to explore and play from dawn until dusk. The start of the holidays meant the chance to dream big. For me, like so many Australian kids growing up in the '70s and '80s, those dreams were dressed in baggy whites and carried a cricket bat. I was certain I'd be the next Australian Test cricketer.

Our farm paddocks became my training ground. I'd sneak off with the old petrol-powered push mower—more noise than efficiency—and carve out a crude cricket pitch in the dry, brittle grass out back. My "wicket" was a rectangle of red clay hauled from the dam and flattened down with the back of a shovel. In my imagination, it rivalled the WACA. It was bumpy, uneven, and entirely lopsided—but perfect.

Our backyard pitch was only good for on-side shots. The offside was blocked by the woodpile, a few big trees, and a scattering of jagged rocks. And just five metres behind the stumps loomed the back fence.

Hook shots and cuts were risky. So, we adapted—we'd field exclusively on the one side, set our catchers there, and become experts in leg glances and flicks through mid-wicket.

At my cousin's place, we built another pitch—flatter, dustier, but just as fiercely contested. We created smaller secondary pitches too, each with its own set of rules, designed for one-on-one matches that honed our footwork and defensive skills. They were our Ashes, our Boxing Day Tests, played barefoot with sunburnt shoulders and intense pride.

Test cricket on the television added to the ritual. We'd crowd around the screen, fanning ourselves with newspapers and keeping tallies in our notebooks. Chappell, Lillee, Marsh, Thomson—they were our gods. The commentators' voices became part of the summer soundtrack, as familiar as the cicadas buzzing outside or the sound of sausages spitting on the barbecue.

Those early days of the Christmas holidays—when everything smelled like cut grass and eucalyptus, when the days felt so long, they almost never ended—were some of the happiest I can remember.

They were made up of sweat and laughter, dust and dreams, the voices of cousins and siblings rising with the heat. They were about cricket, yes—but more than that, they were about belonging. We didn't need much. Just each other, a bat, a ball, and the golden promise of summer.

## Gifts

The weeks leading up to Christmas weren't filled with shopping trips or shiny department store catalogues. We didn't have the money for all that, and truthfully, I never felt we were missing out. Still, as the day approached, I would start to feel the pressure—not from my family, but from myself. I wanted to give and give something meaningful. I didn't have a wallet full of cash, but I had my hands, some tools, and a bit of imagination. I turned to what I had: wood. Offcuts, branches, gnarled roots, and jarrah burls found across the farm became my raw material. Using a battered electric drill, a couple of chisels, clamps, and my trusty chainsaw, I crafted gifts I hoped would last—knife blocks, breadboards, bowls, even small side tables with legs shaped from old grass tree roots. I didn't follow any plans; I just worked with what I saw in the timber and hoped the result made sense. Mum especially loved natural materials—there was something sacred about wood in our house. Each curl of grain or knot in a branch seemed to hold a story.

I know now that some of those early gifts were clunky or uneven, maybe even a little laughable. But to me, they were beautiful. They were mine. I was proud of what I could make with my hands. And even now, decades later, I've seen some of those homemade gifts still in use—quietly sitting in my siblings' kitchens or living rooms, doing the job they were made to do.

When I got to university and money became even tighter, I leaned into these skills. I made jarrah burl tables and sold them through a small craft shop in

Margaret River. It wasn't a fortune, but it helped. My parents noticed this passion and backed me. They encouraged the creativity and practicality in equal measure. Maybe that's what planted the seed that would later lead me to become a technology and enterprise teacher—someone who could pass on the value of making something by hand.

Back then, those gifts weren't just presents. They were proof. Proof that I could contribute something lasting, even when times were tough.

## Celebration

The church calendar marked this time of year with something called *Advent*—a period of reflection, fasting, and spiritual preparation in the four weeks leading up to Christmas. As kids, we didn't fully grasp its depth, but we participated with the same reverence expected of all good Catholics. Every Sunday during Advent, we'd attend Mass with the rest of the community, aware that something special was coming, even if we couldn't always articulate it.

The church would slowly transform. One of the most anticipated arrivals was the Nativity scene—a well-worn, almost antique set at the Margaret River church that drew both reverence and, occasionally, ridicule. As altar boys, we'd sneak glances and whisper among ourselves about the odd-looking figures.

The baby Jesus seemed too big for his manger, the donkey was chipped, and one of the Wise Men leaned permanently to the side like he'd had too much communion wine. Suppressing laughter became a weekly trial, especially under the watchful eyes of the priest, who did not take kindly to irreverence.

As Advent passed and the air filled with anticipation, another event signalled the nearness of Christmas—Dad's work party. This wasn't just a workplace gathering; it was a moment when the adult world relaxed, loosened its belt, and allowed itself a bit of fun.

Dad would mingle with his colleagues and their families, glass of wine in hand, speaking more than he usually did. For us kids, the highlight was simple: endless food, fizzy drinks, and a present from the Secret Santa. It was our first gift of the season and always felt like the curtain-raiser for Christmas.

Then came a tradition we all looked forward to—Margaret River's one night of late-night shopping for the entire year. Shops that usually closed their doors by 5:00pm would stay open into the night, and the town would come alive in a way that felt electric. Kids reunited with their school friends, laughing and racing between stores. But the real chaos came with the water fights.

While some bought cheap little plastic pistols from the local shop that barely managed a squirt, we came prepared. We'd rigged up large detergent bottles—Ajax or Fab—filled them to the brim with water, and fashioned powerful nozzles that could shoot up to fifteen metres. We were little water-bandits, soaking anyone who crossed our path, especially the unfortunate souls with pitiful toy pistols. It was glorious fun.

The streets buzzed with pop-up stalls: chocolate wheels spinning with anticipation, coconut piles waiting to be won. Coconuts were rare treats, strange and exotic in the southwest, with their sweet water and tough, fibrous shells. Dad loved the chocolate wheel—he'd play until he won something. Sometimes it was soap, sometimes socks, sometimes a gift for Mum. He was as much a fixture at the wheel as the wheel itself.

Mum moved between shops and stalls, catching up with friends and quietly gathering the last bits for Christmas—perhaps ribbon, maybe a bottle of something special, or just conversation. Meanwhile, Dad and Uncle Giuseppe would inevitably end up at the pub, raising glasses of homemade wine in the company of other Italian migrants, welcoming the holiday as only they knew how: with laughter, stories, and more than a few toasts.

And then came the highlight for the kids: Santa on the fire truck. Moggy King in a red suit, tossing lollies from the back of the truck as it rolled down the main street, sirens blaring, children scrambling. It was noisy, sticky, and chaotic. It was wonderful. These were the moments that stitched Christmas into the fabric of our lives—not the presents or the perfect decorations, but the messy, joyful rituals of a small town coming alive together.

### Christmas Day Lunch

Us kids could hardly sleep on Christmas Eve, bubbling with anticipation. We'd whisper to each other in our beds, trying to guess what gifts might be waiting under the tree or where our secret presents were hidden. But Christmas Day was the main event—the crescendo of all our excitement and energy.

It began with that magical moment around 8 a.m., after all our early attempts at sneaking into the lounge room were thwarted. You see, Mum and Dad's bedroom was strategically located between ours and the living area—an architectural checkpoint designed specifically to foil our festive espionage.

We'd be sent back to bed more than once, our tiptoeing uncovered by the creak of floorboards or a stifled giggle. Eventually, Dad would ceremoniously open the stained-glass sliding doors, revealing the decorated Christmas tree and gifts—objects of wonder that had seemingly appeared overnight. We always laughed at the half-drunk glass of wine, the half-eaten biscuit, and the chewed carrot left behind by Santa and his reindeer.

After tearing into presents with giddy enthusiasm, we'd settle down for the first proper meal of the day: Christmas breakfast. Mum never held back—toast, crescentina, bacon, eggs, sausage, frittata, cheese, and the strong aroma of coffee brewing on the stove. Sometimes we were lucky enough to get bomboloni, warm and sticky, dusted with sugar and devoured while still hot.

But it was Christmas lunch that truly captured the essence of our family—big, loud, generous, and unforgettably delicious.

**Natural Christmas Tree and Presents were Always a Surprise**

When I was young, the two Palandri families—ours and Uncle Joe's—would come together for this grand meal. It wasn't unusual for 30 to 35 people to gather, a sea of siblings, partners, cousins, and children. The house would pulse with laughter, chatter, and the clinking of cutlery, as if the walls themselves were soaking in the celebration.

Mum—Angelina—and Zia Tilly were the culinary heart of these occasions. Together they would cook for days, filling the kitchen with the scent of garlic, roasted meats, and fresh pasta. Their bond in the kitchen was unspoken and perfect, like two dancers rehearsed through a hundred performances. At the centre of the meal was tortellini in brodo, painstakingly handmade by Mum and Tilly—hundreds upon hundreds of delicate parcels, each filled with seasoned pork and parmesan, then simmered in a rich, golden broth. We all had our tasks—some helped fill, some folded, and the lucky few got to taste the first ones off the boiling pot. It was said that one year they made over 5,000 tortellini, enough to feed the entire neighbourhood.

**Plate of Tortellini e brodo**

Beside the tortellini sat crisp cotoletta, fresh salads with homegrown vegetables, and all the pickled fare our mothers had prepared through the year. There would be roast turkey, pork, and beef, reflecting the Australian traditions that had gradually worked their way into our otherwise Italian table. At first, these meats seemed foreign, but over the years they became part of our own rituals. As our partners and in-laws came from different cultures, our family grew more open, more layered—Italian at heart, but Australian in flavour.

One of the standouts dishes each year was cabbage ripiene—savoury mince wrapped in cabbage leaves, baked in a bubbling tomato and cheese ragù. It was a recipe passed down from Emilia-Romagna, deeply traditional and so rarely made that its annual appearance became a culinary event of its own. We savoured every mouthful, knowing it would be another year before we tasted it again.

The desserts followed with no less drama. Torta al cioccolato, almond biscotti, fruit pies, and cream-filled sponge rolls were all laid out across the table. Then came Mum's specialty—apple pie, served warm with custard or cream, and always gone in a flash. My sisters occasionally tried to replicate it, but they'd be the first to admit that Mum's had something extra—maybe love, maybe magic, or maybe just muscle memory from decades of baking.

By the end of lunch, most of us were in a food coma. Kids would nap in corners or sneak out to play with new toys, while the adults lingered over glasses of wine, espresso, or homemade liqueur. Sometimes there were card games, sometimes family arguments, but mostly there was storytelling and laughter, tales repeated from past Christmases or exaggerated with each telling.

That was Christmas Day in our family—abundant, chaotic, deeply rooted in tradition, and shaped as much by what we brought with us from Italy as what we embraced in Australia. No matter how many years pass, I still remember the warmth of that day, the clatter of plates, the smell of roasting meat, and the sound of my family filling the house with life.

— ◆ —

### Post-Christmas and New Year

We would eventually round out Christmas afternoon with a game of backyard cricket—not just the kids, but sometimes the adults too. I especially loved it when Dad joined us. Seeing him out on the grass, laughing, bat in hand, brought to life stories I'd only half believed. In his youth, he had been a skilled sportsman—naturally gifted in soccer, of course, but surprisingly agile at AFL too. That he took the time to play with us, even briefly, left a mark. It showed a rare glimpse of ease and playfulness in a man who carried so much weight on his shoulders. Christmas Day would taper off with sleepy farewells as relatives packed up leftovers and shuffled back to their homes. Dinner that night was always a patchwork of the midday feast—roast meats cold from the fridge, crusty bread mopped through sauces, and whatever cakes and sweets had survived the earlier onslaught. Boxing Day was sacred for a different reason: recovery. We lazed about, picking at food, playing with our new gifts, and settling in front of the television for the Boxing Day Test. The cricket was more than just background noise—it was tradition, an unspoken rhythm in the slow days between Christmas and New Year.

Dad usually took time off during this period, but it wasn't quite the restful holiday kids imagine. We often found ourselves back on the farm—repairing fences, shifting timber, checking vines—quietly setting the scene for the year ahead.

Then, almost before the dishes were done, New Year's Eve would arrive.

Celebrations were typically held at the Fontana home, where Mum, Zia Tilly, and Zia Marion would reunite to begin the next culinary event. The menu echoed Christmas—platters of pasta, cured meats, cheeses, insalate, and pickles—but dessert was the true point of difference. Zia Marion made cheesecake—something new, something exotic. Neither Mum nor Zia Tilly knew how to make it, so it was treated as a rare treasure. We devoured it shamelessly, fascinated by its texture and taste.

The night wore on with laughter, games, and bocce. Not lawn bowls—this was Italian-style, rough ground, heavy iron cannonballs salvaged from an old military half-track abandoned on our property. Nothing went to waste in our world.

The importance of food, family, and festivity during these holidays is something I carry forward, especially after losing both Mum and Dad. These were more than celebrations—they were affirmations of who we were, and who we still are.

# Part Two

# Le Case e le Comunità (Homes and Communities)

*"La comunità è la casa del cuore."*
*"Community is the home of the heart."*
— Italian proverb

# Chapter 6
# Our Homes (Le Nostre Case)

*"La casa non è dove abitiamo, ma dove amiamo."*
*"Home is not where we live, but where we love."*
— Christian Morgenstern

## From Stone and Snow to Timber and Wine

They say the soul of a family often dwells in the walls that shelter it. For us, those walls were made of stone and timber—materials as strong and enduring as the people who built them. Our homes were never just structures. They were the beating hearts of our lives, built not by architects or contractors, but by the calloused hands of family, guided by memory, heritage, and vision. They smelled of fresh-cut wood and strong coffee, echoed with laughter and argument, and held the warmth of countless shared meals and quiet, intimate moments. To understand who we are, you must first understand where—and how—we lived.

As I know it, the Palandri story in Margaret River began with my grandfather, Giacomo Palandri. He first arrived in 1925 and returned in 1936, eventually purchasing 300 acres of virgin bushland from another Italian migrant, Francesco Tarchini. This land, situated on the eastern side of Caves Road about ten kilometres north of town, was dominated by towering karri, jarrah, and marri trees. Untamed and raw, it was far from the vineyards and polished homes of present-day Margaret River. But it was opportunity—and that was enough.

Nonno, as we called him, worked primarily in the timber industry—cutting sleepers, carting timber, and even helping to build bridges in the region. In those early days, he built a humble one-room shack from jarrah he cut himself, with a dirt floor and a tin roof that rattled in the wind.

When my grandmother, Leonilda (née Vignaroli), arrived in 1940 with their sons Giuseppe and Carlo (my father), the family moved into this shack. My father was 17. Conditions were rough, and Nonna found life particularly hard. The boys, now nearly men, camped outside in ramshackle shelters while the forest pressed in around them. They lived with the basics—no electricity, water from a rain tank or nearby creek, and a diet that depended on home-grown vegetables, rabbits they could catch, and bread baked in an outdoor oven.

Work was scarce due to the outbreak of World War II. But necessity bred resilience. The boys took to clearing the land, learning to cut jarrah sleepers with a broadaxe—an unforgiving skill that demanded precision and strength. They worked long hours for modest pay. My father often said that despite the hardships, Australia was the lucky country. It offered a chance. A future. A better life than what might have awaited them in Italy.

**Sleeper House behind My Father**

By 1948, after nearly a decade of backbreaking work and simple living, they began construction of something more permanent—a granite stone house. Built on the semi-cleared land using stone found on the block, this house was a tribute to their roots. Its thick walls and cool cellar mirrored the houses of Piandelagotti and Savoniero. Only when I visited Italy decades later did I realise just how deeply their heritage was embedded in its design. This stone house was the first of its kind in Margaret River. Two-foot-thick granite walls. A vast cellar. Built entirely by hand. The mortar was mixed in buckets, and the stones, rough and heavy, were laid one at a time. Today, stone homes and feature walls are seen throughout the town, but ours was the beginning. A pioneer house, born not only of necessity but of nostalgia.

**The Stone House 1948**

Initially, the plan was for both Giuseppe and Carlo's families to live under one roof. But families grow, and soon space became tight. Though grand in appearance, the stone house had only three large bedrooms. When my father married Angelina Fontana in 1950, she moved in as well. Suddenly, Nonno, Nonna, Giuseppe, my father, and my new mother were all under one roof. Mum later said it was both comforting and difficult—shared meals and stories, but also tight quarters and clashing routines. Something had to change.

My father was working and had saved money from long shifts at the timber mill. Nonno gifted him 160 acres of the original 300-acre property and retained the stone house for Giuseppe. Across Caves Road, on a plot that bordered Ellenbrook Beach, my father began again. This was the land where he would build our future.

At first, the land was wild and untouched—thick with bush, rock, and undergrowth. By 1951, Ricardo was born, and Carla followed in 1952. The new property still had no house, so the young family squeezed into a single bedroom in the stone house while my father cleared land and prepared to build.

Though the property boasted excellent outcrops of blue vein granite, it was decided the new house would be timber. They simply didn't have the time or energy to split stones again. So, they felled the jarrah and karri trees from their own land and milled the timber themselves. Every board used to build our wooden house was cut by my father's hands. He worked long days at the mill and longer nights under moonlight, preparing the site.

By the mid-1950s, construction began. The first house was modest.

**Wooden House on New Block 1955**

A verandah, one bedroom for my parents, a narrow corridor, a small kitchen with a Metters No. 3 wood-fired stove, and a lounge with a brick fireplace. Two smaller rooms were built for Ricardo and Carla. The toilet and washhouse?

Outside, of course—a true Aussie outhouse. I missed that experience, but my siblings didn't let me forget it. Being the youngest, they always joked I was spoiled. Despite its simplicity, our house was crafted from exceptional timber. The jarrah was rich, red, and old—"old man jarrah" as some called it. Decades later, I salvaged pieces to use in my own woodworking. Even seasoned craftsmen marvelled at the quality. We didn't just build a house—we built a legacy from the land.

As more children were born, more rooms were added. On the left side of the house, two large bedrooms were built—one for the boys and one for the girls. Ricardo's old room became a real toilet and shower.

The original fireplace, once the heart of our living room, was eventually decommissioned when a new leisure room was added to the right side of the house. It hosted our prized pool table—a gift from Mum to Dad, which became a centrepiece of family life. It also revealed a childhood mystery. When the fireplace was removed, I discovered dozens of toys Francesco had thrown down the back. A brother's mischief uncovered years later.

The outdoor spaces grew too. We built sheds, garages, and eventually a winery shed for the small vintages we would try our hand at producing. Each new structure seemed to rise from the ground, shaped by the same hands that tilled the soil.

Meanwhile, the stone house continued to evolve. A verandah was added to the front, then others followed. But what fascinated me most was the tradition of verandahs themselves. Nearly every Italian home we visited had them. Always with chairs. Sometimes a summer bed. These weren't just porches—they were social spaces. Whenever guests arrived, they didn't sit inside—they sat on the verandah.

Why?

I only found the answer in 2023, when I visited Piandelagotti. There, every afternoon, the older villagers sat on their verandahs or out front of the alpine bar, sipping wine, arguing, laughing, sharing news.

It struck me: Italians may not have invented coffee, but they did invent the café. Our verandahs were the bush version of the Italian piazza—a place to gather, to share, to be seen.

Despite their stone and timber, our homes were never about grandeur. They were about family. About continuity. About honouring old traditions in a new land. They smelled of woodsmoke and stew, echoed with the sounds of yelling children, quiet prayers, and spontaneous laughter.

It was in those walls that we felt the passage of time—from quiet mornings to the noise of birthday parties, from Easter Sunday feasts to quiet evenings playing cards.

They gave us shelter. But more than that—they gave us a sense of belonging. We didn't grow up in mansions. We grew up in homes carved from the land and shaped by love.

# Chapter 7
# Fede, Paura e Prima Confessione
# (Faith, Fear, and First Confession)

*"La fede non è l'assenza della paura, ma il coraggio di andare avanti nonostante essa."*

*"Faith is not the absence of fear, but the courage to move forward in spite of it."*

— Anonymous

Religion ran through our childhood like a thread—sometimes golden and comforting, sometimes coarse and scratchy against the skin. Catholicism wasn't just something we believed in; it was something we wore, recited, and feared. It shaped how we spoke, what we ate, when we confessed, and how we understood right from wrong. For us, faith came with ritual, reverence—and an undercurrent of quiet terror, especially when it came to First Confession.

## Meaning

The Catholic Church played a significant role in all our lives. For Mum and Dad, it was more than a Sunday obligation—it was a social anchor, a ritual of belonging. Church was where they could reconnect with others who shared their language, values, and the unspoken burdens of migrant life. Especially in the early years, it was the one place they could engage in conversation that wasn't about timber, livestock, or survival. It offered a kind of community that reminded them of Piandelagotti, where Catholicism had been woven into everyday rhythms.

**Chiesa della Natività di Maria Vergine.**

## Church of the Nativity of the Virgin Mary. Piandelagotti

In their Italian mountain town, church wasn't just for prayer—it was the communal hub. People didn't drop in on each other casually, but they did meet every Sunday. That sacred space became a conduit for friendships, matchmaking, sharing harvest news, or planning the next feast day.

When they settled in Margaret River, they brought that habit and hope with them. Church became a familiar refuge in a foreign place. For Mum especially, it wasn't just about faith—it was about connection. She found companionship among the other Italian housewives, women who were also juggling the unfamiliarity of Australia with the pressure of preserving traditions.

The church carpark and hallways became spaces for whispered advice, shared recipes, and compliments over one another's biscotti, ciambella, and festive cakes. That part of her life—the social fabric of women meeting through faith—comes alive in other parts of this memoir. But it started here, in the wooden pews of the local Catholic church.

For us children, though, the church meant something entirely different. It was a place of mystery and solemnity, a grand stage of marble, incense, and rituals we only half understood. At times, we were dragged along reluctantly, pulled by the ear, with scuffed shoes and crooked buttons, fidgeting through the long Latin mass.

But even as we grumbled, there was something awe-inspiring about the grandeur of the space—the stained-glass windows catching the light just so, the echo of the priest's voice, the deep swell of the organ. It held a strange kind of beauty, and for all the resistance, it also etched itself deep into our childhood memories.

In primary school, Catholicism wasn't just something we experienced on Sundays. It spilled into our classrooms, particularly in the form of weekly Bible studies. We were pulled out of regular lessons—maths, reading, spelling—and

**The Original St Thomas Moore Catholic Church Margaret River**

shuffled into a separate room where we learned about the Old Testament. Stories of giants and floods, pillars of salt and flaming bushes.

David and Goliath. Noah's Ark. Samson's hair. These weren't gentle moral tales. They were epic, frightening, full of divine punishment and miraculous survival. For a child, they cemented the idea that God was watching—closely—and not always gently. We believed that if you misbehaved, swore, stole, or broke the commandments, something bad might happen. Lightning. Disease. Disgrace.

Whether or not we admitted it, those early lessons stitched themselves into our conscience. Even now, part of me still believes, or at least hopes, that doing good earns its reward. That heaven waits for those who behave.

Being pulled out for Bible class created its own kind of tension. It clearly marked the Catholic kids from the others, and not everyone was happy about it. While we memorised stories and learned to cross ourselves correctly, the non-Catholic kids stayed behind doing arithmetic or free writing. Sometimes they teased us. Sometimes we felt a bit smug.

Other times, it created rifts—especially when Catholic kids got access to extra things like church excursions or beach fun days. These weren't always received warmly by those who weren't invited. The divide was subtle but real.

But even with all that, we carried our religion with a mix of reverence and resentment. It was inescapable, yes—but also deeply formative. We didn't always understand it, but we lived it. Every genuflect, every Hail Mary, every moment of kneeling on cold wooden pews—it all became part of how we saw ourselves in the world.

### Sacraments and the Altar Boys

For those who grew up Catholic in the 1960s and '70s—especially in country towns like Margaret River—the sacraments were more than religious rites. They were milestones that shaped the rhythm of your childhood and the lens through which you understood the world.

For those reading this who shared that journey—especially my siblings and cousins—you'll know exactly what I mean when I say Catholicism was less about belief and more about participation.

You moved through the sacraments as if on a conveyor belt of faith: baptism, confirmation, Eucharist, reconciliation, matrimony, and—for a select few—holy orders and the anointing of the sick.

In our family, not everyone made it through all seven. But we came close. One of Mum's sisters became a Mercy nun, which gave our family a kind of honorary ticket to the "holy orders" box, even if the rest of us remained firmly in the laypeople's pews.

Some of the sacraments felt distant or mysterious—like the anointing of the sick, which only occurred at the very end of life. I remember watching in quiet grief as the priest placed sacred oil on my grandparents, on my uncles

**Sister Mary Cabrini (2nd from the left) Mums' Sister.**

and aunties, and later Mum and Dad. It's a solemn moment—the priest's fingers tracing a cross on the forehead of someone you love, whispering ancient words meant to prepare them for the journey into heaven. It feels both sacred and brutal. Final.

I don't remember my own baptism. There are no surviving photos that I know of, which is probably a good thing—me screaming in a too-big gown, drenched in freezing holy water, likely red-faced and furious. But I do vividly remember preparing for my First Holy Communion. In primary school, we were ushered into small classrooms during Bible Study to rehearse for this pivotal moment. We were taught to memorise the Lord's Prayer word-for-word and understand what it meant to take the body and blood of Christ. At that age, the concept was well above our heads. The wafer was thin and tasteless, and the wine—syrupy altar port—was secretly thrilling. For us, it wasn't about sacrifice and divine love. It was about finally being included. We got to line up with the adults, to hold out our hands, to speak the single word—"Amen"—and feel part of something sacred.

**Giacomo and I at Our Communion**

We didn't always grasp the metaphor, of course. The idea of Jesus giving his body and blood for the sins of the world was far too heavy for eight-year-olds. What we did understand was that it meant we were growing up. It was a badge of maturity. And, truthfully, the thrill of sipping wine in church—however small the drop—was enough to make some of us feel like rebels in robes. More than once, rumours circled about altar wine going missing. The cabinet that held the port and wafers—separate from the tabernacle—was occasionally broken into by curious boys. I won't name names, but a few were caught tipsy before mass, and I suspect others never got caught at all.

Once you had taken communion, you were eligible for confession. Reconciliation, as it was formally called, was another rite we approached with a mix of dread and amusement. In those days, the idea was simple: you did wrong, you confessed to a priest, and after a few Hail Marys and Our Fathers, you were forgiven. It seemed almost too easy. The younger you were, the more nervous you felt, especially the first few times. You'd kneel inside a dark, stuffy booth, whisper your sins into a screen, and hope the priest didn't recognise your voice. Of course, in a small town like ours, he almost always did.

That was the tricky part—everyone knew everyone. The priest knew your name, your parents, your school marks, and how much you fidgeted in mass. You'd be there confessing to stealing lollies or thinking something rude about a classmate, and you'd wonder whether Father really forgot your voice once he left the confessional. I think we all felt a bit exposed. But even then, there was something quietly therapeutic about it. Before I understood the psychology of confession, I understood the relief. You got it off your chest, and someone told you it was okay. It was cleansing in its own old-fashioned way.

The final sacrament I received as a child was Confirmation. Like Communion, it came with its own set of lessons and rules. We were drilled in Bible class to learn particular prayers, and we sat small exams to prove we were ready. Confirmation was explained to us as a rite of strengthening—the moment where our faith was sealed, our commitment to God affirmed. But for most of us, the real highlight was choosing a saint's name. We got to pick a spiritual identity—someone we admired or liked the sound of. I chose Luke. I'm not entirely sure why. It was before Star Wars, I promise. Maybe it just sounded noble. Maybe I liked the idea of being someone a little holier, at least on paper.

Beyond the official sacraments, one of the most enduring parts of my church experience was being an altar boy. There were five of us in total—my brother and I, and a few cousins—all roped into the service by equal parts devotion and curiosity. The priest's robes, the solemn Latin, the drama of the mass—it all had a theatrical appeal. Our own robes weren't quite as glamorous, but they made us feel important. We had jobs. Responsibilities. We stood at the altar, lit candles, rang bells. We were part of the show.

The part I remember most vividly was ringing the sanctus bells. It happened when the priest held up the host—the body of Christ—toward the congregation. A hush would fall across the pews, and I would flick my wrist to set the bells jingling, marking the holiest moment of the mass. I took that duty seriously. Too seriously, probably. If I rang too early or too late, I'd cringe with embarrassment. But when I got it right, I felt like I'd done something truly meaningful.

Being so close to the inner workings of the church also meant we got to peek behind the curtain. We saw what others didn't: the storage rooms, the preparations, the leftover wafers. And we heard the stories—whispers of ghosts in the sacristy, rumours of exorcisms, tales of the devil's tricks. For a kid like me, who already had a fascination with horror and the unexplained, this was irresistible. I once asked the priest if he'd ever performed an exorcism. He smiled and said no, but I remember the glint in his eye that made me wonder if he was holding something back.

More than the rituals and mysteries, though, it was the camaraderie that stayed with me. We altar boys shared jokes, snuck lollies behind the altar, helped each other remember lines. We were a team. And in a small town like Margaret River, where church was one of the few place's kids gathered outside of school that meant a lot. Those friendships—some still strong today—were forged not just in faith, but in shared nerves and whispered jokes during the sermon.

Looking back, the sacraments were never just boxes to tick. They were signposts on a winding road—markers of identity, of growing up, of navigating right and wrong. We didn't always understand them, but we lived through them. And like so much else from that time, they stitched themselves into who we became.

## A New Age

I was about twelve when Margaret River welcomed a new priest. I won't name him—his name has since been quietly erased from church records—but his impact on our small community was immediate and unforgettable. Unlike the priests we'd grown up with—quiet, distant, and almost regal in their detachment—this man was gregarious and magnetic. He didn't float above us like the others; he embedded himself right into the lives of the young, blending charm with strategy.

Where most priests stuck to the altar and scripture, this one took a different path. He began organising excursions for the youth—maroning trips, beach outings, and barbecues. It all seemed so innocent at the time. To us, it was exciting. He wasn't just preaching from the pulpit; he was inviting us into his world. And though there was an undertone—one I didn't quite understand then—it felt like someone finally saw us, spoke to us, wanted to include us. He let some of us sleep over at the presbytery. I was one of them. Nothing happened to me, and for that, I count myself fortunate. Others weren't so lucky. The truth only emerged years later, when it was too late for some. But in that moment, before the truth surfaced, he was a revelation.

He reinvigorated a parish that had grown tired. Our small church, once struggling for attendance, found new life. He breathed into it a kind of energy and purpose that hadn't been there before. People began to show up again. Families returned. Faith was on the rise—or so it seemed.

His greatest legacy, however, was not spiritual. It was architectural.

The Margaret River Catholic Church—still a striking landmark today—was his vision. It was modern, expansive, and entirely unlike the austere chapels of our parents' generation. He rallied the town behind him, inspiring a wave of community contribution that, to this day, remains astounding. The land was donated. The stones were donated. The labour was unpaid. People gave what they could—time, tools, materials—and my family was at the centre of it.

You see, we came from a lineage of stonemasons. Back in Piandelagotti, our family had carved homes, chapels, and fountains out of cold stone. When Dad and his brothers arrived in Australia, they brought that legacy with them. And on our property in Margaret River, there was granite. Beautiful, dense, raw granite—enough to build a wall, or a dozen. And so, we gave.

**Notice the Large Granite Feature Wall**

For weeks, we quarried it by hand—Dad, Uncle, cousins, and us boys. We dug and chiselled and lifted, blistering our palms and straining our backs. The stone was hauled, shaped, and delivered to the church site. The feature wall—the one that still draws admiration—is made of that very granite, cut from our soil and carried by our hands. The retaining walls too. All of it, done without a single dollar in exchange. We weren't the only ones. Dozens of others contributed: builders, painters, electricians, all volunteering their time. The priest's charisma drew them in, one by one, spinning the idea that this church was our collective gift to God—and to the town.

As young people, we were pulled into the final phase. My brothers, cousins, and I were roped in to paint, sweep, install windows, and clean. We were proud of our work, especially when our family was mentioned in the parish newsletter as generous contributors. But somewhere beneath that pride, a seed of doubt had taken root. Whispers began to circulate. We heard that not everyone worked for free. Some people—architects, consultants, organisers—had quietly accepted payment. Some profited. We hadn't. Neither had most families who'd poured sweat and time into the build. Slowly, it dawned on me that maybe we'd been used. Manipulated, even.

It wasn't a betrayal I could name at the time. But it began to change the way I viewed the Church—not the teachings or the tradition, but the institution itself. The decisions made behind closed doors. The selective generosity. The control masked as inspiration.

Then came Antioch.

One evening, the priest invited us to a special youth night at the church. We arrived curious, dressed in our best shirts, not knowing what to expect. A group from Perth greeted us. They called themselves Antioch—a Catholic youth organisation with energy, charm, and beauty to spare. Every member of the visiting group seemed impossibly attractive and effortlessly cool. They smiled easily, laughed openly, and seemed genuinely interested in us. Especially the girls. Gorgeous, charismatic, confident—unlike any girls we'd met in Margaret River.

The evening was filled with games, prayers, music, and testimonials. We were told about the joy of belonging, the depth of friendship, the fun and meaning we'd find if we joined their movement. We weren't just invited—we were courted.

At the end of the night, as we left the hall buzzing with excitement, the girls hugged us and—more than a few of them—kissed us on the lips. For a group of hormonal teenage boys, it was electric. We floated home, dreaming of Antioch and all it seemed to offer. But that dream faded fast.

Antioch never really took root in Margaret River. Maybe it was too foreign, too structured, or simply too much hype. The promise of gorgeous girls didn't materialise, and the movement fizzled. But for me, the whole episode sealed something I hadn't wanted to admit. I saw how the Church, even in its youth outreach, could trade in manipulation—using beauty, charisma, and spiritual promises to gather the faithful.

And so began my slow retreat. I didn't stop believing, not entirely. But I stopped trusting. The glitter had worn off the gold. And what remained was something older, heavier, and far more human than I'd ever realised.

## Reflection

It's difficult to categorise my entire experience with Catholicism. It was never just one thing. As a young boy, I saw it primarily as a space where my parents—newly arrived, navigating a strange country—could find their footing among people who shared something familiar. It gave them a place to belong. The rituals and routines of the Catholic Church offered not only spiritual grounding but also the kind of social life that was hard to come by in those early migrant years. They didn't have the luxury of a broad social circle or extended networks, but they had the church, and that was enough.

Coming from a town like Piandelagotti, where the church stood as both a spiritual and communal pillar, it made sense. Faith wasn't compartmentalised there; it was embedded in daily life, in every bell tower chime, feast day, and Sunday gathering. My experiences of Catholicism ranged widely—sometimes it inspired awe and reverence, other times confusion, frustration, even scepticism. It carried with it a deep emotional spectrum: wonder, joy, alienation, and ultimately, reflection.

There was a time in my life when I felt lost, disillusioned with the church. But over time, with age and perspective, I've found myself returning—not necessarily to doctrine or dogma, but to a simpler, quieter sense of faith. A recent visit to Italy brought it home. Walking through Vatican City and standing in the same parish church my parents and grandparents once attended grounded me in something larger than myself. Visiting the cemetery in Piandelagotti, seeing generations of Fontana's and Palandri's who all believed, all carried their faith through war, migration, and change—reminded me that Catholicism will always be part of who we are. It's stitched into our story.

# Chapter 8
# La montagna che ricorda

# (The Mountain That Remembers)

*"La montagna custodisce i ricordi di chi l'ha amata."*
*"The mountain holds the memories of those who loved it."*
— Anonymous

The mountain remembers what we forget. In Piandelagotti, time settles into stone walls and echoing footpaths, where the past lingers not in history books, but in the hush between snowfall and silence. Even after decades and oceans, the mountain holds our stories—of birth and burial, laughter and leaving. My parents may have crossed the world to build a life in Margaret River, but the Apennines never loosened their grip. In every season, in every memory, the mountain calls to us—not with words, but with the weight of where we came from.

**Piandelagotti Main Street**

### The Village That Carried Us

Even after we moved to Australia, the pull of Piandelagotti remained strong—an invisible tether that bound our family to that rugged stretch of mountain in the Apennines. My siblings and I may have grown up with the sea breeze of Margaret River in our hair and rich loamy soil under our fingernails change to, but we knew the rhythm of that faraway village. It was in the way Dad hoed the soil, in the way Mum kneaded dough, in the dialect that shaped their arguments and endearments alike.

They spoke of Piandelagotti often—not with sentimentality, but with matter-of-fact reverence, as if the place were still just a short walk away, and not halfway around the world. We heard about la neve, the deep snow that swallowed fences in winter, and the chestnut trees that dropped their prickly fruit like gifts from heaven. We heard about the barefoot treks to school, the meagre rations during the war, the hours spent cutting wood and tending goats. For us children, it all sounded like folklore—but for Mum and Dad, these were simply the facts of their youth.

**Main Street Piandelagotti in Winter**

The stories repeated until they were stitched into our family fabric. We knew which families lived on which slopes, who was related to whom, which cousin had the best singing voice, and which one had a limp from falling out of a cherry tree.

Even though we'd never met most of them, they became real in our minds. Names like Lina, Ettore, Maria, and Zio Giuseppe danced across the dinner table as if they might knock on our door at any moment.

Each mention of Piandelagotti carried a kind of weight, a quiet pride. It wasn't just a village—it was our root system. And even as Mum and Dad embraced their new lives in Margaret River, they never fully let go of the rhythms and rituals of the mountain. Our childhoods were coloured by that blend of past and present. We ate pasta with chestnut flour, grew vegetables in neatly furrowed beds, and prayed in a language we barely understood but knew was important.

When letters arrived from Italy, written in tight cursive and filled with affectionate blessings, Mum would sit by the kitchen window to read them aloud. Sometimes she would cry—not from sadness, but from the ache of connection. The mountain was far but never gone. Even our silences carried its echoes.

In time, some of us would visit Piandelagotti ourselves. We walked the same paths, breathed the crisp air, and touched the walls that had once sheltered our family. And when we stood in front of the old church or the crumbling house where Dad was born, we understood what he meant when he said, "This land remembers."

## Where Footsteps Still Echo

In 2023, I walked the same narrow lanes that generations of my family had once hurried through—stone-paved paths worn smooth by time and stories. With each step through Piandelagotti, I imagined the footsteps that had come before mine: Leonilda Palandri balancing a bucket of water from the old fountain; Maria Lunardi rising before dawn to knead dough for the day's bread; barefoot children—my ancestors—laughing and shouting as they raced through the village. I saw shadows of them everywhere. In those streets, I could almost hear the rise and fall of voices, in joy and grief, in prayer and in song.

**Snowfall: Clearing the Street for Passage.**

**Where Footsteps Still Echo**

I thought of my mother and father as young children, attending church within metres of each other, not yet knowing one another but already shaped by the same mountain winds and stone chapels. That tiny hamlet had held them, raised them, and laid the foundations for the family they would one day raise together on the other side of the world.

The cemetery brought the past into sharper focus. There, among weathered headstones and iron crosses, I found names I had only ever seen on old letters or scribbled in the margins of family trees—Fontana, Palandri, Vignarioli, Zani, Lunardi. They weren't just names anymore. They were resting places. Markers of lives that had once breathed the same crisp mountain air. I had returned not just to a place, but to a beginning.

We stayed at Albergo Alpino, the inn where my mother was born. A hundred years had passed, but the façade was nearly unchanged—just updated windows and a bit more paint. It was surreal comparing the old photos with the reality in front of us. Mum recalled snowbanks so high they had to climb out the second-storey windows. Now, I watched my son sit on the veranda sipping coffee, exactly where their elders had once gathered to chat and spettegolare—gossip—in that familiar, affectionate way.

The past felt tangible in those moments. Our family's rituals—once rooted in that village—had quietly travelled across oceans and taken hold in Australia. Yet here they still were, breathing in the rhythms of daily life: the sound of sweeping brooms, the scent of woodsmoke, the language of familiarity.

Sometimes, as my son and I strolled the streets, locals would stop us. "Who were your parents?" they'd ask. "Your grandparents?" Each time, I'd watch their eyes spark with recognition, their memories reaching back through decades to connect the dots. That small recognition felt like belonging.

Piandelagotti remains. Its breath is slower now, its streets quieter, but its heartbeat is strong. It lives not just in our memories, but in the living continuity of who we are. And in many ways, as long as we return, so do they.

**Savoniero, Dad's Eventual Village**

# Chapter 9
# Legname e Vino, Margaret River
# (Timber and Vine, Margaret River)

*"Nel profumo del legno e nel gusto del vino, si intrecciano le storie di chi ha plasmato questa terra."*

*"In the scent of timber and the taste of wine, the stories of those who shaped this land are intertwined."*

The scent of fresh-cut timber and the damp earth between vine rows defined the rhythms of life in Margaret River. For families like ours, survival wasn't a romantic notion—it was muscle, sweat, and stubbornness carved into karri trunks and coaxed from the soil. Timber fed our families; vines nourished our future. What began as a small settlement tucked between forest and coast slowly transformed, and so did we. This chapter tells the story of a town growing up—and a family growing with it—through the clang of axes, the planting of posts, and the promise poured into every bottle of wine.

### A New Land, A New Life

Seventeen years old—that's how old my father was when he first laid eyes on Margaret River. But it wasn't the Margaret River we know today with wine-tasting tours, gourmet cafes, and busloads of tourists. No, it was little more than a clearing in the bush—raw, wild, and full of untamed possibility. Coming from the craggy slopes of the Apennine Mountains in northern Italy, where the land was harsh, stony, and snowbound half the year, Margaret River must have seemed like an open canvas.

**Raw Land Completely Different to His Home**

The sun would have been warm on his face in April, so different from the biting chill of his Italian homeland. Around him stood trees he'd never seen before—karri and marri, giants that soared skyward and stood like sentinels. His father had already been there a few years and would have shown him the shack he'd cobbled together with borrowed tools and sweat. Compared to Piandelagotti's rocky, unforgiving soil, the earth here was rich, loamy, and full of promise. Not the burnt red dirt of the north, but a darker, nourishing brown that held the scent of growing things.

Nonno took him to see the coast—the open ocean, the ease of catching fish, and the endless sky above. The land wasn't just fertile, it was generous. And the wildlife! My father would never forget the first time he saw a kangaroo, bounding through the bush like something from a storybook.

They rode horses into the heart of Margaret River, still only a scattering of shops—mostly general supplies, farming goods, and practical things for settlers. No one would've called it a town yet, but it had the bones of something that could become one.

**Margaret River Circa 1940s**

They knew almost no English. My grandfather had picked up a few words in the years before Dad arrived, just enough to get by. But when my father wrote letters to his fiancée, Angelina Fontana, in 1948, they were always in Italian. He might have spoken some English by then but writing it was another matter entirely. His pen still danced in his native tongue. He used to tell me how taken he was with the towering trees. To him, those trees were a sign of good soil. "Where the trees grow tall," he'd say, "the grapes will grow strong." The contrast between the small, stony parcel of land they'd left behind and this new place couldn't have been greater. In Piandelagotti, you struggled for every harvest. Here, the land gave back. Not without hard work—never without that—but you could see the results. You could feel hope in the soil.

This place wasn't easy. But it was easier than where they'd come from. Here, they could plant seeds and watch them grow. They could build, not just survive. The physical work—the language barrier—it didn't matter. Their actions spoke louder. The locals respected that. They didn't need fluent English to prove they were there to stay. Remarkably, they weren't the only ones. Many families from Emilia-Romagna ended up in Margaret River. I suspect this had something to do with the Ship Hotel in Busselton, owned by Amadio Palandri. It became a beacon of familiarity for arriving Italians—a place to find your bearings, to hear your own language, and to meet others chasing the same dream. My father and my Zio Giuseppe were among them, and as it turns out, so were several other Palandri families, all distantly connected to Amadio.

**The Ship Inn, Busselton. Circa early 1900s**

And not just Palandri's—families like the Zani, Zanotti, Fontana, and Piacentini, all from Piandelagotti or nearby. There was something magnetic about this place. Even in my own childhood, when these families would visit, the wine would be opened, the snacks laid out, and before long the house was filled with loud, rolling Italian. It was like stepping into another world. My father would light up when he could slip back into his first language, even just for an evening.

Yet he didn't live in a bubble. He made friends with plenty of Australian families too. The Millers, the Leepers, the Earls, the Blakeys, the Duggans—these names still echo through the history of group settlement in the area. They were farmers too. Hardworking. Weather-worn. Dad respected them. And over time, they respected him too.

He would later build strong ties in the timber industry, and just as firmly in wine. The Palandri family and the Meleri family were pioneers in Margaret River winemaking—producing and selling long before the region was synonymous with wine. Long before anyone had heard of Vasse Felix, Cullen, or Cape Mentelle.

My father and Uncle Giuseppe didn't just work the land—they helped shape the very industries that would define the region. They consulted with the big names later, shared knowledge, shared tools, shared sweat. And they brought with them the work ethic of Piandelagotti—one of hand tools and calloused palms, of long days and quiet pride.

They planted more than vines and fence posts—they planted roots. Not just for themselves, but for the generations to come.

## The Town That Followed Us Home

People often tell me how lucky I was to grow up in Margaret River. To them, it's a slice of paradise—pristine beaches, rolling vineyards, towering forests, and postcard views in every direction. When I casually mention that I'm from there, eyes widen. "You're so lucky," they say, with a wistful sigh, imagining a childhood of barefoot summers and surf breaks.

But I've always said Margaret River didn't grow up around us—we grew up with it. My friends and I used to joke that we spent the first 18 years of our lives trying. to get out, and the rest of our lives trying to get back and for many of us, that's exactly what happened.

I left to study, to work, to live in places as far-flung as Perth, the Wheatbelt, and the Kimberley. Each move gave me something new—opportunity, perspective, sometimes challenge. But always, there was this quiet thread pulling me back. It wasn't just homesickness—it was belonging. Forty years after I first left, I returned. Not for the waves or the wine, but because the place had never really let go of me.

When my grandparents arrived here, it wasn't a holiday destination. There were no boutique wineries or luxury retreats. Margaret River was a dirt road, a few timber buildings, and the smell of livestock and sawdust. Horses and carts still clattered through town. Their vision wasn't framed by ocean views, but by survival, stability, and the hope that their children could thrive in peace.

They didn't come chasing paradise—they came to build a life from nothing.

Over the decades, I've watched this town change and change again—timber to farming, farming to wine, wine to tourism. But underneath the new signs and fresh coats of paint, the heart of Margaret River still beats with the stubborn rhythm of its settlers—ours included.

## Tracks Through Town and Time

During the 1970s, when I was most active as a child, Margaret River was still more of a working town than a destination. It hadn't yet been claimed by tourists, tree-changers, or wine connoisseurs. It was a place defined by community, hard work, and practical needs. For those of us growing up there, Margaret River wasn't a name on a wine label—it was a dusty street, a familiar face behind every counter, and the quiet rhythm of life shaped by the land.

The main street was humble. It had one large general store that sold everything—groceries, hardware, bits of clothing, and even feed for animals. There was a butcher, a baker, and a small petrol station, all run by people who knew your name. The town had a hospital, churches, a school, and a pub, but as kids we rarely noticed those things unless we were dragged there. What caught our attention were the trips into town in the family Valiant—always a tight squeeze—and the promise of a treat if we behaved.

**The Original Margaret River Hotel**

Just ten kilometres south sat Witchcliffe, a smaller hamlet with a kind of rural magic all its own. Darnell's General Store was its beating heart. You could find anything there—from rabbit traps to boiled lollies to fresh produce. It was the kind of shop that felt like something out of *Little House on the Prairie*. Walking through those wooden doors was like stepping back in time. The smells of hessian sacks, kerosene, and sugar mixed in the air. It wasn't just a store—it was an experience.

Some places that are major tourist draws now were, back then, almost inaccessible. Ellenbrook, for instance, was practically in our backyard, but the road that led there was little more than a rough sandy track. Without a four-wheel-drive or tractor, you didn't go down that road. More than once, I remember Dad rescuing stranded surf-seekers who had bogged their cars chasing a wave. Now it's a sealed dual-lane road leading straight to the beach, with signs and parking bays and picnic tables. Back then, it felt like secret country. The centre of town shifted more than once as Margaret River slowly evolved. First, it was that original general store, then came the Wesfarmers Co-op across the street—a curious hybrid of farm supplies and groceries.

**The Original General Store**

Eventually, development nudged everything further down the road into a shopping mall, where a new IGA marked the next step in the town's retail growth. By the late '90s, a full-blown Coles rose where sacks of grain and cattle feed used to sit.

Even as the buildings changed, the heart of the town stayed the same—quietly beating to the rhythm of people who built it with their hands and called it home.

**Then it moved to the Co-op – Groceries and farm equip in one store.**

**(NB: The parking in those days)**

### The Town We Lost

The Margaret River of my childhood no longer exists. The quiet streets where everyone knew your name have been replaced by bustling footpaths and round abouts clogged with hire cars. Once upon a time, the town was a scattered collection of buildings framed by tall gums and patches of soft, wild grass. You could walk straight down the middle of the main street and not meet a soul, maybe wave to one or two neighbours along the way. Today, that same street is lined with boutique shops, wine bars, and cafes—every square metre accounted for, every view neatly manicured.

Back then, Margaret River still felt like ours. It belonged to the locals—farmers, timber workers, teachers, and families who didn't need much to feel rich. The green patches where we used to kick a football or rest our bikes are gone, now paved over or fenced off. The car parks are always full. There's a buzz, a gleam, a sense of polished prosperity—but the spirit of the old town lies buried beneath it all.

Some places have held on. Lloyd's hardware still stands in the centre of town, one of the last remnants of that earlier era. It's weathered and worn, but familiar—a touchstone to a time before tourism found us. As a boy, I knew it as a place that was part barber shop, part toy shop, and part sweet store. Smiler Gale, the barber, would sit us in his big old chair and clip our hair into short crew cuts. The reward? A lollipop, always.

It wasn't much, but it was enough. Those were simpler days—days of patched knees, dusty roads, and long shadows stretching across the paddocks. We didn't know how fast it would all change. We didn't know what we were losing.

But I remember. And maybe that's enough to keep a small piece of it alive.

**The Street Looking at the Tavern Circa 1970s (NB: Street width)**

# Part Three

# Growing Up (Crescere)

*"Growing up isn't just about getting bigger—it's about learning who we are in our hearts."*

*"Crescere non significa solo diventare grandi, ma imparare chi siamo nel cuore."*

# Chapter 10
# Before I Was Born (Prima che nascessi)

*"Our stories begin before us, woven into the lives of those who first loved us."*

*"Le nostre storie iniziano prima di noi, intrecciate nelle vite di coloro che ci hanno amato per primi."*

Before I took my first breath, a world was already spinning around me—full of stories I didn't live but would grow up hearing, echoes I didn't create but would come to carry. I wasn't part of the beginning, but I would spend my life threading myself into its middle, listening for what came before and finding meaning in what was left behind. This is not a story of arrival—it's a story of all that was already unfolding when I quietly entered the scene.

### The Surprise.

They'd sold the pram. The cot was long gone, probably given to a cousin or passed on to another growing family. The baby clothes, the nappies, the lace-edged baptism gowns—all folded up and gone. Mum and Dad were in their forties, the house was already full, and no one was expecting another child.

And then—me.

I've often wondered what went through their minds when they found out. My mother was 44 and my father was 43 years old. Was there shock? Laughter? A pause before the reality settled in. There's is no doubt that I was not planned. I was what they called a menopause baby. Mum and Dad were from a generation that didn't speak much about feelings or intentions, so I've been left to fill in the gaps. And in those gaps, I've sometimes slipped in the word *mistake*. My siblings have teased me with it over the years—not cruelly, but with the kind of dry humour that only comes from love. "You were the afterthought," they'd say. "The bonus baby. The one they didn't see coming." Talking to my brothers and sisters about this brought these same reactions but also some fact about what it was like before I was born.

That's what you get, I suppose, for being Catholic and careless. By the time I arrived, the Palandri family machine had been running for years. My siblings were growing up, moving out, finding their way in the world. Mum and Dad were tired but settled. Life was shifting, and then—here I came, six years behind the youngest, dropping into a family that already had its rhythms and stories. Sometimes I think of my childhood as a postscript. Not in a sad way. More like a quiet coda at the end of a long, rich symphony. The home I was born into was different from the one my brothers and sisters knew.

**The Family apart from Dad before I was Born**

The hard years—post migration, of building the stone house, then a wooden house, of struggling through TB and timber mill injuries, of raising five children on a sparse wage—those were behind us. By the time I came along, there was more space. More time. Maybe even a little more gentleness.

But there was also a sense that I had missed something. The stories I grew up with—of Nonna and Nonno, of the lucerne patch in Cannington, of dances at the hall and Mass at St. Thomas More—were not my stories. They were told to me, passed down in scraps over dinner or in the car or in the quiet moments after family gatherings. I listened to them like they were legends from a world that had closed its gates just before I arrived. The world was already built; I just had to find my place in it. That wasn't always easy. With siblings spread in age and interest, I grew up slightly apart. Too young to join in, too old to be babied. I often wonder if Mum and Dad treated me differently because I came along so late. Were they softer? More fatigued? Did they parent with the same intensity as before, or had the edge worn down? I'll need to ask my brothers and sisters about that.

Some say being the youngest means being spoiled. Others say it means being overlooked.

**I Never Saw the Horses and Never Knew This Life**

For me, it meant learning how to observe. I watched everything. I listened. I learned the family language not by being taught, but by absorbing it. I became the keeper of memories that weren't mine, and I've carried them carefully, trying not to drop or distort them.

And yet, I have to admit—there's a certain power in arriving late. You get to hear how the story went before you, but you also get to add your own unexpected ending. My childhood was shaped by the lives that had already been lived around me. But in some small way, I think my arrival reshaped things too. Maybe I brought back some laughter. Maybe I gave Mum and Dad one last chance to hold a baby in their arms. Maybe I helped remind them of who they'd been, and how far they'd come.

This chapter—before I was born—is one I'll never fully understand. It belongs to others. But that doesn't mean I can't walk through it slowly, ask questions, gather fragments, and see what they reflect about who I am. I wasn't there for the beginning. But I've always been curious about the pages that came just before mine.

### Echoes in the Hallway

My early years were shaped not just by the people around me, but by the space that held us—the house itself. It had a rhythm of its own, like a living thing. It breathed in our silences, sighed in our footsteps, echoed in the creaks of old wood. Our home was modest, made of timber and shaped more by necessity than any grand design. But in its bones, it carried the quiet grandeur of a family's entire history. In its original form, the wooden house had three bedrooms: the master at the front, flanked by a window onto the verandah, and two small rooms out the back. The master bedroom stood apart, separated from the communal living areas by a long corridor that ran straight through the centre of the house, from the front verandah to the back. The hallway was a spine, connecting old and new, memory and presence.

At the back, the two small bedrooms were divided by a narrow back verandah, like an afterthought tacked onto the house. The toilet was outside, and the bathroom was in a shed—a separate structure entirely. We weren't what you'd call modern, built as it was in 1955, but the place functioned. It held us. And in that holding, something sacred occurred.

The living area was the heart of everything. A large kitchen with a big table

**Looking from kitchen to lounge.**

**Looking from lounge to kitchen.**

planted in the middle, surrounded by wooden benches and cupboards that never quite shut properly. At one end of the space was a lounge room, separated by a sliding door. At the other end, the kitchen opened to a *Metters* wood-fired stove, glowing through winter and silent through summer. The lounge had its own fireplace, and the two flames—one for cooking, one for comfort—seemed to represent the twin souls of the home.

Before I was tall enough to see over the bench tops, I knew the kitchen was where everything happened. Mum's presence hovered there like steam from a simmering pot. Her sauce bubbled quietly. Her bread rose in warmth by the fire. The smell of onions and tomatoes mingled with rosemary, a scent that clung to the walls and to my memory. This was where meals were made, and stories were told. Where games were played, and disappointments softened. Where time paused, if only for a cup of coffee or a glass of wine.

Dad claimed a particular seat at the kitchen table—his spot. It backed onto the Metters stove, as if proximity to its warmth grounded him. He didn't say much, but his quietude filled the room more than words ever could. He'd occasionally sit in the lounge room later in life, but back then, this seat was his station. I was told a television appeared in 1964. We didn't even have reliable electricity until 1963. For my older siblings, entertainment meant board games by the glow of a Tilley lamp. *Chinese checkers*, draughts, darts. Books under candlelight. Card games—*Scopa*, *Rummy*, *Canasta*. There was a sacredness in those simple, shared moments, stitched together under a flickering flame.

As a child, I would tiptoe through the kitchen and lounge, cautious not to disturb this quiet ritual of living. My place was the hallway and the front verandah—my own little territory. That hallway became my runway, my racetrack, my stage. With Lego or Meccano spread across the floorboards, I constructed my own stories while walking the length of the hall, back and forth. I often wondered: did my siblings play like this too, once? Did they own this corridor the way I did? In truth, they had grown up in those rooms long before I came along. During the 1950s and 60s, Carla, Lina, and Annunciata shared the bigger back bedroom, while Ric had the smaller room opposite theirs. I never saw that setup with my own eyes, but I could feel it in the air—in the way stories were told, in the affectionate roll of the eyes during recollections. The rooms retained the warmth of those years like old timber holds heat. The house was like a museum of a life I'd missed. I was its newest resident, but also its archivist. I didn't just inhabit it—I read it, like a book already three-quarters done. I listened to its echoes, tried to decipher the meaning in every mark on the wall, every creak in the floor. I was growing up in a house saturated with memory.

Even in its silences, the house spoke. They weren't empty silences. They were filled with the residue of what had been—a laugh down the hallway, a cry in the middle of the night, the scraping of a chair during an argument, the muffled hum of relatives gathered in the backyard. It was a soundscape built from repetition and routine, and even when I didn't understand its origins, I recognised its melody. Being born into a space already so full of life gave me a strange kind of awareness. I knew early on that the world hadn't started with me. That I was walking into a story mid-sentence. And even as a young boy, I felt a quiet responsibility to honour it. I wasn't the protagonist in the family's early tales. But I was the audience—watching, listening, piecing it all together. I wasn't centre stage, but I was close enough to hear the actors breathe. That hallway wasn't just where I played—it was where I figured out how to belong.

## Absence and Arrival.

If there's one thing that shaped my earliest beginnings, it was my mother's presence—unyielding, devoted, and fiercely protective. She was never distant, never dreamy, never diminished by age or fatigue. If anything, the trials of the 1960s had forged in her a kind of iron-willed grace. This was a woman who had crossed continents, carved a home from the wild soils of Margaret River, raised five children, endured the weight of her husband's tuberculosis, and still—against all odds—brought me into the world in her forties. I wasn't part of the original plan, but life had other ideas.

The 1960s began with both joy and fear: the birth of my brother Francesco. Not long after, he contracted meningitis. Today, it's treatable. In 1960, it was nearly a death sentence. With only rudimentary hospital facilities in Margaret

River, it took a storm of effort—relentless vigilance from Mum and Dad, endless prayers, and help from the four older siblings at home—to pull him through. That battle, so early in the decade, left an imprint on the entire household. But Francesco survived. He flourished. And life, in its unpredictable way, moved forward.

Then, in 1964, it was Dad's turn to fall. Tuberculosis struck hard. He was sent to Sir Charlie Gairdner Hospital in Perth, and Mum was left alone to shoulder the weight of the farm, five children, and the daily rhythms of life. I still have the letter she wrote to him from that time. Her English was careful, her words modest. She downplayed the difficulty. "The children are behaving. Carla and Ricky are a great help," she wrote. "The farm is good." But I know what she didn't say. The exhaustion. The fear. The long evenings after the children went to bed, when she sat alone at the table, listening to the wind rattle the walls and wondering how she'd make it through the next day.

By 1966, the roles had reversed. This time it was Mum who was sent away—back to Perth. The pregnancy was complicated. I had turned in the womb, presenting a danger neither Mum nor the local doctor in Margaret River could safely manage. So, she was moved to St John of God Hospital, where she stayed for weeks—some say a month, others recall nearly three—on bed rest. Waiting. Hoping. Trusting the baby would hold on.

That baby was me. My arrival wasn't gentle. A caesarean was required, a serious intervention in those days. I was born small, sickly, and immediately troubled by lung issues. The hospital staff fought to get oxygen into me. I caught pneumonia shortly after birth, and then came asthma, bronchitis, and every respiratory concern imaginable. In the first fragile months of life, I was never far from illness. And yet, somehow, I held on.

Back in Margaret River, Dad—still recovering from the long shadow of tuberculosis—stepped into Mum's place. He managed the farm, held a full-time job, cooked, cleaned, and oversaw five children. But he didn't do it alone. My siblings rallied. Carla, Lina, and Anne took over the housework. They cooked, cleaned, made sure school bags were packed, and the washing was folded. The boys helped on the farm, filled the gap in the paddocks and the sheds. Everyone contributed. Everyone pulled tighter.

That's how I was born—not just into a family, but into a living web of sacrifice and cooperation. Into the kind of love that doesn't shout, but shows itself in effort, in steadiness, in doing what needs to be done.

And when Mum returned from Perth, she resumed her post as guardian with quiet intensity. Every breath I took was monitored. She learned the sound of each cough. She could sense a fever before the thermometer confirmed it. She understood the rhythms of nebulisers and the signals of shallow breathing. She was not just my mother; she was my watchtower.

One of the more vivid memories I have—though I'm not sure whether it's real or reconstructed from stories—is of Mum placing me on her lap each day, laying me forward on my stomach while a man (a local healer of sorts) slapped my back in rhythm to loosen the phlegm in my lungs. I'd cough, wheeze, cry. But it worked. And Mum never flinched.

What others might have called spoiling was, in truth, something else entirely. It was over-care. It was the fierce protection of a mother who had already stared down meningitis, TB, and now the fragility of her youngest child. She wasn't about to face another loss. So, she watched me like a hawk. I slept in her room—her and Dad's room—until I was five years old. Always nearby. Always within reach.

She wrapped me in layers even on warm days. "You'll catch a chill," she'd say, as she pulled up my socks and pushed a scarf into my school jumper. "Don't sit on the cold floor." I was coated in warmth, both literal and emotional. The hot water bottle under the sheets. The soft-spoken "Buonanotte" whispered each night. The soup warmed just for me, served with quiet anticipation. She held me steady while the world wobbled around us.

But even then, she wasn't alone. My siblings, though young themselves, added their own strands to the net. They helped cook, tidied quietly when I was sleeping, distracted me with stories when I was wheezing. Each of them bores a share of responsibility—not because they were asked, but because that was the nature of our family. It's what we did. The house changed around us, too. As Ric and Carla moved into adulthood and left home, new spaces opened, new configurations formed. But the heart of the home remained Mum. No matter how many lefts, no matter how the seasons turned, her presence anchored everything.

And despite all this—despite the weight she carried—Mum made room for joy. She sang to me, Nursery rhymes. She sat at the end of my bed when I was unwell, brushing the hair off my forehead, whispering stories to chase the fever away. I don't remember the details of those moments. I remember the feeling—of safety, of being seen.

Older mothers are sometimes cast as tired, their love worn thin. Mum was never like that. Her love was tireless, even defiant. Structured, vigilant, unwavering. She didn't melt into sentiment; she stood strong in purpose. Every meal she cooked, every sock she pulled up, every curtain she drew shut against the night air—these were her love letters. Quiet acts of protection and resolve.

Looking back now, I see her clearly—not just as a mother, but as a force. The 1960s through every kind of hardship at our family: illness, distance, economic uncertainty. And yet, the centre held. Because she held it.

## Shadows of Departure

It began quietly, almost imperceptibly—the thinning of footsteps, the closing of doors that once remained ajar. In 1966, the year of my birth, the rhythm of the household was already shifting. Ricardo was fifteen and in Year 10, Carla fourteen and in Year 9 at Margaret River High School. Lina was eleven, Annunciata nine, and Francesco six. The three youngest still attended the convent school run by the Mercy Sisters—Frank in Grade 1, Ann in Grade 4, and Lina in Grade 6.

If there had ever been a plan to stop having children, life had other ideas. News of Mum's pregnancy didn't send shockwaves through the household. Instead, it seemed to ripple gently through the family, absorbed with a kind of quiet excitement. The girls were thrilled—a baby in the house was something new, something joyful. Too young to grasp the challenges of a later-in-life pregnancy, they instead saw it through the lens Mum had taught them: family first, and love above all.

Mum had raised her daughters to be capable homemakers. They could cook, clean, and care for others with the same practical wisdom passed down from her own mother. In many ways, they were more prepared than they realised for my arrival. And as for Mum—she was remarkable. The most kind, compassionate, and loving soul I have ever known. There was a strength in her, even when tired, even when the world asked too much.

**The new bedroom built onto the side of the house before I was born.**

## From Stone and Snow to Timber and Wine

By the time I entered the picture, change was already in motion. Electricity had arrived in 1963, transforming the way we lived and worked. Two new bedrooms were built onto the side of the house to accommodate the ever-growing family. Frank was moved out of Mum and Dad's room, and Ric, too, was shifted from his small front bedroom. The girls upgraded to the spacious new bedroom, vacating the older bedrooms that had once brimmed with energy and clatter. What had been cramped suddenly felt expansive. The family was growing—and yet, subtly, it was also beginning to shrink.

One by one, they began to leave.

In 1966, Ric left school to work on the farm, studying Year 11 and 12 by correspondence. By 1968, he secured a job at the R&I Bank in Manjimup, and later that year, he returned to the Margaret River branch. But opportunity called again. In 1969, he left for Perth, chasing independence and a life beyond the boundaries of our small town. Carla followed closely behind. After leaving school at the end of Year 10, she took up a typing job in Cowaramup, then left for Perth to become a secretary. Like many of us, Carla often said that by seventeen, Margaret River felt too small. She wanted to breathe new air, explore new things. She jokes now about stealing Dad's tobacco and sneaking roll-your-owns in the back room. Everyone knew, even Dad, I think.

Their exits weren't dramatic. No long hugs or emotional farewells. Just a slight shift in the air. A voice missing at dinner. A room where the bed stayed made. The clatter of cutlery at the table grew quieter. The house that had once thrummed with energy began to echo. I didn't fully understand it at the time, but I felt it. The air changed. Something was thinning—not love, but presence.

Each room they left behind became a capsule. A drawer of old lipstick. A comb. A forgotten schoolbook or a folded scarf. These weren't just items; they were memories in waiting. Sometimes I'd find myself wandering into those rooms, not to snoop, but to feel closer to them. It was like walking through a gallery of stories paused mid-sentence.

Mum grew quieter. Dad seemed more inward, less animated. He was always a man of few words, but now his silence felt heavier. Mum, still strong, still loving, had begun to stretch herself thinner between work, ageing, and the remaining children at home. I may have been too young to articulate it, but I knew things had shifted.

Still, there was joy. I was seen as a new beginning—a little soul born into the afterlight. Though I was small and often sickly, the girls loved doting on me. Mum, ever protective, especially watched my health. My breathing, my coughs, my exposure to the cold. I became the centre of their vigilance, and in that attention, I found love. Mum would often leave me in the girls' care while she helped Dad on the farm. They were proud of that responsibility. They bathed me, changed me, wrapped me up in jumpers even on sunny days. The house, although quieter, still pulsed with warmth.

By 1971, modernisation had crept in further—the bathroom and toilet were moved indoors, taking over Ric's old room. Carla visited often, now with her boyfriend in tow, adding a new dynamic to the household. Beds were made up with linen that stayed pristine between visits. And in all that rearrangement, I was still growing—shaped just as much by who had left as by who remained.

Lina and Anne were next. They travelled to Busselton Senior High School to complete Years 11 and 12. After finishing, Lina left to study nursing in Perth, later relocating to Geraldton to begin her career. It was 1973; I was nine years old, bunking in with Frank in one of the newer rooms. Because of my delicate health, everyone watched over me—Mum, Dad, and all remaining siblings. Ricardo had married in 1972 and moved to Karratha, then to Darwin, just in time for Cyclone Tracy. Carla had married in 1974. Lina's visits became less frequent. But when they came, they were filled with laughter, stories, and the kind of joy that only grows in absence.

The house kept shifting, breathing out one child at a time. Anne left in 1975 to pursue teaching in Perth, leaving just Frank and me. Frank, though six years older, stayed local, working around Margaret River. He became my closest sibling, my constant companion in those last years of the family home as we once knew it. He would stay my anchor until I too left to study.

By 1977, just after I turned eleven, Annunciata returned for visits with her boyfriend and a group of friends, ushering in yet another new phase. Each visit was an event, each laugh in the kitchen echoing a past that felt further away with every passing season.

I never resented any of them for leaving. I missed them, of course, but I understood. The world was wide, and they were ready. I watched them go like the tide retreating—steady, inevitable, natural.

The wooden house had stretched and grown with us. It expanded when I was born, then slowly emptied over the next twelve years, until only echoes remained. But the love never faded. It condensed—into visits, into Sunday lunches, into the hum of voices when we were all together again.

In their absence, I learned to hear my own voice. In the quiet of those empty rooms, I wasn't lonely—I was learning how to remember.

### Keeper of Their Stories.

I was born into a story already in motion—a novel halfway written, with characters well-formed and history deeply rooted in the soil of Margaret River and the memory of another country. Long before I ever opened my eyes, the family had lived a thousand lives: a migration by ship, a farm built from the ground up, the stone house, the timber house, births, hardship, weddings, TB, and survival. By the time I arrived, the lines had already been inked, the pages turned. I didn't witness the beginning, but somehow, I became the one who remembers.

Not because I planned to. Not because I wrote everything down in a journal or wielded a camera at every turn. It was something quieter than that—something softer. I listened. I noticed. I paid attention to the things people said in passing, to the expressions on their faces when certain memories rose up unexpectedly. Like the youngest often does, I lingered on the edges, watching the scenes unfold, collecting fragments.

That's the strange thing about being the last-born. The spotlight never lingers too long on you. Instead, you learn the rhythm of others. You hear the same stories retold, modified slightly each time—expanded in the warmth of memory or contracted by time. You notice what's repeated and what's avoided. And if you're careful, you start to piece together not just what happened, but how it felt.

For me, this gathering of stories wasn't just a pastime—it became a responsibility. Not imposed, not instructed, but felt. Deeply. Somewhere along the way, I began to realise that if I didn't remember, some things would be lost forever. Some already were. There were voices I never got to hear in full: Nonna's, Nonno's, even Mum and Dad's at certain times in their lives. There were photographs without names on the back, letters tucked away in drawers, silences that could have spoken volumes if only I'd known the right questions to ask.

Still, I caught what I could. Stories were rarely told in chronological order—they came in bursts, in laughter over Sunday lunch, in a sigh while washing dishes, in a passing comment during a car ride. They came in scraps: "Remember when Mum fell off the ladder?" "Ric used to sneak smokes behind the shed." "Lina's kindness always reminded me of Nonna." "Anne? Fierce as ever, always the one to speak up." "Frank? Quiet as Dad, but with eyes that saw everything."

Some stories I had to tease out, nudging gently. Others came unprompted, spilling forth when someone let their guard down or nostalgia got the better of them. What I didn't live, I absorbed. What I didn't witness, I imagined, carefully filling in the cracks with what I knew of the people involved. And perhaps that's how I came to see my place in all this—not as a central figure, not as the hero of the tale, but the scribe. The observer. The bridge between those who were there and those who will come after.

I've often been asked how I remember so much. The truth is, I don't know.

Sometimes a smell, a sound, or the way someone laughs are all it takes to unlock a flood. Other times, it's the absence of someone—the space they once filled—that brings the sharpest memory. I remember Dad's quietness, how it filled a room more than any speech. I remember Mum's way of watching everything without seeming to, of folding care into every sock, every meal. I remember how Frank mirrored Dad's stillness, how Anne's grin lit up a space before she even spoke, how Lina carried everyone else's burdens without complaint. How Carla moved with confidence, and how Ric, half in the world and half outside of it, lived a life of quiet contradictions—stone and wood, bank and bush, laughter and loneliness.

I didn't just collect their stories to preserve them. I collected them to understand. To find myself in them. To make sense of who I was, coming in at the tail end of something so vast and already in motion.

Some stories were light-hearted. Some were sad. Some weren't even stories at all—just impressions, echoes, a certain silence that told its own tale. And when I look back now, I don't see one great family narrative with a clear arc. I see a mosaic. Pieces that don't always fit neatly, that overlap and contradict, that shine differently depending on where you stand. But together, they make something whole.

I never asked to be the keeper. It wasn't a role handed to me. It just happened—one moment, one memory at a time. And the older I got, the more I realised how much was at stake. If I didn't keep them—if I didn't write them down or speak to them aloud—they might vanish. Already, there are things I wish I'd asked Mum. Details I wish I'd written sooner. Letters I wish I'd found earlier. But what I do have, I hold tight.

This memoir, then, is more than a retelling. It's a gathering. A way to carry the past forward, to ensure that our story doesn't get folded away with the old photographs and yellowed baptism gowns. It's not just about Mum and Dad, though they are at its centre. It's about all of us. Ric and Carla, Lina and Anne, Frank and me. It's about how we grew, how we left, how we stayed connected, even when the house emptied out. I didn't build the house. I didn't plough the fields or cook the meals that held our family together. But I was there in the quiet moments after—the echoes in the hallway, the creak of old floorboards, the dust in the photo frames. I was there to remember. And I will keep remembering, as long as I can.

Call it sentiment. Call it duty. Call it love.

But I'll keep telling our stories—because someone must.

**Mid 80s, we built a games room to house the pool table.**

# Chapter 11
# Mischief, Mayhem and Missteps

## (Dispetto, caos e passi falsi)

*"Youth is the time of dreams, mistakes, and first laughter."*

*"La giovinezza è il tempo dei sogni, degli errori e delle prime risate."*

Before I understood right from wrong—or perhaps even after—I understood how to push a boundary. Not out of malice, but curiosity. Boredom. The electric thrill of seeing just how far a young boy could go before someone noticed. In a household built on hard work, Catholic values, and a strong sense of "doing the right thing," I became the outlier: the small one always testing the edge. My mischief wasn't grand or cruel—it was everyday rebellion, stitched into the seams of a sprawling family life. And yet, those small moments—the quiet disobedience, the secret schemes, the innocent lies—form a hidden thread through my childhood. This chapter is about those stumbles. The chaos, the cracked windows, the fibs told, and the knees grazed. The things I got away with. The things I didn't. And the strange, sweet lessons they left behind.

### Blessed, Bronchial and a Bit of a Menace

I've often marvelled at the fact I survived childhood at all—let alone made it to adulthood mostly intact. Anyone who's read the earlier chapters will already know that my childhood on the farm was, in many ways, idyllic: wide spaces, good food, a big family, and days filled with mischief and mud. But just under the surface of those happy memories lurks the reality that danger and disaster were never too far away. Some of those incidents still make me laugh out loud—others leave me shaking my head and wondering how I didn't end up in traction.

One of the earliest stories told about me involves pneumonia. I contracted it when I was very young, and it left a lasting mark on my lungs. From there it was a cascade: bronchitis, asthma, and long stretches of time off school during primary years. This delicate health situation shaped a lot of how I was treated growing up. Mum and Dad wrapped me in wool—sometimes literally. I was always rugged up like an Arctic explorer: two jumpers, a coat, a scarf, and something itchy under it all. Shoes on, always. Heaven helps me if I tried to sneak out barefoot.

But all that caution must have pent up some mischief. Because when I did get my chance for a bit of freedom, I took it. Some might say I became the family pest—annoying my older siblings, poking into their business, and generally causing trouble without ever getting into too much of it myself. Spoilt? Maybe. A survivor? Definitely.

### The Day the Earth Moved (and Nearly Took My Ear with It)

In 1968, I was doing what most little kids do best playing in the dirt, blissfully unaware of danger, consequence, or gravity in all senses of the word. I was lying on the garage floor of our house in Margaret River, face down, probably vrooming a Matchbox car through the dust and inventing a miniature world that lived solely beneath my nose.

The garage wasn't exactly Bunnings. It was a ramshackle wooden shed patched together with whatever was available—oil cans, old cupboards, broken furniture, buckets, tins, tangled cords, and unused windowsills leaning against the walls like forgotten artwork. It was a sacred space of clutter and curiosity—a treasure trove for an imaginative child like me.

And then, without warning, the earth moved.

Hundreds of kilometres away, in a place called Meckering, a massive earthquake struck—6.5 on the Richter scale. Now, in Margaret River, we barely felt it as more than a tremble. But tell that to the jarrah-framed window leaning against the wall of Dad's shed. That tremor was enough to send it toppling over.

I never even saw it coming.

One moment I was building a dirt empire. The next, I was pinned to the garage floor—by my ear. The jarrah frame, solid and unforgiving, had somehow missed crushing my skull by a whisker and instead caught my ear like a tent peg. I couldn't move. I didn't even know what had happened, only that my ear was being introduced to gravity in a deeply personal way—and it hurt like hell. There was no one around. Mum was inside, probably elbow-deep in dinner prep. My siblings were all at school. I screamed until my voice gave out, flailed until I gave up, and then—I think—I passed out.

The next thing I remember is being cradled in my father's arms. He must have heard the commotion or sensed something was wrong. He scooped me up, bundled me into the front seat of the Valiant, and we sped off to Margaret River Hospital. The hospital lights were cold and bright. I can still see that big, articulated surgical lamp looming overhead, like some alien creature. The doctor said I was going to sleep now. I was too young to count back from ten. I just stared at the light and drifted away.

I woke up with stitches—about ten of them—holding my ear together like Frankenstein's lobe. The giggling voices of my sisters echoed faintly in my memory. Mum and Dad were close by, their worry softened by the relief of knowing I'd be okay. I've carried that scar ever since. A jagged little reminder of the day the earth moved just enough to almost take me with it. Not the whole me—just a piece of cartilage. And maybe—just maybe—an angel was watching that day. Or at least nudged the jarrah an inch to the left.

## The Great Egg Gambit

When you're the youngest in a big Italian Australian family, your duties are rarely glamorous. While my older siblings were driving tractors, fixing fences, and milking cows with a maturity that made them seem ten feet tall, I was consigned to poultry patrol. That's right—I was the self-appointed Chicken Wrangler of the Palandri farm. Our chickens weren't the pampered kind you see in today's backyard coops with name tags and designer feed. No, ours were true free-range birds—scruffy, stubborn, and fierce little foragers who ruled the paddocks like feathered outlaws.

When grasshopper season hit, they went on feeding frenzies that resembled scenes from a horror movie—beaks snapping, wings flapping, insect legs flying. And once the sun went down, it was my job to herd them back into the coop before the foxes had their midnight snack.

This was no small task. Chickens, as it turns out, are both agile and deeply unreasonable. They refused to be herded, especially not by a boy armed with nothing but hope and a cracked ice-cream container. They scattered in every direction like feathered fireworks. And catching them? Let's just say I developed cardio fitness long before it became trendy.

My second job was egg collection—a sacred ritual that took place twice daily. Sure, sometimes the eggs were in the coop, nestled dutifully in their straw beds like obedient children. But often, the hens got creative. They laid eggs in flowerpots, behind the woodpile, under the water tank, in Dad's workshop toolbox… basically anywhere that gave me a reason to crawl, scratch, and occasionally swear under my breath. Hunting for eggs became a kind of farmyard treasure hunt—equal parts satisfying and infuriating.

Of course, not all eggs were fresh. Sometimes I'd stumble upon secret stashes that had clearly been hidden for weeks. The smell gave it away. If you've never cracked open a rotten egg, count yourself lucky. These were the kind of eggs that could strip paint. Naturally, in my youthful wisdom, I discovered a second use for them: ammunition.

Frank—my older brother and constant target—bore the brunt of my egg-slinging escapades. On more than one occasion, he'd be walking innocently through the yard only to be struck with a stinky splat of sulphuric justice. To be fair, I thought it was hilarious. He did not. But years later, even he laughs about it. Sort of.

Then there was the Chicken Incident. I was visiting my cousins, who shared similar poultry duties on their side of the family. We decided to "speed things up" by herding the chickens with sticks, because nothing says effective animal management like a group of overexcited ten-year-olds with weapons. Inevitably, one of the chickens zigged when it should've zagged and—whack. Instant fatality. We stood frozen, staring at the feathered casualty. Panic set in. We weren't worried about the chicken—we were worried about Uncle Joe. Uncle Joe had a voice that could stop birds' mid-flight. We knew we were in for it. So, we got creative. First, we doused the dead chicken in diesel (don't ask why, it seemed logical at the time). Then we tossed it into the old copper fireplace and set it alight. Problem solved, we thought. No evidence, no crime. But fate wasn't done with us yet. The next day, we overheard Uncle Joe telling Auntie Tilly about something strange he'd found in the copper. Our ears pricked up. Were we busted?

Apparently, a fox had come in during the night, tempted by the smell of roast chicken. It feasted on the diesel-marinated carcass and died beside the copper. So, when Uncle Joe found it, there was no sign of the chicken—just one very dead, very poisoned fox. We couldn't believe our luck. Not only had we avoided punishment, but we'd accidentally become heroes in the ongoing war against foxes. A fluke, sure—but one that went straight into our catalogue of childhood victories.

Eggs, it turned out, weren't just farm produce—they were the source of great scientific inquiry. One day, my cousin Giacomo (Jimmy) and I got into a debate about their structural integrity. Eggs, after all, are strong along the long axis, right? Jimmy, who had the arm of a young fast bowler, boasted that he could hurl an egg the full length of the paddock and it wouldn't break if it landed just right. Naturally, I called his bluff. With the kind of confidence only eleven-year-olds possess, Jimmy launched an egg with everything he had. It flew like a white missile, arcing dramatically before landing… and bouncing. It didn't break. We stared at each other, then at the egg. Then burst into laughter. Nature had surprised us yet again. Somehow, it had survived.

Looking back now, these weren't just silly moments of childhood chaos—they were our rites of passage. Egg hunts, chicken chases, and prank wars. We weren't always well-behaved, but we were endlessly inventive. So no, I didn't drive the tractor or fix fences in those early days. But I tamed the chickens (sort of), explored egg physics, outwitted a fox, and learned that a rotten egg, well-timed, could bring a lifetime of laughter. Not a bad resume for the youngest kid on the farm.

### Claws, Paws, and Furry Chaos

Throughout my life—and I mean *the entire length of it*—we had a rotating cast of four-legged, feathered, and downright peculiar companions. Not counting the usual cows, chooks, and the odd sheep, our property played host to an ever-changing zoo of dogs, cats, parrots, magpies, frogs, and one wildly confused quail. We didn't call them "pets" as much as we called them "guests who occasionally pulled their weight.". Let's start with the dogs. Back then, dogs didn't live inside like royalty. There were no "doggy beds" or knitted jumpers. They didn't sit on couches or dine on gourmet kibble. Our dogs lived outdoors. Rain, shine, or south-westerlies—they were outside. These were working dogs. Or, at least, they were *meant* to be.

My first dog was Digger—a scrappy little thing, part-kelpie, all heart. She followed me everywhere, tail up, nose twitching, eyes full of loyalty. Then one day, Digger vanished. Gone without a trace. That's when I learned one of life's solemn truths: when dogs sense their time is up, they often crawl off somewhere to die quietly. No fuss, no farewell, just an act of dignity—perhaps to spare us the pain. I missed her terribly.

**Digger and I, My First Dog**

Next came Scotti—a black Labrador gifted by one of Dad's cousins. He was magnificent in size and temperament, a walking marshmallow of affection. The kind of dog you could lie on during a sunny day and drift into a nap. Loyal? Absolutely. Useful with cattle? Not even close. He had no idea what to do with livestock and once came home with a fishing hook lodged in his cheek. We couldn't remove it (there was no vet in Margaret River), so we waited… and waited… until the hook just dissolved or dislodged itself. He never seemed to mind. Just smiled, drooled, and wagged his tail.

After Scotti passed, Dad got serious. "Time to get a *real* cattle dog," he said. He brought home a blue heeler—gregarious, muscular, ankle-biting to the core. Covered in strange white spots, we named him "Three Spots." It was never entirely clear how many spots he actually had. Could've been two.

**I'm saying good morning to Scottie.**

Could've been thirty. But he was a working dog through and through—brilliant with cattle, nipping at their heels like a pro. And then the chickens started dying. It turned out Three Spots wasn't just good at herding. He was also good at *killing*. And when you live on a farm, that's a dealbreaker. One morning I heard the dreaded gunshot from my room. I cried, of course. But Dad never explained it cruelly. "We can't have a dog that kills chickens," he said. And that was that. Quiet. Necessary. Devastating.

Long before I was born, Dad had a different kind of dog—a "roo dog" called Bullet. These were serious animals: part bull Arab, built for speed, strength, and hunting. Bullet, true to his name, was fearless. The story goes that he was out near Ellensbrook with Dad and my uncle when he was cornered by a massive kangaroo. Bullet lunged. The kangaroo struck. The result was awful: Bullet's chest was ripped open by the roo's claws. He died by the riverbank. We never forgot him.

Sometimes dogs just *appeared*. One day a strange creature bounced into our yard. It looked like a greyhound mated with a bulldog. Slender body, huge chest, and lips that sagged like deflated tyres. It bounced, jiggled, twisted, and

**Dad with "Bullet" the 'roo' dog.**

wriggled. It was a total fruit loop—and I loved it instantly. Turns out, he was a Boxer. We kept him for a few weeks until a stranger came to claim him. I was devastated. But four days later—miracle of miracles—he reappeared on our front lawn, tongue out, tail wagging like a helicopter. I wanted to keep him forever. But again, Dad said no. "He's not ours." And back he went. Now, onto the cats. Oh, cats.

We had one long-term cat in my youth. Unlike every other animal on the property—which were banned from the house like they carried bubonic plague—this cat had *privileges*. It sat by the *Metters* stove like it paid rent. It followed Mum around like a puppy and received saucers of milk like it was born into aristocracy. I can't even remember its name. Probably because I never bonded with it.

Truth be told, I've never been a cat person. They have… attitudes. One minute they're purring like angels, the next they're shredding your arms for daring to pat them. This particular cat never attacked me, but I kept my distance. I sensed it was up to something.

On the farm, cats could quickly turn from cuddly companions to predators. Feral cats were a real problem—massive things, sometimes twice the size of your average tabby, and angry. If you tried to rescue one from a trap or untangle it from wire, it would reward you with shredded hands. They decimated native wildlife and were notorious for hunting chickens. They were ghosts in the fields—silent, sleek, deadly.

One year, we began hearing odd noises in the ceiling. Something scratching and mewing. Of course, I was the smallest, so I was the one shoved up into the roof space. What I found was nightmarish: around fifteen feral kittens, hissing, deformed, and vicious. Most had clubbed feet or twisted limbs. Abandoned by their mother, they'd turned feral within weeks. I carried them down in a bag, one squirming mass of claws and teeth. Dad took one look and made the hard call. "We can't keep them. They'll grow up wild and dangerous." I wasn't involved in what happened next, but I knew. Dad placed a brick and the kittens into the bag and quietly took them to the dam. Afterward, he retrieved the bag and buried them. It was brutal, but in those days, there weren't animal shelters or vet clinics just down the road. Life on the farm was often unforgiving. And yet, we still loved our animals. Despite the hardship, the deaths, and the decisions that weighed heavier than they should've on young shoulders, there was deep affection. We gave what we could: food, warmth, laughter, play. We grieved them when they passed. We remembered their quirks.

Today's pets might sleep on heated blankets, get organic treats, and have Instagram accounts. But back then, love looked a little different. It was a scratch behind the ears, a scrap of lamb fat tossed under the table, or a warm spot by the stove. It was digging a grave in the back paddock when it all ended, and telling their story decades later—claws, paws, and all.

## Tractors, Trouble and the End of the Hunt

At around fifteen, we discovered spotlighting. Not the Broadway kind—ours involved tractors, floodlights, and highly questionable decisions made under the illusion of rural genius. We kitted out the old Fiat tractor like it was a military vehicle. A spotlight got rigged onto the mudguard with bits of wire and blind confidence, while the rest of us perched ourselves on the carry-all hanging off the back. That's right—the carry-all. No seatbelts, no helmets, just teenage bravado and an unshakeable faith in our reflexes.

We took great pride in how "safe" we were, proudly declaring that no one had been shot. That was our gold standard of success. We mostly bagged rabbits, sometimes a fox, and—on rarer occasions—an unfortunate feral cat. We thought we were doing pest control. In reality, we were just boys playing cowboy in the dark.

One memorable night, my cousin was driving the tractor on the old property when the headlights gave out mid-hunt. Did we stop? Of course not. He continued driving blind. In no time at all, we managed to wedge the underbelly of the tractor firmly onto a fallen log. The front wheels went over, but the rest of the machine belly-flopped onto the timber like a stunned cow.

There we were: stranded, embarrassed, and forced to trudge home and admit our brilliance to Dad and Zio. Their response was a mix of relief that no one was dead and fury that we'd treated expensive machinery like a joyride prop.

Our final act of spotlighting stupidity came when we "borrowed" Zio Giuseppe's newer tractor instead of the reliable old Fiat. No one told our fathers. And when Zio noticed his shiny machine missing, he thought it had been stolen and launched a manhunt. When he found us—mid-paddock, clueless and caught—he delivered a verbal dressing-down that echoed across the district.

That night marked the end of our nocturnal hunting escapades. Not because we learned a great lesson, but because the tractors were now locked up. Still, we bagged a few rabbits. And a lifetime of laughter.

## "The Bare-Bottom Boys: Cousins, Catastrophes, and Other Country Crimes"

Some cousins are your friends. Others are your partners in crime. Ours were both.

Besides me, there were three usual suspects—sometimes four if Frank got dragged into it. Zio Giuseppe and Zia Tilly lived about a kilometre and a half down the road in the old Stonehouse with their nine children. That gave us a rotating cast of mischief-makers. Little Giuseppe (we called him Joe), Giacomo (Jim), and Domenico (Dom) were the closest in age to me. Joe was a year older, Jim was my age, and Dom was two years younger. On the Fontana side, Daryl was a regular too, one year older than me and full of wildly confident ideas. And then there was Frank—older than all of us and, on most days, slightly wiser, but still young enough to get roped into our harebrained schemes.

The farm was our playground and our proving ground, equal parts adventure and hazard. The equipment we used had seen better decades. Trailers had loose nails, sheds had tetanus threats sticking out at every angle, and our uniforms of shorts, T-shirts, and bare feet wouldn't have passed even the loosest safety inspections. But we thought we were invincible.

Take, for example, the firewood run.

It was a basic operation: cut dead trees into chunks with chainsaws, throw them onto the trailer, jump aboard, and move to the next block. Except one day, as I leapt onto the rear of the trailer in motion, my shorts caught on a rogue nail. Before I could react, they tore right off. There I was, standing in my underwear with an audience of cousins roaring with laughter. The only option? A two-kilometre jog home in my jocks, cheeks burning—both kinds—so I could find a new pair of pants and preserve what little dignity I had left.

Unfortunately, this would not be my final wardrobe malfunction.

Later, while stacking hay into the shed, we found ourselves faced with a glorious pile of loose hay below the 15-metre-high roof. Naturally, the only logical next step was to jump from the roof into it. The others launched themselves heroically. When my turn came, I dangled my legs off the edge, summoning courage, when—once again—a bloody nail caught my shorts. There I was again, suspended midair, this time *by* my pants. Seconds later, gravity won. My shorts ripped free, and I plummeted into the hay pile in my underwear, my cousins in hysterics and my dignity once again swinging from the roof, 15 metres up.

You'd think I'd start wearing sturdier shorts. Or at least stop climbing onto things.

One day, Daryl spotted a large beehive nestled in a tree. The rest of us Palandri boys, seasoned in common sense if not in fashion, backed away immediately. Daryl, on the other hand, decided to hurl a rock at it. It was a direct hit. The hive trembled. Then came the hum—a furious, unified roar of wings. The bees poured out like vengeance itself. Daryl ran. We ran faster.

We sprinted to the cattle trough and dove in like soldiers escaping enemy fire. Daryl didn't make it. As we watched from our watery refuge, Daryl danced, swatted, and screamed his way into history as the only one of us brave—and foolish—enough to pick a fight with a swarm of bees and lose. On calmer days, our activities turned to engineering. Zio Giuseppe built us an epic swing set: two heavy swings hung from thick chains bolted to solid jarrah posts. Naturally, we decided to launch ourselves off these swings at high speed in the hope of landing on an old mattress dragged from the cellar. It started well—graceful arcs, big landings, lots of whooping.

But as always, we pushed the boundaries. Higher, faster, wilder. Someone attempted a mid-air flip. Someone else tried a double dismount. Eventually, the mattress slipped—or maybe we forgot to check where it was—and we began missing our target. Hitting the bare, unforgiving ground knocked some of the wind out of our sails—and out of our lungs. After a few bone-jarring crashes and bruised bottoms, the thrill wore off. We quietly abandoned the aerial acrobatics and went back to more traditional mischief: bothering the cows, trying to ride goats, and seeing who could throw a rock the farthest without hitting something important.

What strikes me now is how little supervision we had. We roamed freely, semi-clothed, armed with chainsaws and bad ideas, protected only by a strong sense of kinship and the occasional divine intervention. Our parents must have trusted either our survival instincts or the fact that the cows would tell on us.

In hindsight, it's a miracle we all made it out intact—well, mostly intact. We may have walked away with splinters, scrapes, stings, and frequent embarrassment, but we also walked away with stories. And let's be honest, nothing binds cousins like a few pant less escapades and a shared mattress landing gone wrong.

### The Fort Over the Creek

One school holiday, around the ripe old age of fifteen, we decided it was time to leave our mark on the farm—not with chores or fencing or shearing sheep, but with something far more essential: a cubby house. Not just any rickety shack cobbled together from leftover firewood and wishful thinking. No, we were aiming for architectural brilliance. A hideout. A sanctuary. A palace of mischief. Armed with Abba-era enthusiasm, hand-me-down carpentry tools, a tractor and an actual chainsaw (yes, a chainsaw—no adult supervision required, apparently), we set out in search of the perfect site. After much deliberation and far too many debates about "load-bearing branches," we settled on the ideal location: straddling the main creek. It had everything—shade, privacy, and two robust trees standing like ancient guardians, their limbs perfectly forked to wedge in our logs.

We hauled, sawed, and hammered our way to greatness. Sturdy logs were locked in across the water, forming a kind of suspended platform that defied all conventional building codes. From the old pig pen—now vacant but once notorious—we salvaged thick, rich Jarrah boards, still smelling faintly of the past. These became the floor of our tree-bridge fortress. Solid until told by Zio that we can't use that timber. We patched together a roof from sticks, boards, and a generous helping of foliage, doing our best to make it waterproof. Miraculously, it worked. The cubby featured a trapdoor entry, lookout windows facing the trickling stream, and enough room for six dreamers to sprawl out and plot their next adventure. It became our place to think, to hide, to be ourselves away from the grown-up world. It stood through storms, secrets, and years of after-school lounging. And remarkably—though the farms are now sold, the animals gone, and we're all older—the cubby still stands. Forty years on, it's a stubborn little relic. Our childhood, still wedged between two trees over a Margaret River creek.

— ◆ —

### The Great Goanna Climb

We were meant to be doing something helpful—responsible, even. That's what we told ourselves anyway. Giacomo and I had been given the task of lighting the bullrushes around the dam, part of the annual "burning off" ritual to stop the reeds from overtaking everything. A rite of passage, really—country kids with fire and no supervision. What could possibly go wrong Now, anyone who's met a bullrush knows they're more than just a plant. They're a jungle of dry tinder, insect hotels, and five-star resorts for all manner of wildlife—including snakes and, as we would soon learn, goannas. The rule was simple: light the match, toss it in, and run like hell. You never knew what might shoot out. On this day, I lit a patch and sprinted. Behind me, there was a cracking sound—and then a blur. Outburst a racehorse goanna. I swear, this thing was as long as a cricket bat and twice as fast. Long claws, flaring nostrils, eyes wild—it was pure prehistoric panic.

Unfortunately for Giacomo, he was the only vertical object in the clearing. Now, anyone with goanna experience knows this: when they're frightened, they run *up*. Trees, fences, haystacks—anything tall. And in the absence of trees, they improvise. That day, my cousin became the tallest available structure. The goanna scaled him like scaffolding—right up his leg, over his torso, and perched squarely on his head, tail flicking in panic. Giacomo didn't scream. He didn't run. He just froze, eyes wide, with an actual dinosaur squatting on his scalp.

Instinct took over. He whacked at it—reflexively, with both hands—until it toppled off and darted for the next tallest thing. I was no help at all, collapsed on the ground in hysterics. Later, we found out the best defence against a goanna is to lie flat. Giacomo learned the hard way. I learned... that I should always let him light the fires.

— ◆ —

### Battlefields and Bike Wrecks: The Games We Called Fun

When you grow up on a farm with a horde of siblings and cousins, imagination becomes your primary currency—and danger a mere side effect. Our games weren't just for fun; they were epic sagas of dirt, bruises, and borderline foolishness.

As we got older, our games graduated from the innocent charm of *hide and seek* to elaborate versions of cricket and football. Those deserve their own chapter. But before sports took over, we were the kings of pretend: Cowboys and Indians, Brandy, tag—you name it, we played it. With a landscape of sheds, haystacks, cellars, and the odd abandoned car, our farm was an amusement park built by nature and neglect.

"Forts" were a recurring favourite. We fashioned bows and arrows out of bendy swamp sticks, convinced we were medieval warriors. The arrows, however, were less Robin Hood and more sad spaghetti—floppy, harmless, and rarely flying more than fifteen feet. Still, they served their symbolic purpose as we flung ourselves behind hay bales or stacks of old timber, shouting commands like generals who had seen far too many Westerns.

One summer, nature provided us with a battleground so glorious we couldn't believe our luck. A winter wash had carved a deep trench across one of the paddocks, unearthing a shimmering bed of golden yellow sand. This trench became our fort, our base, our battleground. Mounds of sand served as barricades, and the yellow grit itself was our ammunition.

We packed the sand into balls—primitive, messy, slightly damp grenades—and lobbed them at one another with theatrical war cries. By the end of each day, we looked like miniature Simpson characters, caked in yellow from scalp to sole. It was pure joy… until Mum and Dad got wind of it. Apparently, causing a small-scale geological disaster wasn't great farming practice. Something about soil erosion and suffocation hazards. Our fort was shut down. We were devastated. No matter. We redirected our creative energy toward weapons manufacturing. Enter: the wooden gun phase.

Armed with scraps from the shed and bits of bent wire, we built guns that could fire rubber bands with shocking force. Some even had working triggers—a mechanical marvel for kids barely old enough to ride a bike. These weren't your average "bang bang" playthings. These were rubber-powered rifles capable of delivering a solid sting from twenty metres away. It took our cowboy games to a new level. No longer did we just yell "You're dead!"—we shot to kill (figuratively, of course), and if you got hit, you knew it.

Of course, not every game involved weapons or trenches. Some involved nature's less aggressive gifts. We'd spend hours stalking frogs, collecting tadpoles in jars, and constructing elaborate aquariums out of plastic buckets and tin wash basins. But nothing beat *gilgie hunting*.

The gilgie, for the uninitiated, is a small freshwater crayfish that thrives in the streams of the southwest. Armed with scraps of meat, fishing lines, and makeshift nets made from old stockings and coat hangers, we'd march down to the Ellenbrook creek and scoop up these slippery treasures. A full bucket meant an afternoon of shelling, a little butter in the frypan, and dinner on fresh bread. It was sticky, fiddly, and utterly delicious. Not every adventure ended well, though.

Take the bike game, for example. We'd found this old skeleton of a bicycle at a cousin's place—rusty but rideable. Naturally, instead of riding it like normal kids, we turned it into a contact sport. The concept was simple (read: stupid). One kid rode the bike full tilt down a gravel driveway. The others hurled tennis balls, footballs, or whatever we could find, aiming to knock the rider clean off. Bonus points if the rider tumbled dramatically or if the bike tangled midair and skidded into the fence.

It started with giggles and minor bruises. But after a few wipeouts that ended in face-first gravel dives and handlebars to the ribs, the fun wore a bit thin. You'd think we'd have learned. We didn't. We just found better helmets—or more likely, thicker beanies. Still, there was something magic about the chaos. We were never bored. Our farm was an endless source of entertainment—trenches to explore, sticks to sharpen, gilgies to catch, and bruises to collect. We didn't need screens or gadgets. We had each other, a stack of old hay bales, and an imagination that could turn yellow sand into gold and danger into a dare. Looking back, it's a miracle we all survived childhood with our teeth intact and no permanent bike-shaped tattoos on our faces. But I wouldn't trade those dirt-covered, mischief-stained memories for anything.

### Broken Things and Bent Pride

On the farm, accidents weren't just possible—they were practically part of the curriculum. Tractors bogged in mud, fences collapsed under the weight of misjudged manoeuvres, and every job ended with some kind of scrape, bruise or mildly traumatic tale. We didn't call them accidents so much as "things that just happened."

One of my earliest near disasters took place in the stockyards, and it still makes my heart skip when I think of it. I was just a little kid, perched with the other children on the railings above a mob of restless steers while Dad worked below. Someone—either mischievous or downright reckless—thought it'd be funny to push me off the fence. I hit the ground in the middle of the yard, dazed and terrified. A steer—big, curious and more than a little annoyed—decided to take a run at me. Dad, seeing what was unfolding, didn't hesitate. He grabbed a fence post-sized chunk of timber and belted the beast right between the eyes. It staggered, stunned, long enough for him to scoop me up and hurl me back over the fence like a sack of potatoes. He saved my life. No drama, no fuss. That was just Dad—always alert, always the protector.

Years later, another mishap left more of a mark on my pride than my body. I was sixteen, newly licensed and still nursing the loss of Dad, who had passed earlier that year. I'd inherited his car—a tangible connection to him, humming with memories. One afternoon I took a drive over to my uncle's place. The road there was gravel and notorious in our family for causing trouble; Dad himself had a few times had a run-in on that same road.

On my way home, as I descended a steep hill, a rabbit darted across the track. Reflex took over—I swerved. That instinctive twitch was all it took. The tyres lost grip, and the car began to slide. I wrestled the steering wheel, trying to correct the swerve, but each attempt only made things worse. At the bottom of the hill I braced for the worst, sure I'd end up in the river. Instead, the car skidded through a fence and came to rest quietly under a tree. I was rattled. My stomach was tight with panic, and that raw grief for Dad came roaring back.

I ran home, breathless, and grabbed Frank and the tractor. Together we hauled the car back out and fixed the fence. The car, miraculously, was mostly unscathed—just some scratches—but my nerves weren't so lucky. The hardest part? Telling Mum. Not because she'd shout, but because I hated worrying her. We patched the car up as best we could, and that car remained a fixture in my life, dented and all.

Not all my childhood tragedies involved moving vehicles. Some were made of willow.

One Christmas, I unwrapped a present that set my little heart ablaze with joy—a brand-new County cricket bat. Not just any bat. This was the bat Dennis Lillee used. Greg Chappell might've swung a Grey-Nicolls, but to me, the County was the crown jewel of Australian backyard cricket. I was about eleven, and Annunciata had brought her boyfriend and his mates down for the holidays. That meant only one thing: an epic Christmas cricket match.

The game began, and I was buzzing with anticipation. I hadn't even had the chance to christen the bat when one of Annunciata's boyfriend's mates picked it up. Now, I wasn't thrilled—this was *my* new bat. I should've had the honour of its first swing. Still, I held my tongue, wanting to be grown-up about it.

First delivery, he stepped forward and missed completely. Second ball came down leg side, and in some wild attempt at a hook shot, he lost grip on the bat entirely. My precious County sailed through the air and slammed—full force—into a nearby tree.

The sound it made was sickening.

I ran over, heart pounding, eyes stinging. My beautiful bat lay on the ground, wounded. A giant dent marked the leading edge. I was crushed. That bat had been a symbol—of growing up, of pride, of summer, and probably a bit of Dennis Lillee swagger. And now it looked like it had gone one-on-one with a eucalyptus.

I didn't speak to him for ages. He tried to apologise, but the bat wasn't just wood and rubber. It had meaning. Eventually, time smoothed things over.

That bat still played in matches, dent and all, and the bloke who broke it somehow became a regular around the family. But even decades later, every Christmas, I'd remind him: "You still owe me a County."

Life on the farm never promised neat endings or perfect gear. But it did offer good stories, scraped knees, and lessons wrapped in laughter or loss. Sometimes both. Whether it was nearly being gored by a steer, fixing fences with Frank, or holding the cracked handle of a once-new bat, I learned that what matters most isn't the break—it's how you carry on after the crash.

### The Craypot Chronicles and the Pajero Predicament

As we got older, a newfound independence crept in. Not that we'd earned it—more like we just gradually pushed boundaries until no one stopped us. And when you grow up in Margaret River, with the bush at your back and the coast at your feet, the only logical thing to do is go exploring. Fishing, surfing, swimming—they became our new pastimes. They weren't the orchestrated "fishing adventures" of earlier years with Dad; these were self-declared missions, sometimes just a group of us kids walking bush tracks in search of freedom and salt air. The coastline was ours to claim—an endless stretch of opportunity, mystery, and half-baked plans.

Our camping trips were loosely inspired by stories of our fathers and uncles, who, as boys, packed whatever they could scrounge into hessian sacks and walked to the sea. We did the same, fashioning a kind of pilgrimage to Ellenbrook. The track was dusty and vague, just a snaking path through scrub, but it led to magic. We'd fish a little, set up a smoky campfire, cook whatever hadn't escaped, and talk about the universe like we were philosophers. Or at least the dumbest, hungriest ones around.

Ellenbrook House became our unofficial haunted headquarters. This old, crumbling stone ruin—half swallowed by time—was equal parts creepy and cool. Stucco walls, wind-whistling rafters, and the ghost of some long-dead settler woman (we were sure of it). At night, we'd sit by candlelight telling ghost stories we were making up on the spot—badly—and trying not to show who was actually scared. Inevitably someone would crack, a torch would be turned on, and we'd fall asleep in a pile of itchy sleeping bags, the surf pounding in the distance like a pulse.

Then there was the Great Craypot Incident. One golden afternoon, washed up on the beach like a gift from Poseidon himself, was a genuine wooden craypot. A real one! To us kids, this was treasure. It might as well have been the crown jewels. Daryl, one of the crew and never short on misplaced confidence, declared it his and tied it to his back with twine and blind optimism. The plan was to carry it home. On foot. Through bushland. In summer. Brilliant.

About two kilometres in, Daryl started to complain. The craypot, now seeming to double in weight with every step, dug into his shoulders. By kilometre three, he'd transformed into a walking moan. Eventually, we all took turns lugging the thing—like it was some sacred relic, or a curse we couldn't ditch. We made it back, scorched, scratched, and slightly broken. That craypot? It sat behind the shed for the next ten years, never used once. A monument to poor decisions and sore backs. Years later, we took one last hurrah camping trip after finishing high school. This time, we drove the battered old Fiat down to the Ellenbrook car park, then walked to our campsite like seasoned pros. We had just settled in when a shiny Pajero 4WD rolled by its owner giving us the smug wave of someone who'd clearly never bogged a vehicle before.

At dusk, a man came sprinting into our camp. Breathless, frantic, red-faced. Turns out, it was one of our Year 12 teachers. A good teacher by reputation, but also one with a particular talent for public humiliation—especially of me. And now, his pride and joy Pajero was sunk up to its axles in beach sand. Karma, perhaps? He didn't ask so much as demand that I get the Fiat and pull him out. I almost laughed. The Fiat? On a beach? I calmly explained that I'd rather face a week of detentions than my uncle's wrath if I bogged the family tractor trying to rescue a Pajero.

"I can take you to someone who's got a proper tractor," I offered. Not good enough. He stomped off, huffing about ruined upholstery and irresponsible youth. Later we heard that saltwater had soaked the car's interior. It was probably ruined. I sometimes wonder if I made the right choice that day. But when I tell the story to my brothers, we always laugh. Maybe not the kindest act—but definitely a memorable one.

These weren't just seaside adventures. They were rites of passage, stitched together by salt, smoke, stupidity, and the best kind of mischief. We were growing up, kind of, and carving out legends of our own. And the coast—wild and wide and waiting—was always there for the next story.

## The Devil in the Garage

It started, as most misadventures do, with curiosity and a box of matches. A few years had passed since the infamous earthquake incident, and I had graduated from shaking walls to playing with fire—literally. This was my experimental phase, the time of imagined inventions and backyard science, of trying to turn nuts and bolts into explosives, all in the name of boyhood brilliance.

On one particularly hot summer afternoon, I was in the garage—a ramshackle structure filled with dry kindling masquerading as tools, hay, and discarded planks—shaving match heads like a tiny chemist with no safety protocols. Somewhere between the scraping and scheming, I must've made an error. Or perhaps I didn't. Maybe the fire started from a spark I didn't see, or maybe I was testing fate, hoping to see just a flicker. What I got was a hungry little flame that leapt like a goanna from a burning bush.

It spread fast. All it took was one pile of shaved match heads and a breath of summer air. In moments, the fire had jumped to the dry grass and loose hay, climbing eagerly up the wooden planks that made up the garage wall. It was chaos—the kind that chokes the air and tightens your chest. I was still a young kid, and suddenly completely out of my depth.

My first instinct was to smother it. I grabbed a hessian sack and tried to beat it back. It laughed at my efforts. I threw handfuls of dirt useless. I screamed for Mum, but she was inside, behind kitchen walls and too far away to hear. Panic had begun its own little fire inside me.

And then—like a blessing—Francesco appeared. He'd been in one of the other sheds and had seen the smoke, heard the commotion, or maybe just sensed that his little brother was about to do something spectacularly stupid again. He rushed over with a bucket of water, and, between his dousing and my frantic sack-smacking, we managed to get the flames under control.

We stood there, panting and blackened, staring at the large smoking hole in the side of the garage. There was no hiding this. The evidence was right there—charred timber, scorched hay, and the smell of singed stupidity. I knew Dad would be home from work in a few hours, and there wasn't a hessian sack big enough to cover what I'd done.

When he arrived, I waited in dread. Mum filled him in, probably with a few added flourishes. But instead of the fiery wrath I expected, Dad sat me down on his knee. His voice was calm, not because he wasn't angry—he was—but because he understood something bigger than my mistake. He explained the danger, the seriousness of fire in summer, and the thin line between mischief and disaster. And while I was still shaken, I felt something settle in me—an understanding that consequences could come not just with yelling, but with measured care. A lesson I carried on with me through my years of teaching other mischievous kids. They never valued walls more than their children. That lesson burned into me more deeply than any flame could.

### Buried Treasure on Wheels

At various points in my childhood, a strange creature would occasionally appear on our farm—not an animal, but something just as untameable: the beach buggy. It would roar in, then sit idle, like an abandoned carnival ride for grown men. It belonged to a friend of Dad's, and though he parked it at our place more than once, not a single Palandri child was ever invited for a spin. It was maddening. A vehicle that screamed *freedom*, yet there it sat—off-limits, untouched, and just beyond reach.

Now, enter Carla. My sister, bright, beautiful, and in love. She'd visit from the city with her boyfriend—later husband—a young engineer with a head full of ideas and a heart full of horsepower. I was about five when I first met him. Carla and he would show up on the weekends, their cars usually worse for wear from the long drive. One memorable Friday, they arrived late and dishevelled, having hit a kangaroo near Cowaramup. The next morning, I spotted the damage and ran inside shouting, "A kangaroo smashed the car!"—a statement that was somehow both innocent and disturbingly accurate.

That wasn't their only vehicular adventure. On another visit, they arrived with a battered Morris Minor on the back of a trailer. It had no roof, no roll bars, no bonnet, no boot—just the skeleton of a car with four fat bald tyres and a cheeky engine barely clinging to life. It was, of course, the buggy's new incarnation.

I was about six and, true to form, strictly banned from climbing aboard. Mum took one look at the thing and declared it a death trap. She wasn't wrong. It skidded across cow patties like a shopping trolley on ice. Carla and her boyfriend and friends would howl across paddocks, tearing up the back trails at Ellenbrook, the buggy swerving wildly every time it clipped a wet patch. Despite their reckless joyrides, it never bogged—the only miracle I ever witnessed from that contraption.

At night, they'd attach a spotlight and head off on kangaroo hunting expeditions. This was the sixties and seventies, when kangaroo shooting was still done in the name of population control, skin sales, or just country-boy tradition. I, of course, was never allowed to go. My participation was limited to standing on the verandah, watching the taillights disappear into the scrub, wondering what excitement looked like from the front seat.

Eventually, as all romantic notions do, the buggy lost its shine. The engine seized, the tyres cracked, and it became more rust than vehicle. It sat in shame under a tree for years—once a rebellious steed, now reduced to yard art.

One weekend, I had a friend from school over. The buggy, now a permanent fixture of our landscape, caught our attention. It hadn't moved in at least five years. So, being enterprising young boys with no mechanical knowledge and too much time, we decided to "fix" it. We attacked the engine and began dismantling with tools Dad had long since hidden from us for good reason. What we did that weekend wasn't repair—it was archaeological vandalism. Carla's now husband, who apparently had harboured quiet dreams of restoring the buggy, was not impressed. We, however, were thrilled.

Years later, after Dad passed and the back paddock was transformed into a sandpit for building contractors, a subcontractor told us we could dump any old junk in the excavation before they backfilled. The old buggy, now more relic than vehicle, met its final fate. We rolled its broken frame into the pit—cowpat-stained tyres, rusted-out chassis, and all—and watched as the earth swallowed it whole.

Maybe one day, centuries from now, an archaeologist will find it and marvel at the crude engineering of rural Western Australians. Or maybe they'll just scratch their heads and wonder what kind of people built this Frankenstein car, and why they buried it under metres of dirt and sand.

For me, it wasn't just a beach buggy. It was a dream deferred, a tale of forbidden speed, and the loudest toy I was never allowed to play with.

## When Nature Throws a Tantrum

We've talked a bit about the sport we played on the farm, and while we loved it, let's be honest—it wasn't always safe. Our makeshift paddock-turned-cricket-oval was an occupational hazard. There were the rocks poking through the topsoil, the freshly hacked dock weed with roots like small landmines, and the ever-present unpredictability of uneven ground. This wasn't Lord's Cricket Ground. This was Margaret River, rural style.

Dock weed was our worst opponent. We only had a push mower, and you'd need the stamina of a marathon runner to clear an entire field. So, we didn't. Instead, we mowed a narrow pitch, maybe five paces long, and left the rest to resemble a wild herb garden. The duckweed would grow up to 30 centimetres high, so unless you hit the ball sky-high, it was lost forever—or until the next goat found it.

One afternoon, we were in the thick of a backyard Test match. Francesca was fielding and Frank—always the overzealous fielder—was sprinting for a high ball. Somewhere between the pitch and glory, he caught his toe on a hidden log tucked beneath the dock weed. He let out a howl that could scare a possum out of a peppermint tree. Naturally, we all burst out laughing. The funnier it was to us, the more furious he became. Red-faced and limping, he picked up the offending log and flung it in disgust across the paddock. About ten minutes later, déjà vu struck. Another high ball arced across the sky, Frank went galloping after it again, and—crunch! He tripped over the exact same log he'd just thrown, having landed it squarely in the path of his own destiny. Same toe. Same pain. Same laughter—this time with tears running down our cheeks. Poor Frank. If misfortune were a sport, he'd have gone pro.

But it wasn't just mischief and stubbed toes that shaped our childhood. Sometimes, the chaos arrived from above—literally. I remember one winter's evening, the kind where nature puts on her full sound-and-light show. Thunder cracked across the sky, and lightning flashed like strobes at an Italian disco. Back then, we had one of those old-fashioned rotary dial phones—the kind you had to wrestle with just to call Nonna. It was bolted to a timber cabinet in the corner of the front room.

Frank, teenage hormones in full swing, was talking to one of his girlfriends—probably whispering sweet nothings in a voice he imagined sounded romantic.

He was seated by the phone, basking in the thrill of adolescent love, while the rest of us sat in the lounge room trying not to gag.

Then, suddenly—BOOM. A lightning bolt slammed into the corner of the house, through the aerial, and straight into the phone. The room exploded in a flash of white light and a deafening crack. Frank was flung across the room like a rag doll in a storm. When the smoke cleared, there was a gaping hole where the phone had been, the cabinet was splintered to bits, and the phone receiver was melted. Frank emerged, dazed but alive—his hair slightly singed and his pride completely obliterated.

None of us knew what to say. We just sat there, stunned, mouths open. I never found out what became of that girlfriend. She might've interpreted the cosmic interruption as a divine warning. And then there was the Great Aerial Collapse. For those too young to remember, tuning into television in rural Australia during the 1970s was not for the faint-hearted. You needed an aerial the size of a small oil rig just to pick up a fuzzy version of the ABC. Ours was a towering metal tripod perched beside the house—probably about 50 feet high, and just as precarious.

One blustery night, while Lina was visiting, the wind picked up something fierce. Around 4 a.m., we were jolted awake by a thunderous bang—louder than any storm or stubbed toe. We raced outside in our pyjamas to find the aerial had snapped halfway up. The top half had come down like a massive javelin, crashing against the corner of the girls' bedroom roof. Astonishingly, the only real damage was a section of ceiling torn open and some plaster littering the room.

Even more astonishingly, Lina's little grey Honda Civic, parked barely a metre away, was untouched. It was one of those moments where you just stop and wonder which saint, angel or ancestor might've been watching over us. Had the pole broken even slightly lower, it could've cut through the house like a tin opener. Instead, it just nicked the edge and spared us. We didn't exactly pray with gratitude, but we did marvel at the absurd luck of it all. Somehow, no matter what mischief or misstep befell us—from cricket injuries to celestial near-misses—we came out the other side with stories, laughter, and maybe just a few more scars.

Looking back now, it's a wonder any of us made it out of childhood without a permanent limp, a police record, or a minor meteorological trauma. Between flying goannas, collapsing aerials, combusting phones, and questionable games involving cricket bats, rusty bikes, and runaway beach buggies, our days were filled with just the right amount of danger, delight and dumb decisions. But these weren't just moments of mischief—they were the glue that bonded siblings, cousins, and friends in a sticky mess of laughter, bruises, and stories we'd dine out on for decades. Sure, we got told off, bandaged up, and occasionally struck by lightning (just once), but through it all, we learned how to bounce back—and sometimes how to duck. Because in a family like ours, missteps were inevitable, but the mayhem was half the fun.

# Chapter 12
# School Years

## (Gli anni scolastici)

*"School is not the filling of a bucket, but the lighting of a fire."*

*"La scuola non è riempire un secchio, ma accendere un fuoco."*

*(Adapted from a quote often attributed to William Butler Yeats)*

School was never just about books and blackboards. For a child of migrants like me, it was where two worlds collided home and Australia, Italian and English, pasta and peanut butter. The classroom didn't just teach us reading and writing; it taught us how to fit in, when to stay silent, and when to speak up. It was a place of laughter and lessons, of scraped knees and sharpened pencils, of nicknames earned and identities shaped. It was where I first felt the sting of being different—and the pride of belonging anyway.

### The Journey (Il viaggio)

Some kids count the days until their first day of school. I didn't even know it was coming.

As the youngest of six children on our farm just outside Margaret River, I had never stepped into a classroom before that day. No kindergarten, no prep classes—just the farm, the family, and the daily rhythm of rural life. My parents, ever pragmatic and grounded in their own old-world sensibilities, decided that an extra year at home would serve me better than any early education. And in so many ways, they were right. By the time I arrived at school, I could read simple words and count to ten. I'd learned not from books, but from the chorus of voices around the kitchen table, from the gentle corrections of my sisters, and from the makeshift lessons carved into the dust of the farm's red-brown earth.

My education had started in the rows of vegetables, in the milking shed, and under the towering trees that shaded our home. I knew the weight of a milk pail before I knew the sound of a school bell. I understood the value of work, of silence, of listening—lessons not always taught in classrooms.

All my older siblings—Ricardo, Carla, Lina, Anne, and Francesco—had attended the convent school run by the stern Mercy Sisters. Their stories painted that school as a place of fear and discipline, where talking too loudly might earn you a corner, a belt, or worse—a cupboard door slammed shut behind you. Francesco, always the performer, would tell of rulers rapped across knuckles, of icy stares from beneath starched black habits. Even Zia Adelina, Mum's sister and a Mercy Sister herself, seemed cloaked in that same silence and solemnity. She visited during Easter and Christmas, but she never sat at the table with us. She existed in our world and apart from it—kind, yes, but distant, as if belonging to another life. Her presence was a reminder of how our Catholic heritage demanded both reverence and restraint.

By the time my turn came, our family had moved away from the convent path. I was to start at the local state school—an enormous change, though I didn't yet grasp what that meant. Francesco was the only sibling still in primary school. Carla and Ric had long since moved to Perth for high school, and Lina and Anne had followed in their footsteps. I was barely awake that morning when the rush began—Lina and Anne scrubbing my face with a flannel, pulling my arms through a too-stiff shirt, buttoning buttons with quick, practiced hands. The toast hadn't even cooled on the plate before I was out the door.

Down the gravel road we went, to the bus stop that marked the edge of the known world. My cousins were already there—Giacomo, who was my age and also starting his first day, and Giuseppe, a year ahead and full of confidence.

While we waited for the bus, we played hopscotch with gravel, chased each other with the awkwardness of school shoes not yet broken in, and showed off our new pencil cases and lunch tins like badges of honour. I remember mine—a small wooden box, the lid smooth beneath my fingers, the inside holding sharp new pencils that smelled like possibility. There was a kind of magic in those quiet preparations.

Then the rumble began. The bus was an orange monster, dusty and growling from its crawl down the road. Behind the wheel sat Mrs. Culcumback, a woman who could have wrangled cattle with a stare. She was as much a fixture of our school life as the chalkboard. As we clambered on board, she bellowed instructions with the force of an army sergeant. "Feet out of the aisle! No yelling! If you miss this bus—you walk!" The rules were printed on a fading sheet above her head like a constitution, and she made sure every kid—especially the youngest—knew them by heart. The back seat was the territory of the high schoolers. Francesco, Anne, and Lina sat there, lording over the bus like royalty. I was sent to the middle, tucked between other wide-eyed primary schoolers, clinging to my school case and a sense of self.

The ride into town was long—thirty minutes or more—and bumpy. The roads curled through bush and farmland, the morning light catching on dew-dusted leaves. We collected other children, many from families like ours—Italians, Croatians, Dutch—each carrying their own version of hope and fear in a lunchbox. I pressed my nose to the glass, watching the countryside shift from open paddocks to tall timber to town streets. What did these other kids eat? What language did they speak at home? Were their fathers also sawmillers and grape growers? I was curious, but also cautious. For the first time, I realised our little farm was just one story in a much bigger book.

The journey was not without its tests. The older boys had a talent for mischief—flicking spit balls, threatening to smear Vegemite on your collar, or hiding your lunch. We'd been warned. But Giacomo and I were protected, in a way, by the unspoken force of family. Our cousins were everywhere—Luigi, Lucia, Elisabetta, Natalia. No one messed with us without risking the wrath of at least one protective older relative. Still, jabs came now and then—taunts about our "wog lunches", about salami sandwiches or olives packed in wax paper. It was my first taste of being seen as different.

Each bump in the road seemed to shake something loose in me. I held tight to the window ledge and let the questions swirl: Would the teacher be kind? Would I be asked to read out loud? Would I be laughed at for my name, my accent, my food? My world had been so small—so safe. Now it stretched wider than I could comprehend.

Arriving at school felt like crossing into another country. The bus lurched to a halt outside the gates, and we spilled onto the gravel path like cattle. Bells rang, children scattered, and teachers barked directions. Everything felt louder, faster, and sharper than home. I remember the smell—a strange mix of floor polish, eucalyptus trees, and something oily drifting from the canteen.

It was overwhelming. Kids ran in packs, their uniforms neat, their voices loud. I stood still, lunch tin clutched tightly, hoping Giacomo wouldn't wander off. The bell sounded again—a clang like a factory horn—and we shuffled forward. I looked for a familiar face. There were a few—cousins, neighbours—but it felt like everyone else had been here forever. I was the stranger.

But I was also not alone. That morning marked a turning point, though I didn't yet understand it. In the blur of schoolbooks and bus rides, I was beginning the long journey from farm boy to student—from Italian son to Australian child. My siblings had paved the way, but now it was my turn. And in that first walk across the schoolyard, something quiet inside me began to grow.

A sense of independence. A curiosity about the world. A subtle, stubborn pride in who I was.

The bus didn't just take me to school that day. It delivered me to the beginning of becoming myself.

## Primary Years

We were the new kids at school, dropped into a sea of unfamiliar faces and unsure how to swim. Giacomo and I stuck close together like barnacles, flanked by our slightly older cousins Giuseppe and Daryl, who were already veterans of this strange, new world. On that first day, all the Grade Ones were lined up outside a classroom, nervous and fidgeting, sizing each other up like little soldiers before a battle.

I recognised a few faces from church, but most were complete strangers—kids who hadn't grown up among salami curing in sheds or grandmothers speaking in dialect. After the sharp clang of a brass bell, we filed inside. The desks were wooden with slanted tops and a storage cavity beneath, complete with an inkwell, even though ink pens had largely fallen out of fashion. I ran my fingers along the grooves etched by countless students before me—initials, doodles, and evidence of lives that had passed through long before I arrived.

Our teacher, Miss Aspinex, stood at the front like a sentry. She introduced herself, calm but firm, and began to call the roll. I sat silently, thankful that my name—Stephen—didn't trip her up. But when she got to Giacomo, she hesitated. The pause was just long enough for some kids to start whispering, others to snicker. Giacomo, brave even then, raised his hand and said plainly, "Just call me Jimmy."

The power of that moment would echo for years. My siblings and cousins would often talk about that first sting of being 'other'—names mispronounced; lunchboxes opened with caution. Jimmy made it easier, more palatable, but part of me knew something had been sacrificed. My cousins always said I got off lightly being the youngest, with my "Aussie" name and my parents too tired to argue about it. Maybe they were right.

Grade One was less about academics and more about learning how to navigate the social web. We played games, shared lunches, and slowly figured out who would become friends and who would always remain strangers. Some of the people I met in that first year are still my mates today—we catch up now and then, swapping stories about those days like battered old soldiers comparing scars.

Most of the kids were third or fourth generation Australian. Some could trace their lineage to the very settlers who founded Margaret River, Busselton, or Augusta. There was a certain pride in that, though it didn't always come with warmth. But for the most part, we found our people.

Not all lessons were in the books. I remember one boy returning from the toilet in tears, having zipped too quickly and caught himself. I made a passing comment—something silly to a mate—and got caught by the teacher mid-whisper. Off I went, straight to the principal's office, where I got my first taste of castor oil. That bitter spoonful became a rite of passage—administered not for illness but for mischief.

We had a parade of teachers in those years, each leaving their mark. Some kind, some eccentric, and some outright terrifying. I never had Miss Carol—who became Miss Craven after her marriage—but she was legendary for her warmth. I ended up instead in Miss Donaldson's combined Year 2/3 class, not due to academic brilliance, but more likely due to small numbers and reshuffled year groups.

Miss Donaldson was elderly, gentle teacher, but she had a temper that could turn on a dime. When she got cross, she'd hurl a blackboard duster at whoever wasn't paying attention. Fortunately, we had learned the art of defence—our desks opened upward, and if you were quick, you could duck behind the lid like a soldier behind a shield. The loud "thwack" of duster against wood was both alarming and hilarious. In Year 4, we had Mrs Miles—gentle, smiling, with a love for stories. She introduced us to Blinky Bill and Br'er Rabbit, reading to us from dusty old hardcovers as we sat cross-legged in the quiet heat of the afternoon. I can still hear her voice lilting through the classroom, the scent of chalk and eucalyptus in the air.

Years 5 and 6 brought Mrs Somerville—a stricter figure with a taste for discipline. She ruled with a ruler, literally, and occasionally knocked heads together (lightly, though it didn't feel that way at the time). She also ran the music program, teaching us to play recorders, tambourines, triangles, and bells with varying degrees of success. She led the choir, too—until my voice broke. On one unforgettable day, I cracked a high note mid-performance. The look she gave me could curdle milk. Minutes later, I was sent to the principal's office another spoonful of castor oil—and was never again asked to sing. Harsh?

**All the Palandri's and one Fontana. Cousins at school.**

Yes. But part of me still believes she cared. In Year 7, Mr Steel took over. Tall, lean, and commanding, he didn't yell often—he didn't need to. We respected him because he held the keys to the sports shed. If you wanted cricket bats or footies, you stayed in his good graces. That final year of primary school had a kind of reverence to it. We knew we were on the cusp of something bigger—teenage hood, high school, independence. Mr Steel helped us walk that line with pride.

Our school had a string of principals, some forgettable, others unforgettable for all the wrong reasons. One would stand outside his office at lunchtime, cane in hand, scanning the yard like a sentry. We would sit in nervous silence, sandwiches untouched. He didn't last long, thank God. The most vivid memory I have of his tenure is his treatment of a boy with clear signs of autism or ADHD—not that we had those labels back then. This boy couldn't sit still, couldn't concentrate, and was often punished for what we now know to be a neurological difference.

It was cruel, but it was the time we lived in. Despite those darker moments, primary school was, on the whole, full of joy. Winter brought out the mischief in us. We'd race on slippery wet grass, ending up soaked to the bone and huddling in front of the fireplaces in each classroom. Those old rooms—creaky floorboards, cracked windows—held us like second homes. Each one had a wood-burning heater, and on cold mornings the smell of smoke mingled with damp jumpers and soggy socks.

Our playground adventures were legendary. In the early years, it was monkey bars and seesaws; later, it was territorial squabbles over who got to sweep the verandah or manage the sports shed. There was pride in being the veranda monitor—pushing the huge broom like it was a weapon of honour.

One of our better principals was Mr Riley. Gentle, insightful, and ahead of his time. He introduced "Uninterrupted Sustained Silent Reading"—USSR, they called it—and he let us lose ourselves in books. I leaned into Biggles books then, discovering a world of pilots and heroism that lit my imagination.

I still have that collection today, their pages yellowed but loved. I can't talk about school without mentioning the milk. Every morning at 11:00 a.m., a clatter of glass bottles would arrive outside our classroom.

The government insisted every student receive a daily dose of fresh milk. In the summer it was warm and souring, in winter it was oddly comforting. Sometimes we drank, sometimes we hid it, sometimes we traded it—but it was always there, a strange little ritual in the middle of our day.

Sport was the great equaliser. Friday afternoons meant two hours of running, kicking, catching, and scoring. We'd gather around the sports board during lunch to see what team we were on.

Rivalries formed and dissolved with the seasons, but what stayed was a love of the game—and of being together. In Year 5, I even had my first girlfriend. I won't say her name—it was a love that lasted only from the lunch bell to the final siren—but she remains a dear friend today, part of a small circle that still catches up, half a century later.

Another lifelong mate was a Dutch Australian boy I shared nearly every year of school with. Together, we got into mischief—including one infamous afternoon where we set off a starter cap in the middle of the oval. We paid dearly for that prank, but we earned our stripes in the process. Primary school shaped me. Not just through its teachers, its punishments, or its lessons—but through the friends, the fights, the laughs, and the long walks home. It was the beginning of knowing who I was, and who I could become.

**Margaret River Primary School**

**Secondary Years**

**1. A School of Characters and Consequences**

High school was a different beast. We were all super excited to walk across the road from the primary school to Margaret River High School. It felt like a rite of passage, like moving into a bigger, more dangerous world. There were new subjects to tackle, more specialised learning, and of course, an entirely new group of kids from places like Augusta, Cowaramup, Karridale, and all the farms in between. With those new faces came fresh friendships, rivalries, and challenges.

At the time, Margaret River was only a high school from Years 8 to 10. So, stepping in as fresh-faced Year 8s meant we were the small fry, staring up at the giants in Year 10. Some of those older students looked enormous, and a few seemed genuinely fearsome. The academic work was certainly more demanding, but I found myself managing it well enough.

Practical jokes were a kind of underground currency at high school. Some of them bordered on brutal. There was the infamous "toilet dunking," where unlucky students had their heads shoved into toilet bowls and flushed. It never happened to me, thankfully, but it did to others—more than once. Then there was the classic flour-in-the-locker prank. You'd open your locker and be instantly doused in a cloud of white, chalky humiliation. In retrospect, it was a bit of a rite of passage.

Some of the teachers made a real impact—on our education and on our psyches. Manual arts were one of the highlights. Woodwork and metalwork weren't just electives; they were initiation rituals. Mr Hatch taught woodwork. He was the father of one of my primary school mates and still a friend to this day. We called him the legendary Mr Hatch. In his workshop, precision was non-negotiable, and rules were enforced with military resolve.

We used calliper rulers that clicked as they extended. Now imagine 15 students flicking them open all at once during a quiet moment—chaos. Mr Hatch would not tolerate that kind of disruption.

If you dared to open one while he was speaking, he'd stop the class, publicly berate you, and in extreme cases, destroy your project. I once saw him take a nearly completed model and saw it into pieces on the bandsaw—all because the student had slipped with a chisel and gouged the workbench.

His disciplinary flair became legend. There were stories—ones I never personally witnessed—of him sending misbehaving students to run laps around the oval while carrying pieces of timber. And when it came to applying wood glue, he had a signature line: "Don't use your index finger to spread the glue—you'll get it stuck up your nose when you pick it."

Then there was Mr Wearing, our metalwork teacher. He didn't mess around either. Operating welders, lathes, and heavy cutting tools demanded focus, and he insisted on absolute attention during demonstrations. Deviating from his method wasn't just careless; it was dangerous. I got to know him even better after school, and we developed a genuine friendship. Still, during class, you did things by the book—or suffered the consequences.

Physical reprimands weren't uncommon. We didn't think of it as abuse back then—it was just school. A rap on the knuckles with a ruler or a clip with a piece of wood was normal. The cane was still in circulation. And while it sounds barbaric now, at the time it was simply part of how school was done.

I also remember my art teacher—just Jenny to us. I had potential in art, I really did. But one single incident changed everything. I had finished my assignment and started a quiet game of noughts and crosses with a mate to pass the time. We got a bit noisy, yes, but instead of a warning, Jenny sent us straight to the deputy principal, Mr Pentridge. He wasn't known for mercy. For our little game, we were given six of the best across the knuckles. That was it for me. My confidence in art crumbled, and I never took another class in it again—not for 30 years.

Thankfully, we had some remarkable teachers in other subjects. Mr Bedford taught social studies. He was a bear of a man with a beard to match but spoke softly and carried immense knowledge. He loved teaching, and we loved learning from him. He had a few quirks, though. If you didn't do your homework, he'd stand behind your chair, reach down to the nape of your neck, and lift you slightly by your hair. Painful? Slightly. Memorable? Very.

Fail a test, and he'd assign you to "the desk" at the front of the room—some sort of academic purgatory. If you didn't improve, you'd be banished outside. Odd methods, perhaps, but he cared. After school, we stayed in touch. I'd see him fishing at Ellenbrook or collecting stone from my family farm for his stonemasonry projects. A teacher and a gentleman.

Then there was Mr Hart, our science teacher. He once gave a very serious talk about the dangers of mercury in thermometers. Just as he was demonstrating their safe use, the school phone rang. He placed a handful of thermometers on a desk and went to answer it. As we all sat silently, one by one, the thermometers slid off the desk and shattered, mercury pooling on the floor like something out of a cautionary tale. When he returned, we had an impromptu hands-on lesson in chemical hazards.

We didn't have the resources for a full curriculum. Languages, for example, were a challenge. Our English teacher, Mrs Spackman, volunteered to teach Italian—even though she wasn't a native speaker. My cousins and I were excited. Finally, we'd learn the language of our heritage. Or so we thought. The rest of the class struggled, and Mrs Spackman, though well-meaning, couldn't quite manage the nuances of Italian. The lessons devolved into cultural chats and food discussions. When Mum or Dad asked what new words I'd learned, I'd reply: "I can cook a pizza now. Lasagne's next."

I found my real passion in physical education. We had different teachers over the years, but Mr Jordan off stands out. He wasn't just a coach—he was a mentor. I opened up to him in ways I never had with any other adult at school. He inspired me, unknowingly planting the seed that would later grow into my own teaching career.

Sports became a core part of who I was. I gravitated toward Australian Rules football and cricket. Cricket was fun, but football was my passion. I played, coached, and stayed involved until 2019. But that's a story for another chapter.

Margaret River High only went to Year 10. If you wanted to pursue university, you had to go to Busselton for senior high school. Many of my mates didn't bother. In the early '80s, there were plenty of pathways into trades or family farms. But Mum and Dad were adamant—I was to finish school. They'd missed out on that opportunity and were determined I wouldn't.

For them, education was everything. It was a ticket to a future they could only dream of for themselves. And even then, I knew I owed it to them to keep walking forward—even if that meant stepping out of the small, familiar world of Margaret River High.

**Margaret River Junior High School 1955.**

## 2. Between Vineyards and Resilience

So, it was off to Busselton Senior High School for Years 11 and 12 and what was then called the TAE—the Tertiary Admissions Exam. It felt like crossing into another world. Gone were the familiar bush tracks and close-knit corridors of Margaret River High; Busselton was bigger, more urban, and filled with unfamiliar faces from far and wide. Students came from Augusta in the south, Yallingup to the west, Nannup to the east, and even Capel to the north.

The catchment was vast, and so was the student body—nearly a thousand teenagers, each with their own story, their own presence.

With that swelling crowd came something else: a noticeable spike in competition and, sadly, bullying. The school had a sharper edge to it, a bustling pace that could be both exciting and overwhelming. Busselton may have had better infrastructure and more specialised subject offerings, but it also had a harder social terrain to navigate. Margaret River had been a rural cocoon; this felt like plunging into the deep end.

Academically, the ante was upped. My pathway was aimed squarely at university, which meant an intense focus on maths, science, English, and the social sciences. There was no time for manual arts or the creative subjects I might have enjoyed. Physical education, which I loved, wasn't part of my coursework. It was all pencils and textbooks and trying to understand complex theories that seemed a world away from the vineyard rows and paddocks I knew so well.

To make things harder, each school day started with a 45-minute bus ride—one way. It wasn't an easy trek. We'd be picked up early, boarding the first bus that made its way through the winding backroads of Caves Road, collecting scattered students like breadcrumbs in the bush. That bus would drop us on the Bussell Highway, where we'd transfer to the main coach that ran from Augusta to Busselton. Sometimes the weather made this routine a drama in itself—howling winds, pounding rain, even lightning. It wasn't uncommon for trees to crash down on the backroads around Willyabrup, forcing delays that meant we'd miss the main bus.

When that happened, we didn't get the day off—not exactly. Instead, we'd report to Margaret River High School, where we'd spend the day with students a few years behind us. Truthfully, those days weren't particularly productive. We kicked the footy, chatted, wasted time. At that age, study wasn't my top priority. I was more focused on my social life, sport, and simply trying to fit in.

Looking back, I realise my studies took a hit. Whether it was immaturity, distraction, or just the difficult transition to a new environment, I didn't perform as well as I could have. But it wasn't all bad. In fact, some of my fondest memories were born in those Busselton years: school balls, socials, interschool sport, and Country Week. For the first time, I felt like I was part of something beyond Margaret River—a bigger social world with real energy and opportunity.

I made some lifelong friends at Busselton, and others I met their deepened bonds I'd started forming in primary school and early high school. It's strange to think now that I still catch up with some of those people—people who knew me when I was still growing into myself. Some teachers from Busselton also reappeared later in my life in an unexpected way: as professional colleagues. The wheel turned full circle when I became an educator myself, eventually returning to Busselton Senior High not as a student—but as its Associate Principal.

That full-circle moment still takes my breath away. Walking those same halls, now in a position of leadership, brings with it a strange mix of pride and humility. I don't take it for granted. Every day I see kids who remind me of my younger self—eager, restless, unsure. I hope that somewhere in the guidance I offer, they can find their path a little more clearly than I did. The bus ride—long and tedious as it could be—had its beauty too. The route meandered through the vineyards of Willyabrup and the green farmland of Metricup, past misty paddocks and stands of towering karri. I'd sit there watching the landscape roll by, half-dreaming, half-dreading the day ahead. Sometimes, those quiet journeys were the best part of the school day.

But not everything about Busselton was rosy. In 1983, during my final year, a shadow fell over everything. My father passed away. I'll talk more about this in my reflections chapter, but it's important to say that his death marked a turning point in my life. At the time, I didn't realise just how deeply it affected me—how it dimmed my focus and shook my sense of stability. Many of my classmates had no idea what had happened. They went about their year, unaware that I was carrying a quiet, heavy grief through every test and every lesson.

That's the thing about school. It can be a place of great promise and growth, but it can also be a stage where we perform—sometimes hiding our most painful realities behind forced smiles and half-finished assignments. No one asked, and I didn't tell. Life just went on, as it tends to do.

In hindsight, Busselton Senior High was a time of contrast. A time of friendship and loss, excitement and anxiety, promise and regret. But it was also a time of becoming—becoming someone who, despite stumbling through adolescence with all its mess and contradiction, would go on to lead, to teach, and to remember.

### 3. Belonging and Becoming

Throughout all my school years, there was an undercurrent I could never quite escape—a subtle, persistent sense of being "othered." Today they might call it casual racism or unconscious bias, but back then, we just swallowed it whole. It wasn't always full-blown hostility, but it was there: the nicknames, the slurs, the jokes made at our expense. If we played well at sport or excelled in something, the response wasn't always admiration—it was a muttered "wog," "ding," "wop," or "greaseball." Sometimes it came with a sneer; sometimes it came wrapped in false humour. Either way, it left a mark.

With four Palandri's and at least one Fontana floating through the same school corridors and sporting grounds, our Italian roots were hard to ignore. We never tried to hide them. How could we? They were in the food we ate, the way we spoke, the families we belonged to. But being Italian in Margaret River wasn't always seen as a strength. In fact, when we did well—on the football field, in class, or even socially—it sometimes triggered resentment rather than respect.

There were no school assemblies condemning racism back then, no diversity posters pinned to classroom walls. You endured. That's what we were taught. And so, I did what so many of us did: I clenched my jaw, swallowed my frustration, and let my actions speak louder than any insult. I played harder, worked better, and tried to rise above it—not just to prove something to them, but maybe to myself as well. I didn't want to be defined by their labels. I wanted to define myself by what I did.

Strangely, despite these challenges, I never carried resentment toward the experience. It became part of who I was. Those moments forged something in me—determination, grit, and an unspoken pride in being Italian, even when others used it to try and put me down. At home, the expectations were… light. Not because Mum and Dad didn't care—far from it—but because their own schooling had been cut short by survival. Their childhoods in post-war Italy were filled with work, obligation, and the need to make ends meet. Education was a luxury neither of them could afford. But they believed in the promise it held for me.

They didn't ask about homework or test scores. They didn't hover over my shoulders. But they worked hard—so incredibly hard—to make sure I had the chance they never got. Their support was quiet, unwavering, and invisible in all the best ways. Still, I was surprised to discover just how connected they were to my schooling in ways I hadn't understood.

Every Saturday, we'd go into town. Mum would shop, I'd be playing sport, and Dad—without fail—would slip into the Margaret River Hotel for a lager with his mates. That was his tradition. What I didn't realise, not until later, was that many of my teachers were doing the same thing. The hotel wasn't just a pub—it was a hub.

And church. That too played a part. Many of my teachers also sat in the pews on Sundays, the same pews where Mum and Dad said their prayers and exchanged Sunday greetings. So, when something happened at school—good or bad—it didn't stay within school walls. There was a whole secret network of passing glances, quiet conversations, and raised eyebrows that made sure Mum and Dad always found out. If I got in trouble, I'd often hear about it before I even got home. Not from a teacher, but from Dad. "What did you do today?" he'd ask in that knowing tone. It was both terrifying and comforting to realise he had eyes everywhere.

One thing still weighs on me, though. My father never got to see me graduate from senior high school. He never saw me step onto the grounds of a university. That part of my life unfolded after he passed, and even now, there's a part of me that wishes he'd been there. I like to think he would've been proud—that the quiet work he did, the sacrifices he made, would have felt worthwhile.

Despite everything—the slurs, the setbacks, the occasional self-doubt—my school years were a time of genuine growth. I learned who I was and who I didn't want to be. I made friends who stayed, teachers who cared, and memories I still carry with me today. I wouldn't trade those years for anything. They were hard sometimes, sure—but they were mine. And they helped shape the man I became.

**Busselton Senior High School Circa 1960s**

# Chapter 13
# From the Paddock to the Coach's Box

## (Dal paddock alla panchina)

*"Sport teaches character, brings people together, and reveals who we truly are."*

*(Lo sport insegna il carattere, unisce le persone e rivela chi siamo davvero.)*

In a family where work was woven into our bones, sport was something else entirely—a joyful rebellion against the demands of the farm and the expectations of our elders. We didn't play for glory or even trophies. We played because the oval gave us space to breathe, to run, to laugh with our mates in ways that life at home rarely allowed. Whether it was muddy boots on cold mornings or barefoot games in the dust, sport became the language through which we found our confidence, our friendships, and a glimpse of a world beyond the vines and the timber yard.

## Chasing the Ball, Finding My Place

My love of sport was sparked long before I understood what competition or teams even meant. Growing up as the youngest in a big, active family, I was surrounded by movement—older siblings and cousins who were always playing, always running, always testing their bodies and one another. There wasn't a day that went by when someone wasn't throwing something, chasing someone, or wrestling in the grass. I didn't just learn how to play—I absorbed it through osmosis.

We weren't coached, at least not formally. But watching was its own form of training. I remember being small—maybe five years old—and going along to my sister's netball games. I was too young to play, of course, so I'd hang around the playground equipment on the edge of the courts. But my eyes were fixed on the players. I noticed how they moved, how they shouted, how the ball sliced through the air. I wasn't just watching I was learning. I saw the value in teamwork, in precision, and in how the coaches managed their players with both discipline and care.

One coach stood out. His name was Kevin O'Keefe. At the time, I didn't know he was an English teacher at the high school, and I certainly didn't know he was Indigenous. What I did know, even as a child, was that he had a presence—commanding, kind, firm. He made the girls laugh and work hard, and they clearly respected him. Years later, when I was a teacher myself in Perth, I ran into Kevin again. To my surprise, he remembered me—a kid loitering by the monkey bars—and we struck up a friendship that has lasted ever since. He became something of a mentor, though he probably never knew it.

Back then, sport in Margaret River wasn't the rich smorgasbord that kids enjoy today. There was no soccer league, no rugby union, no surf squad, no martial arts club—at least not for us. There were two main choices: football in the winter, and cricket in the summer. Tennis existed, sure, but it required proper gear, club memberships, and parental time we couldn't spare. So, the boys played footy and cricket, the girls played netball, and that was the extent of it.

The farm became our playground. In the summer, I'd haul out the old push mower to flatten a strip of grass in the paddock and turn it into a makeshift cricket pitch. Wickets were fashioned out of oil drums or sticks; we dusted off the bat, found a ball—sometimes a regulation one, sometimes a softer indoor version that would swing wildly in the breeze—and off we went. These weren't just games; they were epic battles; our own backyard test matches played under a blazing sun. There were enough of us—siblings, cousins, neighbours—to create decent teams, and the days felt endless.

Cricket never truly took hold of me the way footy did. I enjoyed the games, and I had a knack for fast bowling—good enough to represent the school and Busselton at Country Week. But batting was another story. I didn't realise it at the time, but my eyesight was a problem. I struggled to see the ball clearly, so my performance at the crease was always underwhelming. More than that, cricket devoured time—entire weekends, really—and with the farm demanding our labour, Dad wasn't likely to excuse two days off for a game. Later in life, when I was teaching in country towns, I did lace up for a few matches here and there, but the spark just wasn't there.

Winter, though—winter meant football. And football lit something inside me.

I'd watch my older brothers and cousins for hours as they kicked the footy back and forth, calling out for marks, practicing handballs, taking the occasional hanger. It was a mesmerising dance. I wanted so badly to join in, but I was always told I was too small, not skilled enough, likely to get hurt. Francesco—my closest brother, six years older than me—was already strong, fast, and talented. The gap between us was enormous at the time, and I had a lot to prove if I wanted to be included.

But exclusion didn't stop me. After the older boys packed it in for the day, I'd snatch the ball and head out on my own. I'd kick and chase it, crafting imaginary games in my head, narrating the play-by-play like I was on the radio. I studied the different types of kicks—the drop punt, the torpedo, the old-fashioned punt and dropkick—and tried to master each one. My audience was usually a few cows and maybe a curious magpie, but it didn't matter. I was doing it. I was part of the game, even if no one saw.

And always barefoot. On the farm, we didn't bother with shoes unless we had to. Shoes were expensive, and if they got wet or caked in mud, it was a hassle. Feet, on the other hand, dried quickly. The grass was often wet and cold, especially in the mornings, and more than once I warmed my toes by standing in a fresh cow pat. That might sound grotesque now, but it made perfect sense then. The fields weren't smooth or soft—they were riddled with sticks, rocks, double-G burrs and dock weeds—but our feet toughened like old leather. We played through it, because that's just what you did. I didn't see it at the time, but those early mornings on the farm kicking a soggy football around weren't just about learning a sport. They were about resilience, imagination, and persistence. No coaches, no scoreboards, no drills—just a boy and a ball and a big open space.

Looking back now, I realise those were the first moments where sport began to shape not only my body, but my sense of identity. It taught me to observe, to practice, to try again. It taught me how to belong, even if I had to earn it. And maybe, just maybe, it started to teach me that one day I'd be big enough, fast enough, good enough—not just to join the game, but to lead one.

## The Game We Made Our Own

I learned early on that my father had once played a little football during his early years in Australia. In Italy, he had only ever known soccer, but like many migrants trying to settle into a new culture, he gave the local game a go. Word was, he was pretty good too—good enough to represent the Cowaramup team. But I never got to see him play, not even once. He never kicked a footy with us in the paddock, never joined in the games we invented. I think by the time I was old enough to care, life had already caught up with him. His body, worn from years of hard work and illness, just didn't have much left to offer the field.

But even if he couldn't play anymore, he still loved the game. Every Saturday afternoon, Dad and I would sit down together, turn on the ABC, and watch the WAFL. These were the days before the AFL took over—the golden age of West Australian football. Dad was a staunch West Perth supporter, one-eyed and unapologetic about it. The rest of the family supported Swan Districts, but I quickly chose Dad's side. Supporting the same team gave us something special. It made me feel closer to him, like I belonged to a small club of two.

Dad admired players like Barry Cable, Barry Day, Bill Valli, and Bill Dempsey. His favourite was Valli—a man of Italian heritage whose graceful style on the field Dad always attributed to his roots. "It's in the blood," he'd say proudly, and I clung to that idea with boyish certainty. If Bill Valli could be that good because he was Italian, then maybe I could be, too.

In 1975, Dad took the whole family to Perth to watch the WAFL Grand Final—West Perth versus South Fremantle. For me, it felt like going to the Olympics. The big match-up was between the legendary Bill Dempsey and a young up-and-comer, Stephen Michael. Two ruckmen, both destined for greatness, meeting on football's biggest local stage. But it wasn't just them. Basil Campbell, John Wynn, Maurice Rioli, Stan Magro—all giants of the game played that day. The names echoed through the stands, mingling with the smell of pies, grass, and excitement. It was the pinnacle of Western Australian football, and we were there.

Inspired, I began to play more seriously. On most wintry afternoons, you could find me in the paddock, booting a ball back and forth with my brothers or a few mates. We set up tall wooden stakes as goalposts and imagined ourselves in packed stadiums. I practiced every day, refining my kicks, handballs, and marks with the dedication of someone who had already chosen his sport for life.

By the time I was around eight years old, I joined the Margaret River Junior Football Club—the Junior Hawks, interestingly a club founded in the Year I was born. Back then, the game wasn't sugar-coated for kids. There was no Auskick, no smaller teams or modified rules. We played full matches with eighteen players on each side, just like the adults. It was fast, rough, and absolutely exhilarating. Most of our games took place up at Nippers Oval, and I still remember my first match as clearly as if it happened last week. Because I could kick straight, they put me in the forward line. I was nervous—every kid is during their first real game—but then the ball came my way, and I kicked a goal. My first ever. I can still feel the thrill of that moment, the strange magic of leather hitting foot and sailing through the posts. From that point on, there was no turning back. Football had me.

As I got older, I moved up through the age divisions. In the beginning, we played three local sides from around Margaret River, but soon we were representing our town in matches against the bigger, stronger Busselton teams. It was in that regional competition that I learned the harder lessons of contact sport.

One game, I went up for a mark and pulled off what's known as a "screamer"—leaping high and planting myself squarely on another player's back to catch the ball. It was a textbook mark, but not without consequence. The boy beneath me, completely unaware and unprepared, was knocked out cold. Semi-conscious, he had to be carried off the field. I hadn't meant to hurt him, and I was shaken. But the fallout was worse. The boy I'd landed on wasn't just anyone. He was the school's toughest troublemaker, a bruiser with a reputation. Two years older than me, he was known for his quick temper and his fists. The kind of kid who had been in more fights before recess than most of us had had hot lunches. As he was taken off the field, my teammates started whispering: "You're dead, mate. Monday morning, he'll sort you out."

All weekend; I lived in dread. I didn't want to go to school. I wasn't a fighter—I never had been. This was just a game, and I'd done nothing wrong. But fear doesn't listen to reason. It camped out in my stomach like a knot that wouldn't loosen. And then… nothing happened. Monday came, and there was no confrontation. He wasn't even at school, and from what I later heard, he didn't remember the incident at all. Relief flooded me, but so did a strange kind of sorrow. That weekend had taught me more than just the dangers of football. It taught me about the burden of fear, of being misunderstood, and the way a single moment can twist itself into something far bigger than it ever was.

Still, I never stopped playing. Football wasn't just a sport. It was an anchor, a rhythm, a connection to Dad and to something larger than me. It was where I found confidence, belonging, and the simple joy of being part of a team. It was my game, and in many ways, it still is.

## Beyond the Game

When we started playing in the Busselton competition as a combined Margaret River team, something remarkable happened—we didn't lose a single game for three years. It's easy to see why. We were the best of the best from each of the four Margaret River junior sides. We had grit, heart, and a connection that ran deeper than mere teamwork.

It was during one of the grand finals in that competition that I first tasted what it meant to be truly targeted on the field. An older player from the opposition clearly had his eyes set on me. Twice during general play, when I entered a pack to go for the ball, he came at me low and hard. One time, I felt the sharp, unforgiving pain of a boot catching me square in the groin, sending me sprawling to the ground, gasping while the game raged on. It was brutal and personal. But rather than demoralise me, it made me quietly proud. If someone had to stoop to that level to stop me, I must've been doing something right.

I'd learned early how to play against bigger, stronger players—mainly thanks to my siblings and cousins. Playing with them toughened me up. They never went easy on me just because I was younger or smaller. I had to earn every possession and learn to use the ball smartly, efficiently. That kind of upbringing translated well into competitive football. Most of the teams I played in were above my actual age group. I was constantly punching above my weight—and loving it.

Busselton, being a larger town, had four teams, and their kids were usually older and bigger than us, or at least me. All our matches were played in Busselton, so we'd often hop on a bus, or, if I was lucky, my brother would drive me. I can still remember those early mornings—cold air, nervous energy in the bus, boots clunking down the aisle, our coach leaning in close for a few last-minute tactical words. That half-hour trip was electric with anticipation. And the trip back? That was euphoric. We'd stop for fish and chips, a rare treat, and relive every highlight—who took the best mark, who kicked the miracle goal, who laid the most important tackle. There was a kind of sacredness to those memories, soaked in salt and vinegar, laughter, and camaraderie.

Our team was bonded by something more than shared jerseys. Four of the eighteen on the field were Palandri's—my cousins Giacomo, Giuseppe, Daryl, and me. We seemed to have a sixth sense for each other's movements. We didn't need to call for the ball; we just knew. We covered each other instinctively. Our coach understood this advantage and used it wisely, often shaping plays around that familial understanding.

By Year 10, I was playing Colt's football for the Margaret River Football Club. I was just fifteen. When I moved to Busselton for senior school the next year, I didn't have any of my usual teammates at Colts level. Most of the Busselton kids weren't playing that high yet, and some didn't take it kindly that an Italian kid from Margaret River had leapfrogged them into a senior competition. There were jibes, teasing, and taunts about my heritage. Nothing I hadn't encountered before—but still, it stung in that uniquely adolescent way.

However, when the football started, the tone changed. During school sport sessions and games, they saw why I had been selected. I let my football do the talking, just as I had in countless classrooms and playgrounds before. My performance spoke louder than their prejudice ever could.

During Year 11 and 12, I was proud to be selected for the Country Week football team, representing Busselton Senior High School. Country Week was a big deal—schools from across the state fielded teams across multiple sports and competed over a week in Perth. In both years I played, we had strong A-grade squads, and we won the competition outright. I still remember pulling on that jumper, stepping onto the city ovals, feeling like we carried not just a school but a whole region on our backs.

It was during one of those Country Week tournaments that a scout from East Perth Football Club noticed me. He expressed interest in drafting me the following year. It was a thrilling moment—someone from a professional club had seen potential in me. Though life took different turns later, that flicker of possibility stayed with me.

Forty years later, I found myself back at Country Week—not as a player, but as a teacher. I was supervising Busselton's teams, watching the new generation warm up, run drills, chase dreams.

Walking onto those fields again was surreal. The smell of freshly cut grass, the chill of early morning dew, the colourful chaos of uniforms stretching and sprinting—it all came rushing back. I could almost see my younger self lacing up his boots and listening for the whistle.

Mum and Dad came to almost every Colts match. Dad was vocal—offering feedback after each game, sometimes praise, sometimes blunt suggestions. I always valued his insights. He had a clear eye and a quiet pride, and football became another thread that connected us. Win or lose, he was there. And that meant everything. There was one Colts match I'll never forget. We were playing a team from Collie.

I lined up as a follower—what used to be called a rover—meaning I was on the ball for most of the match, only rotating down to rest in the forward pocket. From the first bounce, the crowd was on me. In local footy, the crowd has the team sheet, complete with names and numbers. So, the heckles weren't vague—they were personal. "Palandri!" they'd yell, followed by every stereotype and slur they could come up with. I'd heard it all before, but that didn't mean it didn't sting.

Still, I did what I always did—I responded with actions. I kicked a couple of goals, shrugged off the taunts, and pushed harder. The more they shouted, the more determined I became. Eventually, they began throwing things from the boundary. But I didn't give them the satisfaction of reacting. I played on, proud, and focused. Because that's what football taught me—not just how to play a game, but how to hold your ground. How to deal with what life throws at you—sometimes literally. How to rise above bitterness, to find strength in silence, and to let your feet, your tackles, and your goals tell the story.

There was—and still is—nothing quite like the feeling of stepping onto the field, smelling the earth, feeling the weight of the ball in your hands. The buzz of the change room before a game, the slap of Goanna oil on your legs, the thud of boots against lockers, the quiet focus before the chaos. These moments stay with you. They become part of who you are. For me, sport wasn't just a pastime. It was a proving ground, a teacher, and a thread that tied my story—my family, my heritage, my identity—into one field of play.

## The Coach Within

I miss the smell of damp grass, the sting of cold air in my lungs, and the distant thump of a leather ball meeting a boot. I miss the rhythm of whistles, the banter from the sidelines, and the nervous anticipation that crept into your bones just before a match began. I miss it all, now that I no longer play—or coach—football.

Over the years, I had my share of coaches—some truly inspirational, others utterly hopeless. In my Colts years, I was lucky to be led by two exceptional men. One of them had played league football for Margaret River and spoke with a fire that stirred something in me. His charisma and belief in our team carried us all the way to the semi-finals, and nearly into the grand finale.

I still remember that semi—how hail rained down on us like frozen bullets, battering our bear arms and necks. Nothing interrupts your flow like ice from the sky when all you're wearing is a thin Guernsey.

Contrast that with some of my early junior coaches. I recall one who pulled me aside before a match and said, "Steve, you know what to do. I've got nothing else to tell you." That was it—no tactics, no strategy, no encouragement. Just a shrug and a push onto the field. Yet, amid all the muddled voices and mixed talents, one coach stands head and shoulders above the rest.

His name was Moggie King.

Moggie didn't play league football. He wasn't technically brilliant. He had a rough, unpolished manner and a gravelly voice that barked more than it spoke. But Moggie had heart. Every game and every training session, he showed up—kitted out, metal studded boots laced, ready to run with us boys. He threw himself into drills, barked instructions from the field, and when things got tough, he never quit. He wasn't there for recognition or status. He was there because he loved the game, and he believed in us. That loyalty—to the club, to the green and gold, to every kid on that field—was infectious.

I never knew why he was called "Moggie". He didn't look anything like a cat. He was stocky, red-faced, with hands like timber offcuts. But he was a local character, someone even my father knew and respected. And although Moggie may not have had tactical finesse, he brought something more valuable: belief. He made each of us feel like we belonged, like we mattered, and like every game—no matter how small—was worth our full effort. My last game as a player came in 1989. I was in my mid-to-late twenties, lining up for Albany Railways Football Club. I'd been battling a knee injury, and it slowed me down just enough for a younger opponent to outrun me all day. I played centre, and we lost. There were no fireworks, no victory lap, no send-off. Just sore legs on Monday morning, the quiet ache of realising the game had passed me by.

The local newspaper summed it up in one brutal sentence: *"Veteran Palandri's colours lowered to champion youth."* I remember reading that line over and over. Not with anger, just with acceptance. My time had come. And though it stung, I knew something else was beginning.

I had already completed my Level 1 and Level 2 coaching certifications and had started working with a junior side from my school. At the time, I didn't know that this would spark a coaching career that would span three decades—thirty years of whistles, water bottles, and pre-game nerves. Thirty years of muddy jerseys and muddy thinking, both needing to be cleaned and sharpened by the final siren.

I coached everything from Aus kick to teenage football, local league teams, regional women's squads, and elite development sides. Some of the highlights included leading the Under-15 State Schoolboys AFL team, a Wesfarmers Under-19 regional squad, and the West Perth Women's Football Team. I was also lucky enough to coach the West Perth AFL Development Squad. But regardless of the level, every session, every match, brought me back to the coaches I had known—the good, the bad, and the unforgettable. I brought all of that to my own style. I borrowed Moggie's loyalty and passion, refined it with tactical knowledge, and wrapped it in care for my players.

Because coaching isn't just about shaping footballers, it's about shaping people.

There's something deeply satisfying about watching young players develop. To witness a shy teenager, grow in confidence, to see them master a skill they once feared, or to watch them step into leadership roles—it's as rewarding as any premiership medal. As a coach, you're not just instructing—you're unlocking something. You see players not only rise to their potential but help each other rise too. That's the magic of team sport. That's why I stayed in it for so long.

Sometimes, I think back to those early days on the farm— barefooted, kicking a heavy, waterlogged footy around the paddock. Dad on the sidelines, my cousins nearby, and the smell of fresh-cut grass in the air.

I had no idea where those kicks would take me, or that they were laying the groundwork for a lifetime in sport. All I knew was that I loved the game. And now, looking back, I see that football didn't just give me something to do. It gave me a voice. It gave me a way to lead, to inspire, and to give back to others what had been given so generously to me.

**Gloucester Park. Home of the Augusta Margaret River Hawks**

# Chapter 14
# Lines in the Water, Stories in the Wind
# (Lenze in acqua, storie nel vento)

*"In every cast of the line, there was more than the hope of a fish—there was a thread to memory, a whisper of the past carried on the wind."*

*(In ogni lancio della lenza c'era più della speranza di un pesce—c'era un filo verso la memoria, un sussurro del passato portato dal vento.)*

Before the sea offered its fish, it offered something else belonging. Long before lines hit the water or waves kissed our bare feet, we felt the quiet pull of tradition, of freedom, of adventure born under the salt sky. Fishing wasn't just something we did; it was something that shaped us. It taught us patience, courage, mischief, and memory. These were not just outings to the coast—they were rituals, each one etching a story into the family lore, passed on with laughter, with pride, and sometimes with scars.

## The Call of the Coast

Some adventures never needed planning—they simply arrived on the wind, hinted at in the crispness of the morning air or the glance exchanged between brothers and cousins that silently agreed: "Today's the day." These moments didn't come with calendars or permission slips. Before responsibilities crept in—before we had licenses, jobs, or a concept of time management—the world often shrank to the size of a trailer hitched to an orange tractor, and the coastline stretched out like a promise. This wasn't just fishing. It was ceremony, instinct, and freedom rolled into one.

There were Sundays, especially in the lead-up to Easter, that bent the normal rhythm of life toward the pulse of the ocean. Between Bunuru and Djeran, the Noongar seasons when the herring ran thick and the heat gave way to the gentler arms of autumn, the air itself seemed to whisper possibilities.

On those mornings, we traded polished shoes and Sunday Mass for bare feet, long bamboo rods, and dreams of the surf. To us boys, no sermon could compete with the thrill of a day spent chasing fish, sea spray on our faces and the wind tugging at our hair.

We'd rise early, before the sun crested the hill, while the rest of the house still slept in its quiet breathing. There was no need for elaborate packing—we'd wear whatever clothes had survived the footy season and a few too many climbs up the mulberry tree. Shorts bleached pale from too many summers, t-shirts worn thin and stained with the good kind of dirt, and no shoes, of course. Shoes were for school or town—not for creek beds or beach tracks.

The first ritual began in the backyard. There, around an old tin drum, we mixed our burley—a porridge of mashed potatoes and pollard, stirred with a thick stick until the mixture gave off a sharp, pungent scent that promised success. We'd take turns mixing, each swirl feeding our excitement.

Next came the garage rummage. Under old tarps and behind sacks of fertiliser lay our sacred tools: bamboo flick rods, tangled handlines, rusty knives that had filleted generations of fish, and sun-bleached tackle boxes full of misfit sinkers and faded lures.

In a final act of stealth, someone would creep into the freezer and 'borrow' a packet of red meat, or better yet, retrieve a stash of grubs or rabbit pieces saved specifically for the occasion. And then we waited.

We'd sit on the veranda, squinting eastward, straining to hear it before we saw it. First, the deep chug of diesel across the paddocks. Then the signature plume of smoke, curling like incense above the tree line. And finally, cresting the rise like some lumbering creature from myth, the orange Fiat tractor appeared.

Uncle Joe sat tall and grinning at the wheel, two kids on the mudguards, and a trailer overflowing with eager bodies—arms flung around each other or grasping onto the timber sides, already jostling for prime position.

The rods stuck out from the trailer like the bristles of some prehistoric beast, and the exhaust coughed and puffed behind it like a dragon's breath. As it rumbled to a halt in the rear paddock, Uncle Joe's booming voice rang out like a rallying cry. More kids clambered aboard. The brave always chose the rear of the trailer, hanging on through every bump and swerve, while the more cautious perched along the edges, ducking the relentless swipes from roadside bushes. We joked—half seriously—that Uncle Joe aimed for those bushes on purpose, letting the scratchy branches teach us a little toughness.

**On the trailer, rods hanging out the back ready to go.**

The road, if one could call it that, was nothing more than a sandy track, a scar worn into the land by years of foot traffic and the occasional tractor wheel. It had once been a horse trail, walked by our fathers and uncles on their own fishing journeys—four kilometres of bush, scrub, and anticipation. Now we followed in their footsteps, carried by diesel and tradition, learning not just how to catch fish, but how to be part of something bigger than ourselves.

**Rough Tracks and Tall Tales (Sentieri accidentati e storie alte)**

The journey down to the coast was never smooth. It wasn't meant to be. That track, beaten into the earth by decades of boots, tractor tyres, and shared laughter, was a rite of passage in itself—four kilometres of sandy stubbornness and raw memory. Every jolt and rattle along the way was part of the build-up, sharpening our anticipation with every bump.

We'd bounce and sway in the back of the trailer, bracing against its timber sides as the Fiat grumbled forward, weaving past trees with twisted limbs and thick undergrowth that reached out to scratch at our skin like ghosts of the bush.

We passed by the cave we never dared enter, half-joking that it was haunted, even though none of us would admit to truly believing it. Then came the remnants of an old homestead, nothing but a crumbling chimney a mulberry tree and the ghost of a garden, once home to Alfred and Ellen Bussell. Their names were etched into the foundations of the region, and we knew the legends by heart.

But the real tale—the one that stirred our imaginations the most—was that of Robert Isaacs and Grace Bussell, who had rescued survivors from the wreck of the *SS Georgette*. It wasn't just history; it was folklore we could see, touch, and feel every time we passed that weathered commemorative rock. To us, the track didn't just lead to the sea—it ran straight through time.

**The Original Ellensbrook Homestead**

**Ellensbrook House after Restoration**

The track, of course, had its own tricks. It would lull inexperienced drivers into false confidence before swallowing their cars whole. Inevitably, Dad would be called upon to haul them out with the tractor. It wasn't uncommon during herring season for him to make that trip two or three times in a week. The recovery missions rarely ended without drama—cars so bogged they practically fused with the sand. Dad would mutter about "bloody townies" as he looped chains through axles and cursed the mess. Occasionally, a bumper would rip off or a side mirror would meet an untimely end against a peppermint tree. It was never intentional—but always a lesson, mostly for them.

One day, our convoy included cousins from Busselton, unfamiliar with the terrain and more accustomed to smooth roads than the sandblasted chaos of our route. They'd joined us on a special expedition, and excitement buzzed through the air. Perched along the trailer's edges, they grinned and laughed—until we hit a particularly wicked dip. One cousin, caught mid-laugh, was pitched headfirst into a prickle bush. His squeal turned into a yelp as he scrambled to untangle himself, face red from embarrassment and scratches. Even Dad and Uncle Joe, usually stoic behind the wheel, couldn't hold back their laughter. It was one of those moments that lived on in family legend, told and retold with increasing exaggeration.

Eventually, the canopy broke open, and the coastline revealed itself like a secret we were lucky enough to know. The tractor would lurch to a stop at the top of what we now call "the lookout," offering a panoramic view of the sea below—wild, foaming, eternal. The reef cut sharp lines into the waves, and the salt air hit us like a slap of exhilaration. We knew we had arrived.

Unloading was a dance. Flick rods, tackle boxes, bait buckets, spare clothes, and yesterday's fish guts for burley—all flung into action. Dad and Zio moved like seasoned field generals, reading the wind and swell, scanning the tides with instinctive precision. They didn't need charts or gadgets. The scent of the air, the texture of the sand underfoot, the rhythm of the water told them everything they needed to know.

We reserved the first bay for the shark line—a heavy, rugged rope baited with the guts from the day before and hurled far into the crashing surf. It was our version of a dare, half hoping something terrifying would bite. The second bay, though, was where the real magic happened. Coral fingers reached beneath the surface, beckoning schools of herring and skipjack. And sometimes, if fortune smiled, a blue groper would strike.

I still remember the day we landed one. It was immense, iridescent blue in the morning light, and when it hit the rock, we erupted—screaming, stomping, high-fiving like warriors after a victorious battle. That fish became more than a catch. It became a tale in its own right, passed on like a treasured recipe or a family secret. Because, in truth, the sea never gave us just fish—it gave us stories.

### Tides of Triumph

By the time we arrived, the older boys and the men already stood at the rocky edge like a picket line, holding their bamboo rods like silent banners. Their eyes were fixed on the sea, their arms in constant, patient motion—flick, pause, flick again. There were no reels, no fancy rods—just three-metre bamboo poles, a length of fishing line tied to the end, and a single barbless hook that made releasing a fish quick and clean. It was simple, time-tested, and deeply effective.

The real drama for us younger kids unfolded much closer to shore, in the shallow tidal pools and cracks of the reef. That was our arena, our battleground. Armed with stubby hand lines, a bucket, and unmatched enthusiasm, we leapt barefoot from rock to rock, peering into each pool for movement. The thrill wasn't just in the catch—it was in the chase. Slipping on seaweed, losing bait to unseen nibbles, shouting when someone snagged something silver—it was chaos, laughter, and learning all in one.

We'd tear the skin from our feet, stub our toes, and lose more hooks than we'd care to admit, but none of that mattered. Each small fish we caught felt monumental, as if we'd bested nature herself. We'd hold up our prize to the sun, proud as champions, before tossing it into a shared bucket. Those fish were never wasted. They were cleaned, cooked, and devoured later that night, often with a story to match.

And while we played at fishermen, we gave the adults the space they needed. Our distractions were their peace. They could focus on the ocean, the tide, and their own quiet rituals without kids underfoot. It was a harmony we all understood, even if it was unspoken. By late afternoon, the trailer looked like a fishmonger's stall—herring, trevally, the odd tailor or skippy, and occasionally, a shark or groper if luck had really tipped our way. We loaded it all in, weary but beaming. The ride back home was slower, the bumps less jarring, the laughter quieter. Our skin burned from the sun, our clothes crusted with salt, but our hearts were full.

**Flick rodding off the rocks.**

At home, the catch would be emptied onto the lawn, gleaming in the fading light like scattered treasure. The older boys and trusted cousins would take up knives—scaling, gutting, and sorting with the practiced ease passed down through generations. Waste went to the chooks, who squawked and scratched until even bones vanished like magic.

And then came the smell—fresh fish sizzling in cast iron pans, mingling with garlic, oil, and the slow rise of voices retelling the day's adventures. Stories of the one that got away, of cuts earned and cousins who fell into bushes, and of course, whispered retellings of the old myths: the ghosts that guarded the creek and cave, the shadow in the cave, the tree that moaned when the wind blew just right. But those are tales for another time.

# Chapter 15
# Sausage, Tomato Sauce and Stewing
# (Salsicce, Salsa di Pomodoro e Stufato)

*"The kitchen of a family is the heart of the home: where time slows down and memories simmer."*

*"La cucina di una famiglia è il cuore della casa: dove il tempo rallenta e i ricordi si cuociono a fuoco lento."*

There are some smells that never leave you—garlic browning in oil, fresh basil torn between calloused fingers, the sharp tang of tomato simmering on the stove, or the rich, smoky scent of pork being transformed into something eternal. These weren't just aromas—they were announcements. "It's sauce day," someone would call. Or "Get the mincer ready." These days were more than cooking. They were rituals, carried out with sleeves rolled high and voices raised higher, where children learned to stir before they could write, and every meal was a story layered in meat, memory, and tomato.

### Frozen in Time, Served Warm

Once, during my student years, I landed an odd job aboard the *Achille Lauro*—a grand ocean liner docked in Fremantle during the excitement of the America's Cup. My role was simple: help sell art to curious onlookers. The perk? A daily buffet lunch worth fifty dollars. By any measure, that should've meant something lavish. But I remember being shocked by what was served up as "Bolognese"—a sad plate of pasta laced with watery tomato sauce, barely a trace of meat or flavour. I knew better. I had grown up in a kitchen where even leftovers had soul.

When I spoke about the food onboard, someone suggested something I'd never considered: that immigrants often preserved the cuisine and traditions of the time they left, freezing culture like a snapshot in a bottle. While Italy evolved, our families—clinging to the past for comfort—kept those traditions alive, unchanged, on the other side of the world.

At the time, I hadn't thought of it that way. To me, the food I grew up with was simply food—home. My mother's cooking was legendary in our household, a daily symphony of sauce, spice, and love. But not everything came from Mum's hands. The men of our family claimed their own culinary domains. Sausages, bottled tomato passata, stewed fruits and vegetables—these weren't just chores, they were acts of heritage. Each dish held meaning. Each task was a ritual. And every mouthful reminded us of a time when food wasn't easily bought but painstakingly grown, prepared, and shared. It wasn't just sustenance. It was memory, frozen in time, and served warm.

### Blood, Spice, and Brotherhood

These days, Italian sausage-making is a bit of a trend. Everyone has their "Nonna's recipe," even if their Nonna was born in Footscray and couldn't boil water. I don't mind. In fact, I smile when I hear people throw around ingredients like fennel seed, chilli, or even xanthan gum with confidence, as though they've uncovered some ancient secret. Let them have their sausage day—I say good on them.

At least they're trying to keep something alive. But I'll tell you now: the recipe we used, passed down from our ancestors in Emilia-Romagna, arrived in Australia in the early 1900s and remained unchanged for generations before that. What made it special wasn't some secret spice—it was the hands that made it and the stories that came with every link.

In Piandelagotti, they knew how to make a sausage. Ours was possibly one of the first Italian sausage recipes prepared in Margaret River. Our pigs—big, stubborn beasts—were fed from the leftover whey and scraps of our dairy. These pigs weren't raised for sale; they were for us. And they were notorious for eating anything, which made them more than a little terrifying for a young barefoot boy wandering too close to the sky.

I'll never forget the day I misjudged the risk. Playing chasey with my cousins near the pig pens, I leapt over the fence—quick and agile, I thought—and landed squarely on a protruding nail. It drove straight through my right foot. The pain was instant and searing, but what made my heart freeze was the sight of the pig raising its snout, sniffing the blood, and turning toward me with a grunt. My cousins howled with laughter as I limped and scrambled out, my foot trailing blood through the mud. One cousin pointed and howled, "Look! He's licking the nail!" Sure enough, the pig had sauntered over to the bloodied board and was giving it a thorough clean. That was the last time I underestimated pigs.

But come July, one pig met its end in the name of tradition. Winter was chosen carefully—not out of cruelty but necessity. The cold helped preserve the meat, kept flies at bay, and slowed the inevitable decay. It was sausage season, and the whole family knew what that meant.

The day began before dawn. Around 4 a.m., we'd gather in the early dark. What came next may seem graphic to some, but for us, it was just part of life. The pig was slaughtered quickly and respectfully. Its organs were removed with care; blood was drained and collected. Only the lungs, bladder, and urinary tract were discarded. The rest—every inch—had purpose.

That's when the children came in. We didn't help with the kill, but we found other forms of "fun." The discarded organs made excellent toys, if you can believe it. We'd spear the bladder or lungs with handmade wooden spears and listen to the grotesque squelches and hisses they produced. A bit of mischief, a lot of laughter, and eventually we'd be told to toss the lot into the chook pen. And here's something city kids would never guess—chickens are carnivores. They'd strip a carcass to the bone, no problem.

Some years, there'd be a kangaroo in the mix too. This was a local twist—one born from necessity and practicality. Roo meat was lean and dry, the perfect balance to fatty pork. It also brought a distinctly Australian flavour to an Italian tradition. We didn't use kangaroo every year, but when we did, it was a welcome variation. I know how it sounds now—hunting kangaroo by spotlight, using it for food and dog meat—but back then, it was just what we did.

The slaughtered pig would be cleaned and sectioned. Cheeks were removed and salted to make *guanciale*, a fatty cured meat perfect for pasta—most famously, carbonara. Every part had its place. The liver, kidneys, heart, even the skin and hooves were minced with spices and blood to make what we called "blood sausage." A cousin of black pudding or haggis, it was rich and earthy. I never had the stomach for it myself. The thought of intestines and brains in a casing made me squeamish. But Dad and my uncles? They loved the stuff, and would eat it with gusto, red wine in hand, declaring it "real food." Those sausages were made early, while the rest of us prepared for the main event—our beloved pork sausages.

Lunch was a feast. While ribs and bones were brought to the kitchen, kids who weren't gut-deep in mincing duties grilled little portions of the spiced pork on sticks over open flames. We'd sneak pinches from the mixing box, roast it quickly, and sample it like connoisseurs. Quality control, we called it.

But the real heart of the day was the production line. And it ran like a war machine.

The youngest kids separated skin from meat. Older cousins trimmed fat. The seasoned ones diced slabs into manageable chunks, all thrown into a massive wooden box—our version of an industrial prep station. Then came the hand mincers, heavy and stubborn. We'd take turns cranking them, ten minutes at a time, sweating and laughing as pork turned to fine mince. Up to 500kg of meat passed through those grinders.

All the while, my uncle barked orders like a foreman at a quarry. His voice boomed across the room, his massive hands—better suited to building stone houses—waving with exaggerated frustration. "No, no! Too much fat!" or "Cut deeper, you blind bats!" But we loved it. His bark was worse than his bite, and his booming presence added to the theatre. Meanwhile, Dad sat outside, elbow-deep in salted water, carefully cleaning the *budellini*—the sausage casings. Each metre had to be blown out, rinsed, and untangled. A meditative task, in its way, but demanding patience and precision.

When the mince was ready, it was spiced. Not with supermarket sachets, but with garlic, salt, and red wine from our cellar. The exact proportions were a closely guarded secret. My father would taste a bit raw, rolling it thoughtfully on his tongue, and nod. Sometimes he'd pass a bit to us boys. "Try this," he'd say, "Tell me if it needs more garlic." We'd roast it, or just eat it raw—something unthinkable today, but back then, it was part of the ritual. Stuffing the sausages came next. The skins were stretched onto the mincing tube, and the mix was pushed through, cool and heavy, forming long ropes of salsiccia that would be twisted and hung to dry. We were proud of those strings, looping them over broomsticks or wire hooks, letting them air-cure in the shed. Each one was a badge of honour.

By nightfall, the kitchen was filled with steam and the smell of charred meat. We'd feast on ribs, grilled chops, and fried bits of everything else. The older men would sip more wine than perhaps they should've, and we kids—exhausted and full—would either sleep on the couches or be bundled into the car for the ride home.

One year, I remember Dad insisting we drive home through the storm. The rain fell in thick curtains, and we barely made it past the gate before crashing into a tree. No one was badly hurt, but the silence in the car told its own story. Another year with bridge washed away he drove the valiant into the river. Later, I'd come to realise the crash wasn't just about weather or bad luck. It was about the quiet danger of mixing tradition with a few too many glasses of vino. Still, no one ever suggested skipping sausage day.

These weren't just events—they were chapters in our family story. Hands stained with spice and blood, laughter echoing in the shed, the bark of an uncle, the quiet diligence of a father, and the eager, clumsy help of kids trying to be part of something bigger than themselves. It wasn't about the sausage, not really. It was about memory. About making something together that you couldn't buy. Something that spoke of homeland, of survival, of stubborn, delicious continuity, still happening now with new kids and new uncles.

## Bottled Sunshine: The Ritual of Tomato Day

I was born too late to witness the full glory of the *Emilia-Romagna* tomato season in our backyard. But I grew up in the echo of its rituals, catching glimpses of something sacred passed from generation to generation. In our family, food wasn't just nourishment—it was history in motion. And no tradition embodied that more than *salsa di pomodoro* day.

The kitchen had always been Mum's domain. But when it came to tomato sauce—*real* tomato sauce—the men took charge. It was a ritual, a performance, a collaboration that turned the ordinary into the extraordinary. And though the vegetable garden that once overflowed with Roma tomatoes had long been scaled back, the spirit of the season remained.

The tomatoes had to be perfect—ripe, meaty, and bursting with sun. Roma tomatoes were the chosen kind, rich in flesh and low in seed. My parents would scan markets or our own small plot for the best of the bunch. And when the time came, we'd gather buckets and head out to pick them, just like in the old days, though the rows weren't quite as long and the harvest not as abundant.

We'd bring the tomatoes back to the *Capan none*, the shed that housed all of our family's practical traditions. There, the transformation began. Children, cousins, aunties, uncles—we all had our place in the assembly line. Someone would quarter the tomatoes, slicing away the vine nibs with swift flicks of a knife. Others would rinse them, filling barrels with clean water, letting the fruit bob and swirl in preparation.

Zio Giuseppe was in command, as always. He'd bark instructions like a general, his booming voice ricocheting off the shed walls. "No! That's too much waste!" he'd shout at someone trimming too generously. Or "Faster! These tomatoes won't boil themselves!" It was half-serious, half-theatre, but completely vital. His presence gave the ritual weight, even when he exasperated us.

Dad, in contrast, was the silent artisan. He'd sit near the firepit, inspecting each quartered tomato with the calm of a monk. His role was to oversee the copper cauldron—*il rame*—set into the fireplace at the back corner of the shed. This ancient vessel was the heart of the operation, and it held the bubbling essence of a hundred years of tradition. Once cleaned and drained, the tomatoes were dumped into the copper and left to simmer for hours. The fire beneath was tended carefully. The smell that followed was impossible to describe—deep, earthy, sweet, and tinged with the sharp promise of garlic and the perfumed lift of fresh basil. You couldn't walk past the capannone without being pulled in by your nose.

By nightfall, the tomatoes had broken down into a pulpy, fragrant mass—the *must*. That marked the end of day one. We'd cover the copper and retreat into the house, where Mum and Zia Tilly would have laid out a feast to celebrate the work done. Wine flowed, laughter rose, and stories circled the table. It wasn't just about preserving tomatoes—it was about preserving connection.

Day two was bottling day. It started early. The shed was quiet but purposeful. Bottles and jars—dozens upon dozens—were washed and sterilised in great steaming vats. The fire was rekindled to warm the copper and soften the must again. Then came the sieve.

It was no small sieve, but a large, metal mesh contraption balanced over a deep basin. The must was ladled in, and strong hands—usually Dad's or one of the older boys'—would press the mixture through, squashing skin and seed against mesh, coaxing out the silken red liquid beneath. The scent intensified as the thick puree collected below, now concentrated with flavour and memory.

There was pride in getting it just right. The sauce had to be smooth, rich, and aromatic. The garlic and basil—steeped in early—added complexity without overpowering. You could taste sunshine and history in a spoonful. And there was always someone with a slice of crusty bread nearby to test the consistency. "Too thin," someone might mutter, and adjustments would be made.

The bottling itself was delicate work. Funnels guided the sauce into jars and bottles; each one handled like it contained treasure. Which, to us, it did. We sealed them tightly, wiped them clean, and arranged them in neat rows on the shelves of the Capan none. Sometimes there were fifty bottles. Other years, closer to a hundred. However many we made, they were shared between the families—especially with the kids who had moved out, who would light up at the sight of a jar brought down in a care package. Even the leftovers had their place. The skins, seeds, and rejected bits of tomato were tossed to the chickens. And those birds, omnivores to the core, would peck happily at the scraps—yet another link in the chain of nothing going to waste.

What amazed me was that the men, usually so far removed from kitchen life, claimed this process with pride. It wasn't just Mum's food that fed us. It was Dad's hands, stained red from hours of stirring. It was Zio Giuseppe's voice echoing in our ears. It was the sweat, the timing, and the attention. That, too, was home.

And in the end, it wasn't just about the tomato sauce. It was about showing that tradition lived not only in memory, but in action—in rituals repeated, in generations working side by side, in bottles lined up neatly in a shed, glowing red like captured sun.

— ❖ —

## A Stew for All Seasons

In many families, it would have been the mother or the aunt who took charge of the stewing, preserving, and pickling. But in ours, it was different. Mum and Dad divided the kitchen by flavour—she claimed the sweet, and he, the sour. Where Mum was queen of fig jam, stewed peaches, and poached plums, Dad reigned over pickled onions, vinegar-soaked olives, and giardiniera in jars with hand-cut carrots and chillies.

The orchard fed much of this quiet production. Apricots, apples, figs, pears, and peaches passed through Mum's hands like seasonal scripture. She'd simmer the fruit in sugar syrups until it softened just enough to surrender. Then came the sterilised jars, the boiling seals, and finally, storage in the *capannone*—that magical shed cupboard we children raided with stealth and precision. We never could resist. Jars would mysteriously shift to the back of the shelf, slightly lighter than before, their seals imperfect. We blamed the mice. Or the heat. Anything but our sticky fingers.

Her fig jam was the crown jewel. After months of resting, it fermented just enough to take on a sharp, almost alcoholic perfume—dangerously close to becoming something illicit. We'd spread it thick on bread before school, half-hoping for a little rebellion with our breakfast.

Dad, on the other hand, was methodical. He would spend hours slicing vegetables into ribbons, curls, or rounds—his tools varied, each one offering a different shape, a different texture. Carrots were often crinkled or diced into perfect coins. Cauliflower florets were carefully separated, and chillies were trimmed with surgical precision. His giardiniera—vivid, tangy, and fiery—was a thing of art. Arranged in clear jars, surrounded by golden vinegar and spice, they were more than pickles; they were memories sealed in glass.

Pickled onions were his favourite. Sourced from our own vegetable garden, they were peeled, blanched, and steeped in his mysterious brew of pickling liquor. Every evening meal, unless pasta was served, was crowned with one of these sharp little jewels. The ritual was unspoken—reach for the jar, fish one out, savour the crunch.

Learning to sun-dry fruit with Dad became its own rite of passage. We'd gather ripe figs and apricots, slice them with our worn pocketknives, and place them flesh-side-up on wire-mesh trays. On hot days, the trays would go on the roof of the shed—higher meant hotter, and hotter meant quicker. But the temptation was always too much. Every day, a little less fruit remained. Birds were the official culprits, of course.

Mum's jam-making days were sacred. The stovetop would hiss and bubble as she stirred pot after pot of fruit and sugar, the air thick with the perfume of ripeness. Her hands moved with quiet certainty—jars sterilised just so, lids sealed with a satisfying pop, and everything tucked neatly away. Watching her, I learned what care looked like—not showy or loud, just deliberate and full of love.

But stewing was not only about fruit. Dad took vegetables and turned them into something enduring. His giardiniera—those spicy medleys of carrot, cauliflower, chilli, and onion—found their way into meals year-round. A splash of colour on the table, always sitting beside the cheeses, the cured meats, and the olives. They offered sharp contrast to rich stews and roasted meats, balancing the plate like punctuation in a sentence.

These pickled and preserved foods weren't made for show or even celebration. They were made to last—to feed, to nourish, to honour the work of hands that planted, picked, chopped, and stirred. They were made because that's how you made things last. They were part of a rhythm we lived by, even if we didn't recognise it at the time.

And in that rhythm, we found comfort. Mum and Dad didn't just cook—they handed down a way of life. They taught us to transform what we had, to preserve not just food but heritage. Today, even without them beside us, we still do the same. The methods might shift slightly, but the heart remains.

All of my brothers and sisters still make sausage. Still dry fruit in the summer heat. Still reach for the vinegar bottle when preparing vegetables. These aren't just acts of remembrance—they're acts of continuation. Through them, the Palandri story simmers on.

# Chapter 16
# The Brothers and Sisters
# (I Fratelli e le Sorelle)

*"What binds us is not just blood, but the stories we've shared and the silences we've understood."*

*"Ciò che ci lega non è solo il sangue, ma le storie che abbiamo condiviso e i silenzi che abbiamo capito."*

*"They say the roots of a tree grow strong beneath the soil. For us, those roots are named Ric, Carla, Lina, Anne, and Frank."*

We were a farm family, stitched together by soil, sacrifice, shared meals, and muddy boots. Each of us was born into a different moment in the family's journey—from stone house to timber, from Nonna's quiet hands to the bustling noise of growing up Palandri. This chapter is a tribute to my siblings—one photograph, one memory at a time. Some moments captured in black and white, others in vivid colour. These are the threads that form our shared tapestry.

### Ricardo Giuseppe Palandri

### (b. 1951 – eldest child of Carlo and Angelina)

**L. Ricardo. R. Mum and Dad with Ricardo**

## From Stone and Snow to Timber and Wine

He was the first—a blonde-haired boy with serious eyes and a watchful stance, born just a year after Carlo and Angelina were married. Ricardo Giuseppe Palandri arrived in 1951, in the era before the timber house was even built, when the family lived shoulder-to-shoulder with Nonna and Nonno in the old stone house. In family folklore, Ric—calm, unshakable Ric—is remembered as the quiet force of the Palandri siblings: steady, dependable, and eternally even-tempered.

My older sisters still tease him about being the "spoilt one." Maybe it's because of the countless childhood photos. Or maybe it's because of the infamous Briggs & Stratton engine accident in the dairy—an incident that nearly took him from us. From that moment on, perhaps unconsciously, we all knew Ric was special, watched over.

As he grew, Ric became a figure of quiet confidence. He was a keen hunter and fisherman, always disappearing into the bush or down along the rugged Margaret River coastline, pioneering tracks and campsites the rest of us would later claim as our own. The stories of his early adventures—the giant fish caught; the secret hunting spots found—are now family legend.

Of course, no story is complete without a misfire. Literally. One afternoon, in what was meant to be an innocent round of target practice, Ric let off a shot that ricocheted off a shed and struck Carla. Some say it hit her in the arm. Others, more dramatically, claim the forehead. Either way, Carla survived, and the tale has grown arms and legs with every retelling. Ric married a Margaret River local and together they raised two children who now have children of their own. His work took him far from home—Darwin, Karratha, the red dust and cyclones of the north. He was living in Darwin when Cyclone Tracy tore through the city in 1974. Like much in Ric's life, he endured quietly, returned to the southwest, and kept going.

Mum once told me a story from Ric's primary school days. A boy had been picking on him, day after day. Ric didn't say a word about it. Until one day he'd had enough. He punched the bully square in the nose. That boy later became one of his closest lifelong friends.

In all my years, I've never once heard Ric raise his voice in anger. He has always been the ballast in our family boat, steadying us in storms, quiet in his strength—so much like our father in that way. His life, in many ways, has reflected Dad's: rooted, humble, and deeply reliable.

### Carla Palandri (b. 1952)

**L. Mum with Carla R. Rick and Carla**

Carla was born in 1952, the first girl and second child of Angelina and Carlo. Like Ric, she spent her early years in the stone house and moved into the wooden house around age three.

Carla has always been the quiet achiever. She carries herself with understated grace, someone who absorbs life deeply and acts with quiet conviction. I didn't overlap much with Carla during childhood—by the time I was forming memories, she was already off in the world, shaping her own.

She moved to the city, fell in love, and married a university student—an engineer born overseas. I remember when they visited the farm, and he attempted to drive his Mini Minor down to Ellen brook. One of the creek crossings had no bridge, only two timber poles across the gap. True to form, one of his mates tried drive across, missed the pole, and plunged the Mini into the river. Dad, shaking his head, had to tow yet another car out of trouble.

I really looked forward to Carla's visits back to the farm. She always brought a little magic with her—sometimes in the form of a matchbox car, or a shiny new Tonka toy. Those small gifts meant the world to a younger sibling, and they left a lasting impression. More than the toys, what she brought was a reminder of the broader world beyond the farm and the love that pulled us back into it.

Through her, I began to understand how deeply my parents valued hospitality—how they welcomed everyone, folded them into our traditions, and made them feel part of something old and important.

As the first girl, Carla learned—almost instinctively—the quiet subtleties of our family cuisine and the rhythm of how we raise our children: close to the land, close to the heart. On those weekends she came home, I remember her lying in the sun on the front lawn with my other sisters, dousing herself in Reef oil and flipping like they were all Sunday roasts, basting to perfection. In Perth, she kept up the habit—Carla was eternally tanned, a golden thread tying the city back to our sunbaked fields.

Her quiet confidence shows up in unexpected ways. She once picked up a golf club for the first time—and won the tournament. She married her engineer, raised two children, and now enjoys the love of grandchildren. Her accomplishments are never announced—they're simply lived.

## Lina Palandri – (b. 1955)

**L. Lina Playing. R. Ric, Carla and Lina**

Lina was the second girl born to Carlo and Angelina, arriving in 1955. By then, the wooden house had been built, so unlike Ric and Carla, Lina never lived in the stone house with Nonno and Nonna. Hers was a different kind of childhood—one that straddled the old and the new, tradition and transition.

As a baby, Lina had a shock of red hair and bright blue eyes, and for a time, she was the apple of Mum's eye. Always active, social, and endlessly generous, Lina had an effortless way of connecting with others. Her kindness and selflessness are legendary in our family. Even today, she's the one who remembers birthdays, offers a bed to anyone in need, and gives without ever expecting anything in return.

Lina had a strong sporting streak too—netball was her game, and she played with the same energy and heart she brought to everything. Like the rest of us, she never backed away from hard work on the farm. I've mentioned before how Frank once accidentally pegged her with a stick (accidentally, he says). Whether she laughed it off or got him back is unclear—knowing Lina, it was probably a bit of both.

She loved sunbathing on the front lawn with Carla, slathered in Reef Oil under the harsh West Australian sun, skin bronzed and carefree. Those sunny weekends, all of us gathered at home, are memories stitched into the fabric of our lives.

When she left home, Lina took off for Europe with a backpack and a sense of wonder. She returned months later with crates—yes, literal crates—of gifts for the family. A testament to her giving heart. She had soaked up the culture, walked through history, and still thought of each of us along the way.

Lina eventually moved to Perth and trained as a midwife—a profession that suited her to the bone. Her warmth, composure, and ability to bring comfort in moments of pain made her the perfect person to guide new life into the world.

She was present at the birth of many nieces and nephews, and for some of the great-grandchildren of our mother, she's simply called Grandma Lina. No one in the family would argue that she earned that title.

I remember a time when Lina came home and spoke to Dad about a plot of land in Grace town, overlooking Cowaramup Bay. The asking price? $3,000. Dad, ever cautious, advised her against it. These days, that same block would fetch well over three million dollars. We still joke about it—one of life's near-misses.

Lina was also known for her faithful grey Honda Civic, a fixture of family life for years. Whenever she came home, you'd find it parked faithfully on the front lawn, as familiar as the house itself.

She's been many things to many people—a daughter, a sister, a midwife, a second Grandma—but to all of us, she's a cornerstone of our family. Strong, steady, endlessly kind.

## Annunziata Virginia Palandri (Anne) (b. 1957)

**L. Anne as a baby. R. Carla, Anne and Lina**

Anne was the last of the girls born to Angelina and Carlo—a firecracker from the beginning. With quick feet and quicker wit, she was athletic, sharp, and unafraid to speak her mind. She played netball with flair, earning awards for her agility and determination. Among the siblings, Anne was known for her fierce spirit, but also for her warmth—the kind that shows up when it counts.

Like her sisters, she was taken under Mum's wing, learning the delicate arts of Italian cooking, homemaking, and all the rituals that bound our family together. Some say she was the favourite—during Lent when the rest of us got Milk and Rice soup, Anne somehow scored a plate of hot chips.

When Polenta with ragu was served up and the rest of us scrambled with forks and elbows, a special portion was already set aside for Anne.

She was worldly and protective, and on my first day of school, it was Anne who smoothed my collar and made sure I was ready for the world. That said, she didn't suffer fools—and I must have been one on the day she chased me off my bike and threw it into the creek. I still don't know why. Maybe it was just an older sibling warning, maybe it was justice for something I hadn't yet figured out.

Anne was the fastest of us, which is probably why she got stuck with milking the mad cow—her quick feet were useful when dodging hooves and flying kicks. Eventually she moved to Perth, studied Early Childhood Education, and found love among a big, noisy group of friends who embraced the free spirit of the 1970s. Her husband came from a large family too, and together they built a life of laughter and community.

Settling in Bunbury, Anne raised three children of her own. They've since had children too, and now Anne has stepped into the role of Nonna, passing down our family traditions—quietly, lovingly, the way our mother once did for her.

### Francesco Palandri (Frank) (b. 1960) – *The second son at last*

**L. Carla holding Frank. R Steve and Frank**

By the time Frank came along, the rhythm of family life on the farm had been well established. He was the fifth and final child or so they thought—my closest brother—and from the beginning, there was something steadfast and grounded about him. Even as a boy, Frank embodied the enduring values that had sustained our parents through war, migration, and the hard graft of building a life from scratch in Margaret River: loyalty, work ethic, and an unspoken devotion to land and family.

Frank never left the soil for long. Unlike some of us who ventured far for study or work, Frank stayed close to home. He lived much of his life on the farm, steeped in the world our parents created, working alongside Dad in the timber mill, and later carving out his own path managing a large vineyard and wildflower farm. To this day, even though the original family farm was sold to an American entrepreneur over two decades ago, Frank still tends to its land, refusing to let go. That's who Frank is—the keeper of tradition, the quiet custodian of our roots.

In many ways, he carried the torch that Ric first lit. He became the family's great angler, a seasoned fisherman who passed on his passion not just to his children, but to every boyfriend and stray visitor that entered the Palandri orbit. He would take them out on fishing trips, show them how to read the tides, cast a line, gut a fish. It wasn't just about the sport—it was about connection, about teaching others what mattered.

And like Ric before him, Frank also had a deep love of the bush and the hunt. I remember Frank in his element—boots on the ground, eyes sharp, completely at home in the paddocks and forests of our region. He had the calm sensibility of a natural outdoorsman, someone who found peace in the quiet hum of nature and satisfaction in the hard-earned fruits of manual work.

But Frank's life wasn't all dirt and diesel. In the 1970s, he was a young man of his time—muscley, athletic, and quietly cool. He loved his cars: his first, a sleek GTR XU-1, followed by a WB Panel Van, and later, a black Toyota Celica that turned heads. There are tales—some best left out—of nights at the Margaret River Drive-In, a setting for mischief, movies, and mayhem.

But through it all, Frank kept his feet planted firmly in the values Mum and Dad instilled in us: integrity, humility, and pride in honest work.

Frank was also a sportsman, a natural athlete like Anne. He played footy for the Margaret River Hawks, not just as a player but as a coach and mentor. There was a moment in time—our heyday—when five Palandri kids suited up for the same club. Frank led the charge, the older brother setting the example on and off the field.

He eventually married a local girl and together they raised four wonderful children, each a reflection of his quiet strength and deep moral compass. His eldest now has children of his own, making Frank a grandfather—though I suspect he wears the title with his usual humility, never one to boast. He simply shows up, every day, the way he always has.

Mum and Dad would be proud. Frank never went to university, but he earned his education through the land—through seasons of sowing and harvesting, through storm and fire, through patience and resilience. He learnt the most important lessons from experience and passed them down without fanfare. Sausage making on family weekends, fishing on Good Fridays, Christmas feasts in the old style—Frank anchors these traditions like a rock.

To me, he has always been a guide. I leaned on him more than he probably realises—his steady nature, his quiet humour, his loyalty. He never raised his voice, never sought attention, and yet, in so many ways, Frank is the centre beam of our family. The one who stayed. The one who kept the land close. The one who reminds us, in everything he does, where we came from.

**The bunch plus Mum (grown up)**

# Chapter 17
# Show Day

## (Giornata della fiera)

*"There was magic in the dust, laughter in the air, and pride in every exhibit."*

*"C'era magia nella polvere, risate nell'aria e orgoglio in ogni esposizione."*

There was one day each year when the paddocks were quiet, the chores were set aside, and the whole town seemed to glow with possibility—that was Show Day. It was our carnival, our catwalk, our country fair rolled into one. Boots were polished, dresses ironed, and nerves bundled with excitement as we loaded up our entries—cakes, calves, zucchinis the size of babies—into the back of the truck. For us farm kids, Show Day wasn't just a break from routine; it was the grand stage where our muddy, hardworking lives met the shine and spectacle of the Margaret River community. And for that one day, we belonged to something bigger.

It would come around once a year, the annual Margaret River Agricultural Show. We would anticipate the day in early November when the days were starting to be warm, the sun was shining, and the air was turning. Every year the marker to the build-up to show day was the culmination of hay season. We would structure the cutting, raking, bailing and collection of hay being complete before the coming of show day, it was a law. As I got older this became harder and harder because of the slight changes in climate. Nowadays it is not uncommon to have rain on show day, and this is not what you want when bailing and storing hay.

School would have us prepare for the show early, so we would know many weeks in advance that on the actual day some of our art or craft works would be on display for the town to see. We would spend a lot of time anticipating and preparing something so that our parents could see something from their child displayed in the show ground pavilion. In the early days the pavilion just an old wooden shed on the edge of the town oval, separating the netball court from the main football ground. It was a creepy dank shed often with broken windows. At all other times of the year, we would hide in, and I believe some of the town kids would use it to drink, smoke or have a secret liaison with their girl or boyfriend, not a lot of drugs or worse were around in those days. By and large it was just an abandoned old shed, but on show day it was tizzyed up with cakes, scone and vegetables all set for display and hung with simple art works or craft works from all local schools. We were generally encouraged to do something for the Primary and secondary school displays at the show. All in anticipation for the grand show day. Locals would display their own crafts, cooking, art works, preserves or garden vegetables. There would always be a stall in the shed for the judging of the early wine industry.

Some farmers would display their stock, cows, bulls, sheep and poultry not much else at Margaret River in those times. Wool, milk and milk products would be classed, and animals would be assessed for the quality of their meat or milk production. I could never work out what it was that the so-called experts were assessing. However, this would generally take place on the Friday before the actual show day so that on Saturday they could parade the winners or best at show on the main oval, slap a place ribbon on the winning items in the pavilion. On show day log chops and wood cutting competitions would also take place. I never saw my father compete in the log chopping, but I heard that he was exceptional, must have been all the cutting and clearing of big trees from the farm, not to mention the hand hewing of sleepers from the hard jarrah logs with a broad axe. Early photos of him younger show a broad shouldered, muscle bound young Italian man.

Eventually show day would come, we would be up early getting ready and trying to find any change that may be floating around. Mom would dress us up in our best clothes, because it was an outing, and she would always present us at our best when we went to town. We never had a lot of money, but Dad would give us $10.00 each for the day. I remember the early days, going with Anne and Frank, by this time Lina, Carla and Ric had left the house and did not come back for the show day. We were all very excited as this was a big outing for us, we would meet our friends, and all our cousins would be at the show as well. For us the anticipation of a fun day and for my parents having the opportunity to meet with other farmers and friends. We would all pile into the Valiant and make our way to the town football oval where everything would be happening. Parking was difficult because most of the farmers from around the town would be in attendance, so invariably would secure parking a fair way from the entry gates. On the walk we could hear the sounds, crowds laughing and cheering, music and sounds of the merry-go round and sounds of livestock. As we got closer the smell of hot chips, donuts and BBQ wafted to us, and the sights glimpsed through the fence surrounding the show ground, side show alley, and stock on the oval and carnival tents surrounded by people. At the gate we would pay our entry fee, not out of the $10.00, but Dad would pay for the family. We would scan the vista, looking for friends, cousins or people we would know. Eventually we would inevitably meet with our cousins, dad and Uncle Joe were in partnership so they would look at the displays together, farm equipment, tractors, all the goodies that could be seen. In those days, like us kids came to the show in their Sunday best clothing. Everyone was dressed neatly; it was a small town so any time in town you represented your family and word travelled fast if you looked bedraggled.

Once we were all together, we would all go to the pavilion, doing a race as we went, what games were there, what rides and what could we arguably win on any of the sideshows. The pavilion would be full of stuff and most of the time we wanted to see who scored highest in the school displays. Did any of our art or craft works come a place. Generally, we didn't get anywhere, even though I often wondered how the winning pieces won. Little did I know that it's not what you had done, it was generally who you were. Yes, nepotism was alive and well in those days as well, we were just too naïve to work it out. My mother never put stuff in, I guess that was in her nature. She was an outstanding cook, but all I can guess is that she didn't want to be put above other people, her humility was amazing.

Eventually we would find our way to side show alley. It was small and very rural, limited games and limited prizes. There was the chocolate wheel, and my father and Uncle would often be there. There were the cork rifles, smiling clowns and a variety of darts and ball games. The prizes were interesting, for a few shows if you won you received a coconut as a prize. We had never seen coconuts before so they were completely novel to us, but we discovered that in your winnings you could not only get a drink but also something to eat. Soft toy prizes were not the go in those days, so coconuts it was. Rides were also limited, no bumper cars, ferris wheel or roller coaster just a few merry goes rounds and swings. We enjoyed the simple show, eating hot chips, fairy floss, candy apples and hot dogs, drinking cooldrink from the local bottler and having fun. Ten dollars went a long way and was a lot of coconuts. We cousins competed at a few of the games, acted older and sat in the tractor displays, visited the animal stalls, talking big to each other and generally running about with friends the whole day. We would end the day buying a showbag each, all of us would save some money so that we could get a showbag that maximised not only lollies that we liked but also a toy that we could use. Liquorice based bags were my favourite and we would love the opportunity to get a small plastic toy with the lollies.

Eventually we would all be rounded up, not wanting to leave but show bags in hand and prizes still with us, possibly a couple of coconuts to have later and we would go back to the valiant and prepare to go home. Stories would be told of the achievements, games that we won or the behaviour of some of our friends. We would almost be asleep before we got home, and when we did, we would share out the show bag goodies among brothers and sisters and prepare for the night. Sometimes we would have to do some chores like feed the cows or light the heater or stove for hot water and cooking or just chop some wood in preparation for the week ahead. We would often share our experiences of the day as a family over dinner.

Dad would talk about the machinery and livestock he saw; Mom would comment on the cooking and preserves, and we would share who we talked to and what we had done. It was a special day each year for the family a day of bonding and relaxation at the conclusion of hay season. It allowed the whole family to refresh and was important for our community.

But as all thing's times change the show like the town had an awakening about to happen. The embryonic wine industry changed the landscape of the show and the town itself. The tourism industry bought more money to the town, and the passage of time destroyed this innocent, family, community time, gone now are these more peaceful, simple times. The show today, no longer has animals, wood chops or the dank shed made pretty, it is commercialised with bigger rides, less family activities and more junk food.

In our late teens because we went to school at Busselton Senior high school, we were allowed to attend the Busselton show. This was a complete step up from the Margaret River show of old, it was much bigger, bumper cars, Ferris wheels, roller coaster and much larger rides all designed to make you sick. We would generally go on Friday night so to our eyes it seemed to take a step away from an agricultural show and almost had become a fairground. Lots of lights lots of noise and lots of people. The social structure was also different. It didn't seem like a family affair with mum and dad 's bringing along their little kids to have a fun day. The show was full of adolescence young and old teenagers all with various agendas, some were there for the rides and of course the sideshow games, others were there for their social life looking for boys and girls of similar age to meet up with, and others were there with their girlfriends. The night was generally very exciting. Bumping into a lot of school friends and watching many people converge on one small area. again, I was lucky enough to share this experience with all my cousins and my older brother Frank. We also met our girlfriends there and the night for us was like a date. We kept to ourselves played a few games went on a few rides and just try to enjoy ourselves. A sour note for the night was to watch younger people get into arguments and sometimes physical fights. This unfortunately became a trend for the Busselton show and families didn't really want to go because unfortunately there were just too many fights. It obviously wasn't the wholesome family environment that our original Margaret River shows were. However, we still enjoyed the experience as if it was a rite of passage. Having a good time, getting some show bags and enjoying time with some special people. (Girlfriends.) was something special.

At a roundabout, the same time of our lives We were lucky that one of our uncles was the Head of the Agricultural Society of Western Australia, which meant that he was on the organising Committee for the Perth Royal Show. We all knew this, and we were always in awe of the prime Agricultural Show of Western Australia. We were. invited to the Perth royal show, end my parents were not interested but they allowed us all to go, I guess as another rite of passage. A trip to Perth was definitely a treat, and we were able to stay with one of my sisters. Because we were invited guests, we were able to get into the show for free. Another bonus was that our uncle got us rolls of tickets for the rides. so, we could go on any ride at any time of the day for no money. The money that we did have was to purchase show bags and play any games. The other bonus for us was to see the state demonstrations in all the pavilions. It was a far cry from Margaret River and of course Busselton, which didn't really have an agricultural section in the show. this was the prime showcase for the best agriculture in the state of Western Australia. It had all the major tools, tractors loaders bulldozers even a section of vintage tractors and vintage machinery. It had displays from every major region of the state, showing what was great about that part of Western Australia. The arena shows were incredible, sheep hurting, cattle dogs, equestrian events. The yards were full of every breed of cattle every breed of sheep and even every breed of goat and pig. There was a dog pavilion, a poultry pavilion and of course cat pavilion. Even pavilions that will put aside for things like emus, Ostrich and of course fish or aquaculture. Any type of farming or any type of animal or any type of crop there was a display for it. I personally really enjoyed any display that had anything you could eat. There was the milk/dairy pavilion, a meat pavilion cooking every type of meat available. And of course there was an education pavilion, that showcase the education department of Western Australia.

If you were there to look at anything to do with agriculture, the list of things you could see was endless. It didn't stop there because they were pavilions that dealt with household goods, electrical goods, roofing and carpentry goods. It was one stop shop. But for Young Teenagers, sideshow Alley was the main attraction. Every ride and side game that you could think of was present. Hot chips, doughnuts, waffles, candy, apples, burgers and pies fried chicken and anything else you could think of was also available, it was a very at Wonderland For a country kid like me. The added factor that we had free tickets to any ride we wanted to go on was a bonus, Albeit short-lived. A Few days later, we will be back on the farm, back to being with family and away from those expensive distractions.

When I look back on this, I think those times were too good to be true and when I tell other people about our adventures, my cousins and I at the Royal show in those early days they look at me and say how lucky I was because of the family that I had in the right place at the right time. Now I go some 45 years later to the old Margaret River show and I'm sad because it's lost that simple attraction that was there so long ago. Time moves on and now the Margaret River show although small and backwater is trying so hard to become the fair ground playhouse at the Perth Royal show is, and that's a shame because what the show was once about was family and good wholesome fun.

**The Old Show displays before My Time**

# Chapter 18
# The Fire, The Devil

## (Il fuoco, Il Diavolo)

*"Sometimes the flames that threaten to consume us reveal the shape of who we really are."*

*"A volte le fiamme che minacciano di consumarci rivelano la forma di ciò che siamo davvero."*

## From Stone and Snow to Timber and Wine

There are events that burn themselves into memory—not just because of what happened, but because of how they made you feel. The fire was one of those moments. It wasn't the first blaze I'd seen, and it certainly wasn't the last, but it carried heat that lingered long after the flames were gone. Fear, awe, anger—and something else, harder to name—flickered through us like the embers in the bush. Then came the whispers of curses, old stories, things better left unspoken. It was then; someone first mentioned the devil.

They said it came out of nowhere—but fire never truly does. It waits, lurking in the rustle of dry summer grass, in the brittle bark of old trees, in the quiet forgetfulness of a cooling fire pit or the casual flick of a cigarette tossed to the wind. That summer of 1974, the Devil didn't roar into our lives. It whispered. By the time we heard that it had become a living wall of flame, tearing across the farm with terrifying speed, reaching for our home, our land and our lives.

I must have been about eight years old, still in primary school, too young to grasp the science of fire behaviour but old enough to feel the weight of fear when adults shifted their eyes and lowered their voices. That year, the summer heat was unrelenting. Day after day, the land baked. The grass turned gold and brittle, and everything crackled underfoot. The dryness seemed to make air flammable, and in the silence between the cicadas, you could sense something's waiting.

Looking back, I don't remember whether we had completed the spring burning-off—those carefully planned, controlled fires we used to reduce the fuel load before the real danger arrived. It was one of the seasonal chores on the farm, done with discipline and caution, always under watchful eyes. But memory play tricks, I can't be certain if it had been done that year. What I remember is that on that day, nothing seemed unusual. The sun rose like it always did, and I boarded the rambling yellow school bus with my cousins, the same as every other morning.

My brother Frank was already in high school by then, while Anne and Lina—my closest sisters—had moved out. At home, things were quieter. Dad was working for the Adelaide Timber Company, having recently left the hardwood mill at Cowaramup for a position in the new pine mill in Margaret River. It was a promotion, a transition from brutal cutting jarrah and karri to a lighter, more manageable pine. The industry itself was changing. The great hardwood forests were dwindling. Future, seemed to belong to plantation pine: fast-growing, sustainable, and suited to the emerging demand.

For Dad, it wasn't just forestry trends, instead, his hands told their own story. Years of working, the bench had taken their toll, and tuberculosis had furthered the damage, leaving him with two fingers on his right hand, permanently disabled. It affected his grip, his dexterity—his identity, even. The move to softwood milling was not just practical but necessary. The pine mill was more modern, less physically punishing, and being closer to home meant less travel and more time with us. He had spent a period in Pemberton, another timber town, where hardwood was still abundant. But Margaret River was where he wanted to be and so did us.

By the early '70s, Margaret River was beginning to evolve. The timber industry that had built the town was making space for something new: vineyards, tourism, and surfing. The first wave of a new culture was washing in—though that culture, in its earliest form, was raw and rough. The surfers who came weren't always clean-cut sportsmen. Many drawn by a different kind of escape. Some were drifters, some were seekers, and a few seemed touched by something darker; drugs, disconnection, a sense of rebellion. For a conservative Catholic family raised on hard work and tight-knit community, it was both curious and unsettling.

Still, on that day, we were unaware of what was coming. The fire didn't begin with a bang—it crept. By the time, word reached us heads turned toward the hills, and smoke began to smudge the sky, it was already too late to prevent what was coming. The whispers started about where it had begun, who had seen what, whether someone had failed to burn off properly, or it was arson, fate, or worse. That's when, a neighbour called it the Devil. And once that word was spoken, it stuck.

None of us really knew how it started, but once it did, there was no stopping it. Some say it began with a cigarette, flicked carelessly from the window of a passing tourist's car along Caves Road. The grass was waiting—parched, pale, whispering with the wind. That was all it took, a flicker, a spark. The tiniest offering, and the Devil stirred.

The fire took root in the long roadside grass, timid at first—licking the earth, testing. But dry shrubs lay nearby, and with each breath of wind, the flame found new hunger. It wasn't long before it leapt, wild and wanting, into the first paddock. Who first saw it, I couldn't say.

Perhaps a neighbour, or a passer-by with better sense than the one who lit the match. But I like to think someone did the right thing—drove down to our house and warned Mum, who was alone.

By the time Mum got a call through to Dad at the mill, it was already too late. The Devil had awakened, and it was hungry. An entire paddock was swallowed in a fury of crackling flame. The wind, fierce and easterly, drove it forward. The dry leaves and trees that surrounded us—normally a shield of comfort—became fuel. The fire curled upward, clawing into the sky, no longer hiding in grass and brush. It had grown bold, moving with a purpose now.

Dad left work immediately and rushed home. His brother—Zio Giuseppe, Uncle Joe—was close behind, arriving with a Fiat tractor, a cultivator, and a chainsaw. Word spread quickly, as it does in farming country. Within an hour, neighbours and farmers began to arrive, from all around, some with tractors, others with bulldozers or and hand sprayers, strapped to the backs of Utes. Everyone knew, if the Devil won't stop, he would not be content with just one property, he would feast.

The fire had started just south of our driveway. That much was clear. By the time our family and neighbours were in place, the flames were clawing toward the bush. In Australia, the bush is always a risk, but in late summer, it's a powder keg. Eucalypts are beautiful, but treacherous brimming with oils that make even green leaves flammable. They don't just burn, they explode. What we faced was not a simple blaze—it was a monster.

The wind pushed fire toward our home, whereas men fought back with what they had. There were no water bombers then, no helicopters, but locals; fathers, sons, and neighbours, armed with shovels, cultivators, chainsaws, and grim determination. Uncle Joe ploughed the earth, circling the house over again with his cultivator to create firebreaks—strips of bare dirt where Devil would find nothing to feed on. Dad was at the front line, cutting down trees with his chainsaw before fire could reach them. Every fallen tree was a victory—a slowed step; a breath gained.

But it was losing work. The Devil didn't care for our resistance. He hissed and leapt from tree to tree, roaring and sneering at our efforts. It was like watching a medieval army face a dragon, hopelessly outmatched. The fire danced and grew, impervious to hand sprayers and soil. It wanted more.

We kids knew nothing of this at first. It was just another hot summer day at school. The kind where the bitumen melts under your feet and flies stick to your arms. We were still laughing and talking when a message came over the PA: Frank, my older brother, was to meet us at the office. That was odd. Later, we were told that the school bus wouldn't be taking us home—it was too dangerous. Our parents had been contacted. That's when worry settled in. Soon enough, Uncle Joe pulled up in the old blue Ford Falcon. We piled in—older kids up front with him, younger ones, including me, in the back. They threw a tarpaulin over us, and off we went. It didn't feel like an ordinary pickup. There was urgency. There was tension. We couldn't see what was coming but feel it in the way adults avoided our eyes. As we turned off Bussell Highway and headed toward Caves Road, the air thickened and sky changed. What should have been bright blue, turned in a dull, smoky brown. Then we saw it—the Devil in full form. As we turned off Bussell Highway and headed toward Caves Road, the air thickened and sky changed. What should have been bright blue, turned in a dull, smoky brown. Then we saw it—the Devil in full form. The trees on either side of the road were burning. Towering flames arched over the bitumen. We were told to lie flat in the tray under the tarp as Uncle Joe drove right through it. I can still remember the sound. Not a crackle, not a roar—something in between. A scream made of heat. Ash fell from the sky like snow, hissing as it hit the tarp, the paint, our skin. The air was thick with smoke and the smell of burning eucalyptus. It wasn't just fire. It was fury.

When we reached home, it was like stepping into a war zone. The paddock around the house had been completely cultivated—bare earth ploughed in wide circles. Behind it the bush split in two: part of it blackened, skeletal, dead, while the other stood silent, like a congregation spared by divine mercy. The sun was still visible through the haze, a red eye in a bruised sky. Everything smelled of smoke and heat. We weren't allowed outside. I didn't know where Dad was. No one would say.

I sat by the window, trying to decipher the muffled voices of the men outside, the murmurs of neighbours who came and went. My heart pounded with every siren I thought I heard in the distance. We were children—useless in the face of such chaos. All we could do was wait. In the years that followed, I would hear many theories about that day. Who started it? How it spread? What could've been done differently? However, none of that mattered in the moment. Except the fire, the land, and people who stood between the two—and the silence that followed, like breath held too long, waiting to exhale.

Night fell, but the Devil didn't sleep. The fire kept fighting, crawling and clawing across the land with a fury, no darkness could quell. Power lines were down, lights had failed, and there was little we could do inside the house except wait, wonder, and worry.

Soldiers—volunteers, neighbours, firemen—came and went, their faces streaked with soot, voices low and strained. They spoke little, but what they shared made it clear: the beast was still on the move, devouring everything in its path I overheard talk of a desperate strategy—one smaller fire ignited in front of the larger blaze, an attempt to starve the monster by offering it fuel only to it off later. But the Devil didn't fall for tricks. It had climbed into the crowns of trees, leaping from one to the next, feeding on gum oil and wind. Each time a tree succumbed, the sound was unlike anything I'd heard—an unholy shriek, a crashing fall, and then a low roar as flames claimed their prize. It felt personal, as though the Devil was taunting us. There were no stars that night. The sky was thick with ash, smudged brown and angry red. All around us, the men came and went, streaked with black, some barely recognisable. They grabbed quick mouthfuls of bread or a cup of tea, then trudged back toward the flames like soldiers in a losing war. I think I briefly saw Dad once. He looked furious, exhausted, hollow-eyed. He'd spent the day felling trees to slow the fire's leap from crown to crown. Only he and his brother—my Uncle Joe—had the skill and nerve to do it properly. Not even the forestry experts dared take on the task.

That injustice stayed with him. It made him angrier than the fire itself—watching others stand back while he risked everything to hold the line. He wasn't one for grand speeches, but you could see it in his stance, in the set of his shoulders: this wasn't just a fire. It was a fight for something deeper. Mum tried to pretend it was just another night. She put us kids to bed early, probably to get us out from underfoot, while she and the other women set up makeshift kitchens, brewing billy tea, buttering bread, and offering whatever they could to the fire front crews. Their efforts stretched long into the night. They never asked for thanks, just did what needed to be done.

I could not sleep, laid in bed and stared at the ceiling, ears straining to hear any change in the wind, meaning, fire might double back. Might take what it had left behind—our house, our trees, and our story. I wanted to help, desperately, but I knew that boys don't fight Devils, they wait and hope their fathers come home.

And then morning came. The Devil had stopped—burned out, they said. Not defeated, just… spent. It had reached the edge of the fuel line, its hunger finally outpaced by the terrain, much of it stone. Where cultivated breaks and controlled burns had taken root, the beast had no more to consume. It had run its course. The air was still heavy, but now with smoke and silence, that follows a storm to realise what's gone.

We stepped outside, the house, the earth was raw ploughed but not blackened, a defensive scar. But beyond that line, the world had changed. The bush to the north, once thick and humming with life, was a graveyard. Charred tree trunks stood like scorched monuments, stripped bare, bark less, leafless. There were no birds, rabbits, underbrush and or sound. Just the crunch of ash underfoot and the smell—acrid, oily, unforgettable.

One blackbutt tree stood alone in the middle of the paddock. Towering and proud, it had always been there—a landmark, a reference point. The fire hadn't knocked it down, but it had gutted it. Hollowed it from the inside. It stood, still and silent, but was dead. A grey ghost against the smoke-stained sky. To this day, it still stands. A petrified relic frozen in time, reminding me of that faithless day. Now, when I see news reports of bushfires—every summer without fail—I remember that feeling.

The helplessness, the scale, the absurdity of watching good men try to hold back a living force with tools better suited to gardens than war. Shovels and tractors against a monster made of heat and wind and hunger. I think of our neighbours, soot-faced and weary, fighting on through the night with no promises and no guarantees.

Questions still echo in my mind.

Why was it only my father and Uncle Joe who knew how to fell the trees? Why did others hesitate? Was it lack training, lack of tools—or just fear? None of it made sense then. And even now, it's hard to say.

But what I do know is that life came back, slowly, stubbornly, nature healed. Green shoots poked through ash. Kangaroos returned. The bush made room for itself again, as it always does. And somewhere in that cycle—of death and renewal, of fire and growth—I saw something human too.

A lesson in humility. A respect for fire, not just as destruction, but as part of the land's memory. Afterwards, we began to burn every year. Not just on our farm, but all-around Margaret River. It became law, routine, gospel. No one forgot what happened when the Devil was let loose. And no one wanted to see it dance like that again.

# Part Four

# Reflections

# (Riflessioni)

*"We do not remember days, we remember moments."*
*"Non ricordiamo i giorni, ricordiamo gli attimi."*

— Cesare Pavese

# Chapter 19
# The End of Days
# (Gli ultimi giorni)

*"Grief is just love with nowhere to go."*
*"Il dolore è solo amore che non sa dove andare."*

There comes a time in every family story when the noise softens, the laughter settles, and the silence begins to speak. For us, it arrived slowly, like dusk creeping over the valley—first a shadow, then a quiet absence, and finally, a hollow space where once there was certainty. "The end" didn't arrive all at once; it came in whispered conversations in hospital corridors, in worn slippers by the back door, in the way Dad stirred his tea just a little slower. These were the years when goodbyes began—sometimes with words, sometimes without—and when I first understood that even the strongest roots, eventually, return to earth. This chapter is not about endings so much as it is about *honouring*—the final acts of love, the last echoes of a generation, and the quiet courage of letting go.

Being the youngest of six children in a unique Italian family didn't feel strange at the time—it was just the way life was. Ours wasn't your average household, and ours wasn't your average extended family. Two Palandri brothers had married two Fontana sisters. Two Italian families migrated to Margaret River in a time shaped by war, scarcity, and hope, and together they built a life so tightly interwoven that it was hard to know where one household ended and the next began.

I had five siblings and nine first cousins, and we grew up in each other's homes. We played in each other's paddocks, fought over the same scraps of food, and shared everything from bicycles to secrets. It was all I knew. It was a joyful chaos, stitched together by shared roots and endless cups of coffee poured from the same enamel pot.

This story really began with our grandparents—the originals. The first Palandri's and Fontana's to make their way to Western Australia. Giacomo and Leonilda Palandri. Giuseppe and Maria Fontana. But I barely knew them. Nonna Leonilda passed in 1970, before I was old enough to know her. I've had to rely on my older siblings to piece her together for me—what she was like, how she spoke, how she laughed. Nonno Giacomo died in 1972. I do remember him, but only in vague impressions. To me—and to many of my siblings and cousins—he was a stern figure. Grumpy. Distant. He didn't speak English, and by the time I came along, he didn't seem all that interested in trying to connect with the youngest of the brood. That connection was lost in the short time we had. I remember his funeral at the Margaret River cemetery. I remember standing there, not really understanding what it meant—that death wasn't a pause, but an ending. I don't recall feeling much. Not because I didn't care, but because I didn't yet know what to feel. Nonnina Maria, my mum's mother, passed away before I was born. I never met her. Everything I know about her lives in the stories told to me—through my siblings' voices, my mother's memories, and the photographs we now treasure.

Nonnine Giuseppe, Mum's father, lingered the longest. He passed in 1977. He was probably the grandparent I knew best—if "knowing" someone with dementia can ever be called that. He didn't really know who we were near the end, but he was warm and kind and always seemed to be working. There was something gentle about him despite his difficult past—his service in World War I, his migration from Italy, the hardship of starting over in a new country.

**Nonno Giacomo & Nonna Leonilda**

**Nonine Giuseppe and Nonnina Maria with Family**

Looking back on those years, I had no sense—none—of how fleeting life really is. It never occurred to me that one day my mother or father would go. That my uncles and aunties, always so present and strong, would slowly vanish from our gatherings. And yet, here we are.

Today, I stand among my marvellous extended family as one of the older Palandri's still left. Only one aunt remains from that generation—the migration generation—and she's a Fontana by birth. Zia Marion, the wife of Ricky Fontana, my mother's youngest brother. The rest—those who came from Italy, who spoke in thick accents, who cooked by feel and built their lives from the soil—are gone.

We are now the first generation of Australian Palandri's. The keepers of memory. The witnesses to both the flourishing and the fading. And this chapter, though hard to write, is a way of remembering that. A way of honouring those last, quiet years.

## When the Pillars Began to Fall

Throughout the pages of this book, I've often mentioned that I'm the youngest in my family—a so-called "surprise" arrival, the product of a time when late-in-life births were uncommon and, in many ways, risky. By the time I started school, both Mum and Dad were already deep into their middle years. And not just any middle years—these were worn, weathered years shaped by migration, by the hardship of building a farm from scratch, and by raising five children before me.

It didn't take long before I began noticing Dad slowing down. He had minimal use of his right hand, a lingering consequence of tuberculosis and the physical toll from his years at the timber mill. The changes weren't dramatic—just small shifts: Dad no longer coming down to Ellenbrook to fish with us, preferring instead to supervise farm work rather than demonstrate it. Still, for a proud and hardworking Italian man, these subtle retreats must have weighed on him. The frustration of losing his freedom, the creeping fatigue, the wear on a body that had already endured war, scarcity, and years of wine and cigarettes. By the mid-70s, the doctors had ordered him off the smokes. In the late '70s, he was put on a strict diet and banned from drinking. These were signs—quiet but clear—that his health was slipping. He retired from the mill in the early '80s and focused more on the farm, but even that became difficult. Machinery broke down, and so did patience. I remember how easily frustration found him. And I noticed how, when I left early in the morning for Busselton Senior High School, he wasn't always out of bed. So, I made a habit of ducking into his room before leaving—grabbing his comb, nicking a handkerchief—just an excuse to say good morning. Just to see him. That small act became a quiet ritual, something that gave me a sense of connection at the start of my day.

My brother Frank told me recently that just three days before Dad passed, he returned to the mill. His old boss had asked him, specially, to come in and show a new worker how to work the saws. Of course, Dad said yes. He did the three days. But Frank noticed that it took something out of him. He came home tired. More than usual. He went to bed early. That's who Dad was. Hardworking. Loyal. A man who would do anything to help out a mate. His passing came too soon—I only had sixteen years with him. I wasn't old enough, mature enough, to grasp the full scope of what he had taught me. I never saw him as the young, strong sleeper-cutter I'd heard about. That man existed only in photographs.

**Dad in His Youth, Possibly at A Ball**

The saddest part? On the day he passed, I was late for school. And for the first time in a long time, I didn't go into his room to say good morning. I skipped the ritual. I didn't think much of it at the time. But I've thought about it nearly every day since.

— ◆ —

## The Quiet After

If Dad's passing left a hole in our family, it tore something far deeper in Mum.

It was May 12, 1983. I was in the middle of my mock exams at Busselton Senior High—final rehearsals before my TEE later that year. I had no idea what had happened while I was at school. When I got off the bus that afternoon and began the long walk up the hill, something felt off. Frank was walking down to meet me, which he never did. As we got closer, I saw he was crying. I'd never seen Frank cry—not even when he cut his leg with a chainsaw, not even when I pelted him with rotten eggs. That sight alone knocked the wind out of me.

Through his tears, he choked out the words: "Dad died." I froze. I couldn't speak, couldn't think. I just walked. When we reached the house, I saw Zia Tilly and Zia Marion already there. Mum was in the kitchen, frantically cooking—preparing something, anything, as if keeping busy could hold off the truth.

I went to hug her, seeking reassurance, but she was caught up in her movements, lost in a loop of disbelief and distraction. It was Zia Tilly who told me what had happened. Dad had gone for his usual morning nap, and when Mum tried to wake him, he was already gone. Quietly. Peacefully. No struggle, no sound—just gone.

The others had been notified. My brothers and sisters were on their way. We were expecting the Palandri and Fontana men to arrive soon, the old guard stepping in as they always did. But I still couldn't believe it. I wandered out the back, trying to make sense of it all, stuck somewhere between shock and denial.

Eventually, I worked up the courage to go into his bedroom. There he was—still, silent, lying as if in sleep. I'd never seen a dead body before. The absence of life was immediate, chilling. He was cold to the touch. That morning, I hadn't gone in to say good morning, hadn't grabbed his comb or stolen a hanky. It was the only morning I broke the ritual. I've regretted it ever since.

**Mum and Dad before Dad's passing**

Mum and Dad had built everything together—a life, a home, a family. Every corner of the house held their fingerprints. Every groove in the floorboards bore the imprint of their shared journey. And now she was walking through it all alone.

No more calling out across the paddocks. No more evening's dancing in the lounge after the kids had gone to bed. No more quiet moments over coffee. The routines that once defined her days now echoed with absence.

After the wake and funeral, after the eulogies were spoken and the guests had gone, it was just Frank, Mum, and me. I searched for the eulogy but all I could find were a few lines from the priest. It didn't feel like enough. Not for a man like Dad. Gentle. Selfless. A quiet force who gave so much to the town and to those around him. But I was too young to have a say, too young to stand up and speak for him the way I wish I had.

Mum tried to carry on. That was her way—stoic, practical, hands always busy. But something in her changed. Her steps were slower. Her movements softer.

The kitchen still smelled of coffee and simmering sauces, but there was a sadness in the way she stirred the pot, a silence in the way she moved between rooms.

She still cooked. She still made beds and tended the garden. But something essential had gone missing—like her rhythm had been thrown off balance. Her cooking began to change, too, subtly over time. It was hard to name at first. Maybe less salt, less flavour. Maybe more memory than appetite in her dishes.

We organised a trip to New Zealand for her—not long after Dad passed. Lina and I went along. Mum had always dreamed of travelling, but I knew she wished Dad was there to share it. Even on that trip, she wasn't truly present. Her mind drifted. Her heart remained with him.

I think, in some quiet way, she poured her grief into us. She became more protective—especially with me, the youngest, and the one still at home. What some might have once seen as "spoiling" was something different now. It was over care. Fierce. Focused. Her love didn't weaken; it became sharper, more concentrated. And behind it, I now understand, was fear—fear of losing more.

I remember how she would linger longer at the kitchen table, cradling her cup of coffee. Sometimes she'd stare out the window, not at anything, just… somewhere else. Not sad exactly, just suspended in memory. Maybe she was picturing Dad out in the garden, calling out like he always did. Maybe she was back in the early days of the farm, before the hardship, before the sickness.

She would tell me sometimes that she still felt him. She'd be lying in bed and see a spark, a flicker of light on his side. She believed he was still there. And to be honest, so did I. That presence lingered. Not haunting. Not spooky. Just… there.

Years later, I was visiting Margaret River with Frank when the new owner of the house invited us in for coffee. Frank accepted. I couldn't. I said no. I wasn't ready to walk through those rooms again. I took a walk instead. Visited our old stomping grounds. That was enough.

Mum never spoke much about how she felt. She didn't need to. Her grief lived in the way she moved through the house. She never rearranged their bedroom. She never touched his chair at the table. It was like she was holding space for him, always. And yet—she endured.

**My Beautiful Mother Always Smiling**

Eventually, I moved to Perth for study. Frank had married and moved out too. Mum was alone in that big farmhouse. She was a woman of fierce love and even fiercer loyalty. Her resilience wasn't loud—it was sewn into her routines, her recipes, her refusal to stop.

But we noticed things slipping. Zio and Zia involved her in everything they could—Zio would drive her to town for shopping—but something wasn't right. Her meals weren't balanced. Some days she ate only bread and jam. She was forgetting things. Important things.

The dementia crept in slowly, then more noticeably. We realised she could no longer live alone. Anne and her husband offered to take her in—they lived in Bunbury, and on weekends, they'd bring Mum back down to Margaret River so she could stay in the house again. We created a rotation. Each of us took turns driving her back. It gave her comfort, even if she didn't always remember why.

She still spoke of Dad. Still claimed to see him. That never changed. Uncle Joe—Dad's brother—took his passing hard too. I think it scared him. But over time, even he softened. When we brought Mum to visit, Zia and Zio were always kind. They understood.

As her dementia worsened, I began to see how much she had truly carried all those years. The sacrifices. The burdens. The love. If Dad was the backbone of our family, Mum was its pulse.

**Lina with Mum, she never stopped smiling even after the loss of Dad and the Dementia.**

And though her steps were slower and her eyes sometimes vacant, she never let the family fall apart. She held us together. Even when she forgot names. Even when she slipped into silence.

Mum survived Dad by twenty years. And though the final decade of her life was clouded by dementia, she was still, at moments, that amazing woman who had once left everything she knew behind in Italy to build a life—full of passion, resilience, and love—in a place thousands of kilometres from home. Even in her quietest days, she remained our mother. And she never stopped loving him.

### The Legacy

With the passing of my father in 1983 and my mother in 2003, it felt as though the original flame of our family legacy had begun to dim. They were the first of their generation—the ones born in Italy, who had carried the memory of the old world and built something new here—to pass on. Outside of my grandparents, both Palandri and Fontana, Dad was first, and Mum was next.

Mum was the first to leave us among the Fontana family, only Renata—also born in Italy—followed in 2010. The rest of Mum's sisters, who were born here in Australia, passed not long after: Adelina in 2010, Olga in 2022, and finally Zia Atilia in 2023. Mum's only brother, Ricardo, also born in Australia, died in 2021. And Zio Giuseppe—Uncle Joe—my father's brother, passed away in 25 Years after Dad in 2008. That's when the loss started to truly settle in. It wasn't just the grief of losing loved ones—it was the realization that a whole generation had gone. The migration generation. The ones who remembered the boat ride. The ones who remembered the snow in Piandelagotti and the stone walls of Savoniero. The ones who still spoke Italian in the kitchen and kept rosaries in their pockets. The ones who didn't just tell stories of the old country—they *were* the story.

In that way, the death of my parents marked the beginning of a different kind of mourning—the loss of a living link to the past. They were the bridge between old world and new, and when they left, the connection thinned. There were questions I never thought to ask, recipes I never wrote down, traditions that faded before we knew they were fading.

And now, we—the children—stand as the first fully Australian generation of Palandri's. The keepers of the stories. The holders of memory. We try, in our own ways, to preserve the legacy passed down to us. To teach our children the songs, the recipes, the reverence for family. We still gather around long tables with bowls of pasta and bottles of homemade wine. We still speak of the mountain village, of the farm, of the laughter that once echoed in those rooms.

But we're also different now. We are a product of two worlds. And so, we carry the burden and the blessing of being translators—between the language of our ancestors and the rhythm of modern Australia. We hold both in our hands.

Both of my sons were lucky enough to visit the farm while their Nonna was still alive. They were little then, too young to understand who she truly was—especially as dementia had already begun to take her from us. But they were there, walking the same earth, breathing the same air I had breathed as a boy.

Even after her passing, we returned often. The farm was still ours then. And just like I had once done with my brothers and sisters, my boys explored the paddocks, scrambled over the rocks, wandered through the bush. I showed them how to whistle with a gum nut, how to flick them with a stick across the wind with perfect spin and surprising distance.

They rode the old orange Fiat tractor, wrestled the steering wheel with their small hands, and learned the stubbornness of machinery with no power steering. Of course, there were mishaps—my eldest falling off a granite rock, splitting his lip, smashing his teeth, carrying the scars still. My youngest walked straight into the bumper bar of the Fiat, face-first. But that, too, was part of the experience. Part of the place. Just as it had been for us. I gave them gilgie ing, fishing, creek walks, and the creaking moans of the old wooden house at night. We passed on the traditions born from necessity—catching fish on Good Friday, making sausages, celebrating Easter and Christmas the way Mum and Dad had taught us. These were the rituals that held us, that shaped our childhood, that we all—my siblings and I—have tried so hard to honour.

More recently, my eldest son and I travelled to Italy. It was the first time for both of us. We did the usual—Rome, Pompei, Florence—but I was determined that we visit Piandelagotti, the small mountain town where it all began. We stood in the cemetery where our ancestors were laid to rest. We entered the same church my parents would have prayed in as children. In that church—and in every church we entered on that journey—we lit a candle. Quiet flames for lives that shaped ours. Silent tributes for the ones who came before.

The house and farm are no longer owned by Palandri's. It's quieter now. The voices have faded. The furniture has changed. But the story—that story—has not ended. It lives in every meal we cook, every laugh around a crowded table, every grandchild who bears their name or their stubbornness or their love of the land. The foundation stone is still there. The roots still grip the soil.

Even when the snow falls. Even when the leaves fall.

**The Bunch Again and the Legacy**

# Chapter 20
# Echoes of a Life (Riflessioni adulte)

*"What we once enjoyed and deeply loved we can never lose, for all that we love deeply becomes part of us."*

*"Ciò che abbiamo amato profondamente non lo perdiamo mai, perché tutto ciò che amiamo diventa parte di noi."*

— Helen Keller

There comes a point in life—not marked by any birthday or milestone—when you begin to look back more often than you look forward. Not with regret, but with reverence. You see your parents not just as Mum and Dad, but as people. You remember your childhood not just as a time, but as a place, layered with sounds and smells and shadows. And in quiet moments—over a glass of wine, in the garden at dusk, or holding your child's hand—you realise just how much of your story is made from theirs. This chapter is not just a reflection. It's a return, a reckoning, and, in its own way, a thank you.

### The Quiet Realisation

There comes a point in life when you begin to reflect more than you plan. It often happens in still moments. You find yourself sitting at the kitchen table, fingers wrapped around a warm cup of coffee, staring out the window a little longer than usual. The house is quiet, the world hushed, and that's when memory comes—uninvited, but welcome.

Sometimes, in those quiet spaces, I think I hear Mum's voice again. It wasn't always the accent you'd expect—there was something in it, a soft American twang that only those close to her would pick up on. She'd inherited it, somehow, from her father, who spent over ten years working in the United States across two visits. It wasn't overt, but it would slip in—especially in the way she said certain things. Instead of "yuck," she'd say "yak," in that unmistakable tone. We called them "Nonna-isms". If the topic of conversation was food or gossip or anything she didn't like, there it was: a little 'yak' and the wave of her hand.

My father was different—quieter, more contained. A patient man who didn't speak unless it was necessary, but when he did, it stayed with you. Every time I pull on a pair of King Gee pants or any form of work gear, I think of him. He was always dressed ready to work, from the moment he woke. It wasn't for show—it was who he was. I see that same steadiness now in my eldest son. Courageous, quiet, strong. Steadfast in a way that reminds me not just of Dad, but of all the men of that generation who led with actions rather than words.

Sometimes I catch little flickers of Mum too—in the way my children insist on sharing their food, or the tilt of their heads when they laugh or smile. And that's when it hits you: the line between past and present isn't fixed. It softens. It blurs. And suddenly, your parents are with you again—not in body, but in gestures, in phrases, in the everyday rhythm of your life.

I find myself saying things like, "If you're going to do something, do it properly," or that old favourite of Mum's: "Y is a crooked letter and can't be straightened." I used to laugh at that one. Now I hear myself saying it at school, and it makes perfect sense.

Their legacy lives not in grand stories, but in the smallest things. The way I move, the way I speak, the values I pass on. Even the strangest sayings and habits—they're part of the fabric now. Woven into me. And through me, into my children.

### Who They Were, Who I Became

As a boy, my entire world revolved around Mum and Dad. I only had sixteen years with my father—those early, formative years when a boy is still trying to understand himself through the eyes of his father. With Mum, I was gifted a much longer time—thirty-seven years. I came to know her more deeply, though the last decade of her life was shadowed by the slow and painful erosion of dementia.

My father was the second eldest boy in his family, and the youngest to emigrate. He was born in Italy, and people say I looked like him when I was a child. He was never overbearing—he had a calm presence, patient and thoughtful, always quietly observing. Though he'd had more schooling than his older brother, he never held that over anyone. It showed, though, in the hundreds of handwritten letters he sent to my mother during their courtship—letters full of affection, humility, and careful thought. He was strong and fit, intelligent and measured, and deeply respectful—especially toward his brother, and toward all elders.

Mum, also born in Italy, came through migration with optimism rather than bitterness. She grew into her new life with grace, finding joy in simple things. She was always quick with a smile, quick to make a friend, and made everyone—neighbour or stranger—feel like they belonged. Her warmth made our house feel like a home. She worked hard too. She helped clear the land, raise the animals, grow the garden. She weathered the rough patches of life with a kind of cheerful resilience that still amazes me.

Together, they were the centre—the axis of everything. But now, as a man, I see them differently. Time has revealed things I couldn't have known as a child. I see not just parents, but full people—flawed, tired, strong, and endlessly brave. When I think back, I realise how much they kept hidden. The stress behind Dad's quiet moments. The fatigue behind Mum's bustling. The love they both expressed through action, not words. And now, as a father, a teacher, a storyteller, I recognise them in myself more than ever.

I grew up with one foot in two worlds. At home, we were unmistakably Italian—loud meals, strong expectations, church on Sundays, and the smell of hot bread rising in the kitchen. Outside, we were Australian kids—playing footy in the paddock, riding our bikes down gravel tracks, watching *Skippy* and *Countdown* after school. It wasn't always easy to straddle those two realities. At school, I wanted to blend in: Vegemite sandwiches instead of salami rolls; cricket over calcio. And sometimes I did. But home was different—home wrapped you in culture and memory like a second skin.

When Dad was still alive, I remember nights when the house would be filled with visitors and not a single word of English was spoken. Italian flowed like music through the kitchen. After Dad passed, that changed. Mum switched almost entirely to English. She rarely spoke Italian again. My older sibling's say they picked up some Italian in those early years, but after our grandparents passed, there wasn't much need—or space—for the language anymore. At school, speaking Italian—or even having an accent—was enough to draw laughter, suspicion, or worse. Racism didn't need a reason. It found you anyway.

Now, as an adult, I no longer see those identities as opposites. They're not in conflict—they're in conversation. I still make sauce the way Mum did, and when I take on a job, I make sure it's done right. That sense of diligence, of honouring your work, came from them. My daily life is different to theirs, of course. I work indoors. My job doesn't involve physical labour or long days in the paddocks. My children grew up seeing both parents' work. The old image of the stay-at-home mother is one they've only heard about. But still, their values echo through mine.

The world I inhabit now—modern parenting, cultural blending, technology, choice—was foreign to them. But their example still guides me. In small ways, I try to keep their traditions alive in my own family. A shared meal. A quiet Sunday. A phrase, a habit, a story. I hope that when my sons become fathers, those values will find their way into their homes too. That something of Mum and Dad will live on—not through relics, but through rhythm. Holding onto both worlds—Italian and Australian—isn't just possible. It's essential. One without the other would be incomplete. I am who I am because of the tension and the harmony between the two. And in learning to live between them, I've come to understand myself. And my parents. At last.

## Fatherhood and the Mirror

Becoming a father cracked something open in me. It didn't happen in a single moment—it unfolded over time, with every scraped knee, every midnight fever, every small hand reaching for mine in the dark. Suddenly I understood what it meant to worry constantly, to hope fiercely, to give everything of yourself without ever expecting anything in return.

I found myself doing things I swore I never would—raising my voice at dinner, insisting on tradition, shielding my boys from truths too heavy for their young hearts. And in those moments, I heard my own father. I saw Mum's fierce protectiveness in how I held them when they were sick. I felt Dad's quiet strength in the way I stood beside them in silence, offering more comfort through presence than words. Raising children didn't just make me a father—it made me a son again.

It pulled me closer to my own parents in ways I hadn't anticipated. I started to understand not just what they did—but why. Even when I was angry, I'd often speak with calmness. I rarely raised my voice with my sons or with students at school. And I realised that came from Dad. He seldom yelled. He led with understanding. Somewhere along the way, I'd absorbed that quiet discipline and made it my own.

My wife would sometimes say I romanticise things too much—that I focus too much on the good and gloss over the bad. But that was Mum's way. She was endlessly optimistic, quick with a smile, quick with a kind word—but the first to defend her children if she felt we were being wronged. I can see that trait in myself now, especially in how I speak up for her and the boys when I sense injustice.

There were little rituals, too, carried from one generation to the next. Every night before bed, I kissed my father on the cheek. I asked the same of my sons, and they did it without question. Mum would always say, "Night, night, sweet dreams, good night." A sing-song farewell that marked the close of every day. I passed that on too. They weren't just habits. They were a language of love. A rhythm of reassurance. You only begin to understand their weight when a small child wraps their arms around your neck, and in doing so, places the world squarely in your hands.

Without even trying, I began to parent in ways I didn't realise I'd learned. The way I prepared food. The way I shifted gears when one of my sons got sick, stepping in with quiet over care—the way Mum and Dad had done with me and Frank. The way I'd check their clothes before leaving the house, making sure they were clean, warm, and proper. That was Mum. I heard myself say things like, "What you do on Sunday, you see on Monday"—a classic Nonna-ism I never thought I'd repeat. But there it was, as natural as breathing.

And yet, there were also things I wanted to do differently. Growing up, life wasn't always easy. Our parents carried burdens we didn't see. Dad, especially, kept his emotions close. He loved us deeply, but words weren't his tool. That was common for men of his generation. But I wanted something different for my boys. I told them I loved them—loudly, clearly, and often. I told them when I was proud, and when I wasn't, I let them know it didn't change a thing. I made space for softness. For mistakes. For conversation. In doing so, I wasn't rejecting my father's way—I was building on it. Evolving it, not erasing it.

There's something humbling about watching your child mirror the generations before them. I see Dad's steadiness in my eldest son. The quiet way he moves through the world. His sense of responsibility. The way he manages frustration without letting it own him. And I see Mum's warmth in my younger son—his laughter, his instinct to share, his kindness without agenda. These moments stop me in my tracks. They remind me that I'm not just raising children—I'm continuing a story that began long before I was born.

When they were younger, I brought them to the old farm. I wanted them to experience the same freedom I'd had as a boy. Chasing gilgies and frogs in the creek, climbing granite rocks with scratched-up knees. They drove the old Fiat tractor—with no power steering and stubborn gears—and felt the weight of history in their hands. There were accidents, of course—busted lips, scraped shins, bumper bar bruises—but that was part of it. They were learning resilience. And they were learning it in the very place where resilience was born for me.

Years later, I took my eldest to Italy. We visited Piandelagotti. The mountain town where Mum and Dad's story began. We walked through the cemetery. We stepped into the same church they once prayed in. We breathed in the beginning. He stood there, taking it all in—not as a tourist, but as a descendant. He didn't say much. He didn't need to. I could see it in his eyes: understanding, respect, connection. The story had come full circle.

That's when I realised: being a father isn't just about raising children. It's about being a bridge—between generations, between cultures, between what was and what might be. I am the son of migrants. My boys are the sons of a man still learning how to honour two legacies at once. And somehow, through all the noise and love and effort, we carry it forward.

That's the work of fatherhood. To pass on what matters. To let go of what doesn't. To see your parents in yourself—not with resentment, but with deep, abiding gratitude. And to know, when your child echoes a gesture or repeats a familiar phrase, that something sacred has taken root.

— ❖ —

### The Questions That Remain

Now that I sit here writing this memoir, I realise just how much I didn't know. There are questions I never asked—not because I didn't care, but because I thought there'd always be time. I thought the stories would wait, quietly stored away in the minds of my parents, ready to be shared when I was finally ready to hear them. But time has a way of outrunning us, and life moves quickly. I was young, too distracted, too caught up in the day-to-day to understand how fragile memory is, how easily it disappears.

I wish I'd asked more about Mum's home—the village in the snow, Piandelagotti, and nearby Savoniero. What did they look like when she was a child? What did it sound like when the church bells echoed through those narrow mountain valleys? What did it feel like to leave that place behind? Did she look back when the ship pulled away from the dock? Could she have imagined that she'd never see it again?

I wish I'd watched her more closely in the kitchen—not just as a hungry observer, but as a student. Why did she stir the sauce that way? Why did the bread always rise best by the stove? Why did she fold the tortellini with such care and precision, as if each one mattered? I watched her, of course, but I never took the time to learn. Never wrote anything down. And I suppose part of that was being a boy in a household where boys did farm work, not cooking. Still, I wish I had pulled up a chair and asked her to show me.

With Dad, I wish I'd listened more deeply. He didn't speak often, but when he did, his words had weight. He told stories about the forest, about the mill, about how to sharpen tools just right. I wish I had asked him what it felt like to shape a jarrah sleeper from a raw tree trunk, or what it meant to walk the bush alone with an axe and a plan. I didn't know then that his body was already beginning to betray him. I wish I'd asked how he endured the pain, the fatigue. Did he ever wish for an easier life?

There were deeper questions too—the kind that can't be found in a recipe or a story about timber. What was it like when they first met? What did Dad think the first time he saw Mum? Did she know then that she would follow him into a life of hard work and faith in Margaret River? What were their fears? Their private dreams? Did they talk about the future, or just keep moving forward?

I didn't know about the letters until I started this journey—those beautiful, handwritten notes in Italian that none of us could properly read at the time. We made assumptions. We thought we understood. But the truth was so much deeper. Their love story, captured in ink and patience, was something you'd expect to see in a film. Full of sincerity, respect, hope. I wish I had asked about those letters while Mum was still here to hold them in her hands.

But regret doesn't shout. It whispers. It finds you in the quiet—over the stove, in the garden, in the stillness of a Sunday afternoon. It's in the family photos we struggle to label, the forgotten names in the margins, the recipes we try to recreate by memory alone. There is so much we'll never know—about war and peace, migration and loss, resilience and love.

Still, these unanswered questions aren't empty. They're part of my inheritance too. They keep me leaning toward the past, yearning to fill in the spaces. And maybe, just maybe, my children will one day do the same. They'll read these pages and find something of themselves in the wondering.

Because sometimes, the questions we don't ask are the ones that lead us back to who we are.

## What We Carry

Our family never had much in the way of wealth. We were never rich in the traditional sense. There were no heirlooms locked in safes, no inheritances set aside in trust. But we carried something else—something less tangible but far more enduring. We carried rituals. We carried them in the pasta we rolled by hand, in the fig trees we propagated and refused to cut down, in the stories passed on over dinner. We carried resilience. We carried the smell of slow-cooked sauce and the way Mum's kitchen felt like a chapel—warm, sacred, and familiar. We carried history in our bones and stories in our mouths. Their legacy was never in what they left behind—it was in how they lived. And we, the first fully Australian Palandri's, are now the custodians of that old-world strength.

When I think about what we inherited, it's not a list of possessions—it's a rhythm, a way of being. A belief in effort. In care. In family. Our inheritance lives in the way we knead bread with our palms, how we prepare food with patience, how we make a place for others at the table, and always overcook—because you never know who might show up hungry.

It's in the fig trees that still grow wild in our gardens—every family has one. And every family makes jam from it. It's in the rituals of Good Friday, sausage days, tomato days, and the long afternoons spent preserving what we grew with our own hands. The conversation always circled back to whether this year's batch was better than the last. It's in the way we tell stories—not just with words, but with our bodies: a gesture, a pause, a raised eyebrow, a flick of the wrist. The kind of expression that speaks louder than language.

Sometimes I wonder what my sons will carry forward. They live in a different world, one where tradition competes with distraction, where convenience is king. But even in that chaos, I see glimmers of continuity. My eldest is drawn to churches. When we travel—especially in Italy—he lights a candle in everyone. Not because he was told to, but because he feels something ancestral in those moments. A connection he can't explain. They still call her Nonna, even though she's gone. And when they ask for pasta, they don't mean spaghetti from a jar—they mean aglio e olio. The simplest dish. Olive oil, garlic, parsley, and cheese. It was my father's favourite. Now, it's theirs.

They ask questions now—about recipes, about the way we used to do things. They ask how to make sausages, how to stew fruit. They want to learn how to season, when to stir, what to taste for. My youngest enjoys wine and is often curious about our family's involvement in the Margaret River wine story. He wants to know which blocks we worked, what grapes we picked, which rows of vines carry our fingerprints.

From a young age, we brought both boys into the heart of those rituals. Sausage day was foreign to them at first. Raw. Confronting. They stood under the tin roof of the shed, rain drumming overhead, while we cut meat, mixed spices, and fed casings through a hand-cranked mincer. At first, they watched. Then they helped. Now, they show up ready—shoulders square, hands steady, knowing the tools, the timing, the texture. They know the smell of a good mix. They know how it should feel when the skins are filled just right. That knowledge isn't written down. It's passed hand to hand.

We still celebrate Easter, Christmas, and birthdays. The food has changed a little—adapted to include the traditions of my wife's family—but the spirit hasn't. On Good Friday, I taught the boys to fish. But more than that, I taught them how to clean, cook, and serve what they'd caught. These weren't just survival skills—they were acts of reverence.

Birthday cakes come and go, but one stands out. When Zia Lina bakes the rich, dark chocolate torta Mum always made for us, it feels like time folds back in on itself. It's a taste that holds history. Unfortunately, that recipe was never written down—and I never learned it. That's one of my regrets. Some legacies slip through the cracks. But even so, when we eat that cake, Mum is with us.

It's not perfect. It's not seamless. But it's there.

We carry our parents' legacy not through grand gestures or ceremonies, but through repetition. Through habit. Through instinct. We carry it when we offer someone the best seat in the house. When we clean up before guests arrive. When we welcome people into our homes, even when things aren't tidy, or time isn't on our side. When we put others first—not because it's expected, but because it's what we saw modelled every day.

This legacy isn't about nostalgia. It's about continuity. It's a thread that stretches across time, sometimes frayed, but never severed. And it's our task—mine, my siblings', my children's—to tend that thread. To mend it when needed. To weave it into new lives, in new ways, without letting go of its source.

We've had to let go of some things. The language. The accents. The exact smell of the old kitchen after a gathering. But the essence remains. The values. The rituals. The reverence. That's what we carry. Not perfectly. Not always consciously. But we carry it, still.

And as long as we do, they're still with us. Mum. Dad. Nonna. Nonno. Not gone—just transformed. Folded into our habits, stitched into our routines. Alive in the way we gather, the way we cook, the way we hold each other close.

## The Road Ahead

Life continues. My children grow older; the years move faster. The road ahead isn't so much about where we're going—it's about how we choose to walk it. The farmhouse is no longer ours. The fig tree still stands, but the hands that planted it are long gone. The shed where we once made sausages is quiet now. The vines we helped grow belong to someone else. Still, I return. Sometimes with my feet, sometimes only in memory.

When I walk through vineyard rows, I think of my father's broken, calloused hands pressing into the soil. I hear Mum's laughter in the voices of my sisters. I stand beneath a tin roof and feel the wind stir—a whisper that sounds like her voice. These moments remind me that this memoir isn't just a record of history—it's a love letter. To my parents. To my siblings. To the land. And to those who will come next, holding these same stories in their hands, reshaped but still sacred.

Time does what it always does. It moves forward, no matter how tightly we try to hold on. Children grow, faces change, and the sharp edges of memory blur into softer outlines. The stories we tell are repeated—sometimes distorted, sometimes embellished—but their truths remain intact. They evolve, yes, but they endure.

We still visit my parents' grave. It's become a ritual—a moment to mark time, to acknowledge their absence while honouring their presence. Mum was adamant she would rest with Dad. They share the same grave, a fitting end to a love story that began across oceans. And in true Mum fashion, she insisted the gravestone be red granite—different, bold, and unlike anything else in the cemetery. My father, quiet and humble, would have chosen grey. But Mum's sense of style prevailed. That granite says something—about her eccentricity, her creativity, her desire to leave something just a little unexpected behind.

Mum had a mind that never stopped turning. She could take a piece of wood and make something beautiful and useful. I remember her egg holder—it was a piece of art, with balance, motion, and function all in one. And she never let go of her dream to one day live in a round house. She spoke of it often, even while Dad was still alive. I don't know where the idea came from—maybe a memory from her childhood in Italy, or maybe just one of those whimsical ideas that never quite fade. It wasn't about practicality. It was about imagination.

When I think about the road ahead, I often turn to my sons. I wonder what they'll carry forward—not just from me, but from the deep roots behind us. I hope they inherit more than recipes and family rituals. I hope they carry with them the quiet strength of my father, the warmth and optimism of my mother, and the knowledge of where we came from—not just Piandelagotti, not just a farm or a vineyard, but a way of being that values effort, generosity, and connection.

In 2023, I travelled to Italy with my son. When we arrived in Piandelagotti, I watched him strike up conversations with ease, laughing and listening, making others feel comfortable, showing respect and reverence to his elders. In that moment, I saw both my mother and father in him. The way she used to welcome people, how she made them feel heard and the quiet respect my dad had for his elders. It gave me hope that the past lives on, not as a burden, but as a quiet gift.

I don't expect my children to live the same way we did. Their world is different—busier, noisier, more disconnected. But I hope they understand that real wealth lies not in what we accumulate, but in what we share. I hope they'll keep lighting candles in churches we visit—not out of obligation, but from an instinct to remember. I hope they'll keep asking questions, keep cooking meals, and keep speaking names that might otherwise fade.

There will come a time when I am no longer the one telling these stories, but the one remembered in them. A voice in the background of a home video. A name scrawled on a recipe card. A phrase they hear themselves saying and wonder where it came from. I don't want to be remembered in reverence—I want to be remembered in familiarity. As someone they knew, understood, and loved—even after I'm gone.

That's the road I want to build for them. One paved with memory, not nostalgia. With values, not rules. I don't expect them to repeat our traditions exactly. I want them to reinterpret, blend, and evolve them—so long as they do it with care, with gratitude. That's how traditions survive: not by being frozen in time, but by being reimagined, tenderly.

This memoir is more than a record of what was. It's a conversation with what will be. It's a bridge between generations. A reminder that our stories don't end with us—they echo. They change form but not meaning. Each new child born into this family carries a fragment of that echo. Every shared meal, every moment of laughter, every time we pause to remember—that's where the story continues.

I may never know what pieces will remain. Maybe it will be a saying, or the way someone folds a tablecloth. Maybe it'll be the instinct to offer a second helping without being asked. But something will last. Because love, the kind that's honest and unadorned, always finds a way forward.

There's a saying: to improve the future, you must understand the past. That's what this memoir is. A statement of the past. A document of lessons learned, stories lived, values tested and passed down. If one of my sons—or perhaps one of their children—reads this one day and understands a little more about where they came from, then it's done its job.

And it's not just my children. All my siblings, all the cousins, all those who still carry the Palandri name—they've gone on to forge families of their own. What's striking now is how many in the younger generation no longer have Italian first names. Perhaps that's a response to childhood teasing, the pressure to fit in, or the subconscious drift that comes with cultural integration. When I think about Mum and Dad naming me Stephen—not Stefano—I see it now as a sign. A quiet nod to a changing world. A choice rooted in love, yes, but also in adaptation.

So, no—I don't fear the road ahead. I walk it with gratitude. With humility. And never alone. I walk it with the memory of those who came before me—and with the hope of those who will come next.

In the small snow covered village of Piandelagotti, nestled in the Italian Apennines, the Palandri family cultivated a life of simplicity, tradition, and resilience. After war and hardship pushed them to seek new beginnings, they found themselves carving a future from towering forests and fertile soils of Margaret River, Western Australia.

"From Stone and Snow to Timber and Wine" is a deeply personal memoir of migration, family, faith, and food. Spanning generations, it captures the laughter, the struggles, and the enduring customs that held one family together as they bridged two worlds.

Through richly woven stories – from love letters and fishing adventures to sausage days and Christmas feasts, this book honours the spirit of those who came before and the legacy that lives on.

www.ingramcontent.com/pod-product-compliance
Lightning Source LLC
Chambersburg PA
CBHW030230100526
44583CB00013BA/649